THE
KING'S
Beast

STORY & ART BY

Rei Toma

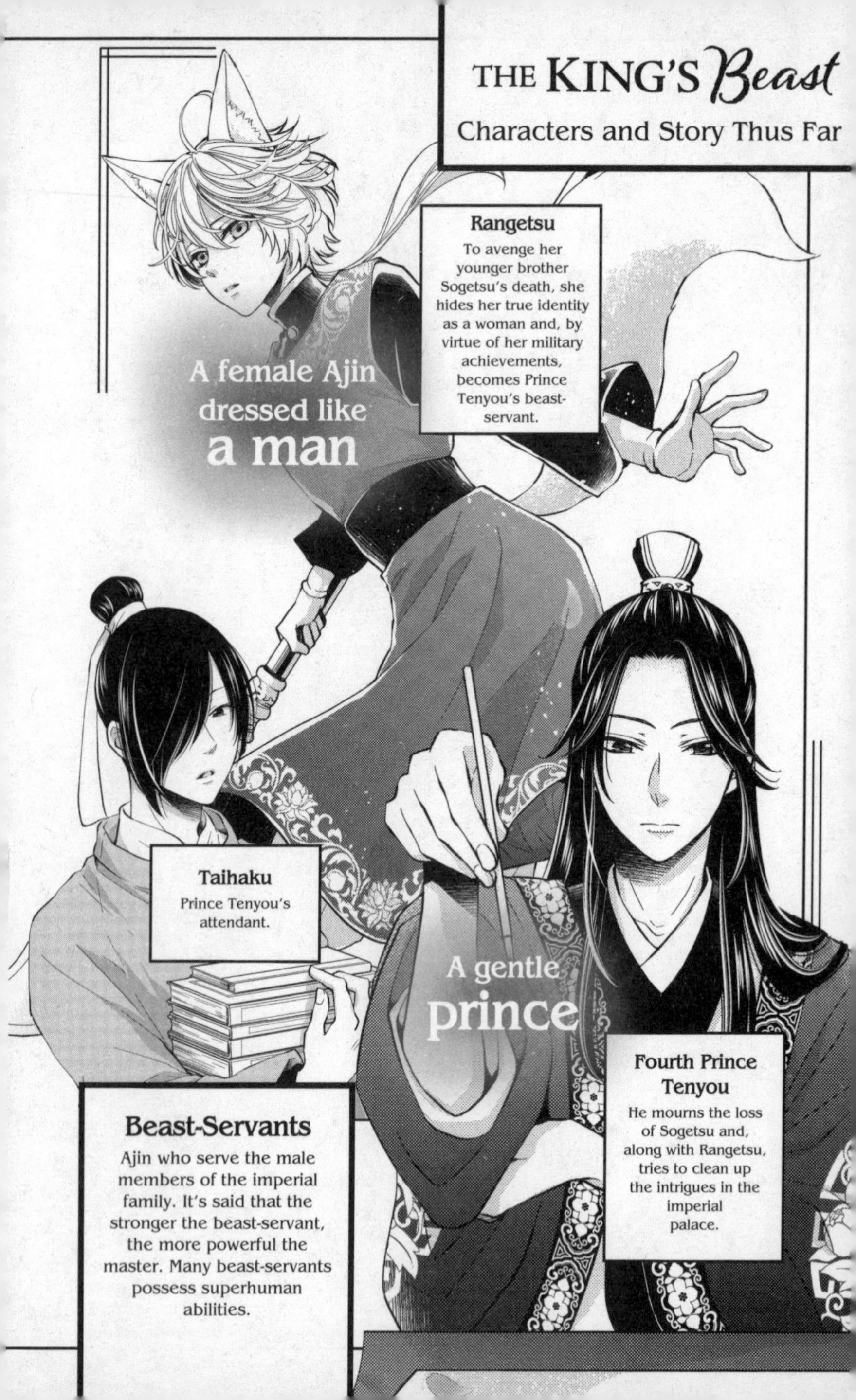
THE KING'S Beast
Characters and Story Thus Far
Rangetsu
To avenge her younger brother Sogetsu's death, she hides her true identity as a woman and, by virtue of her military achievements, becomes Prince Tenyou's beast-servant.
A female Ajin dressed like a man
Fourth Prince Tenyou
He mourns the loss of Sogetsu and, along with Rangetsu, tries to clean up the intrigues in the imperial palace.
A gentle prince
Taihaku
Prince Tenyou's attendant.
Beast-Servants
Ajin who serve the male members of the imperial family. It's said that the stronger the beast-servant, the more powerful the master. Many beast-servants possess superhuman abilities.

Prince Tenyou's Brothers and Their Beast-Servants

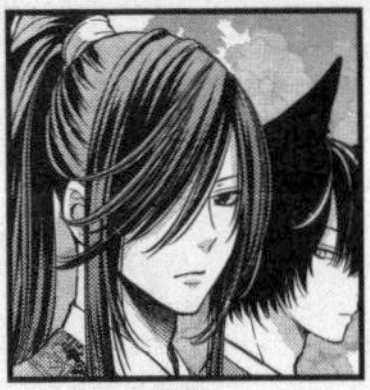

(??)

The third prince. Still shrouded in mystery.

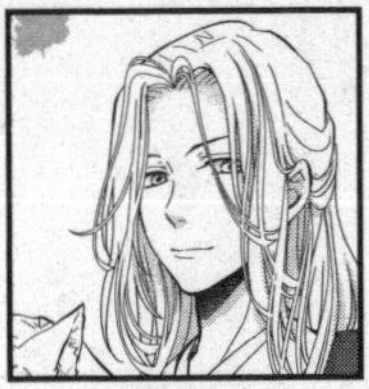

Reiun

The second prince. Intelligent and bored by his own idleness.

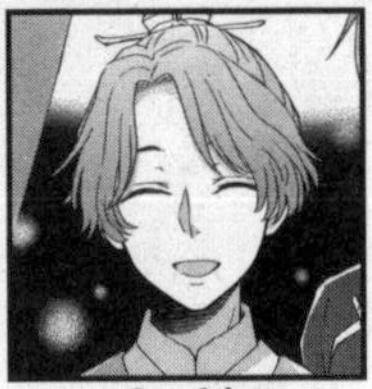

Oushin

The first prince. He is sickly and passive.

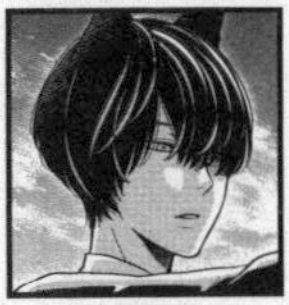

(??)

The third prince's beast-servant.

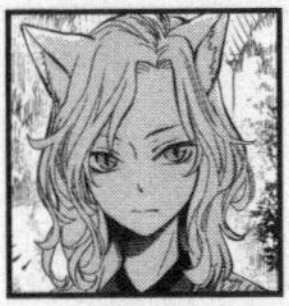

Youbi

Prince Reiun's beast-servant.

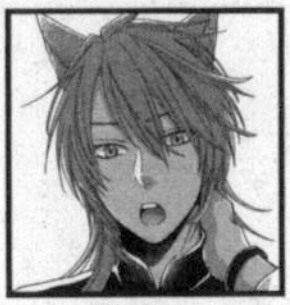

Teiga

Prince Oushin's beast-servant.

The Assassination of Sogetsu

Sogetsu, Rangetsu's twin, was brought to the imperial palace to serve Prince Tenyou as his beast-servant after it was discovered that he had special abilities. He was brutally killed soon after.

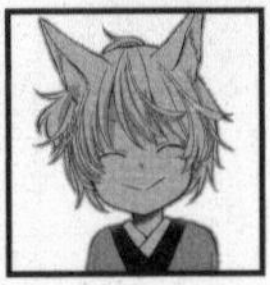

Sogetsu

Summary

In a world where humans rule the half-beast Ajin, Rangetsu disguises herself as a man and proves herself in battle to enter the imperial palace and become the Fourth Prince Tenyou's beast-servant. She seeks revenge for the death of her brother Sogetsu.

Rangetsu feels hopeless when she discovers that her prime suspect, Prince Tenyou, is not the mastermind behind her brother's murder. But at the same time, she realizes that the prince is the only person who has mourned Sogetsu's death. Tenyou regrets the young Ajin's death and asks Rangetsu to value her own life. Rangetsu tells Tenyou that she is willing to sacrifice her own life to avenge her brother's murder.

Upon seeing Rangetsu's determination, Tenyou starts to question the other princes, starting with Second Prince Reiun and his beast-servant Youbi. Prince Tenyou vows to find Sogetsu's killer and see the perpetrator punished even if it antagonizes his brothers. Furthermore, he's prepared to put his life in Rangetsu's hands.

THE KING'S *Beast*

2

CONTENTS

◆◆◆

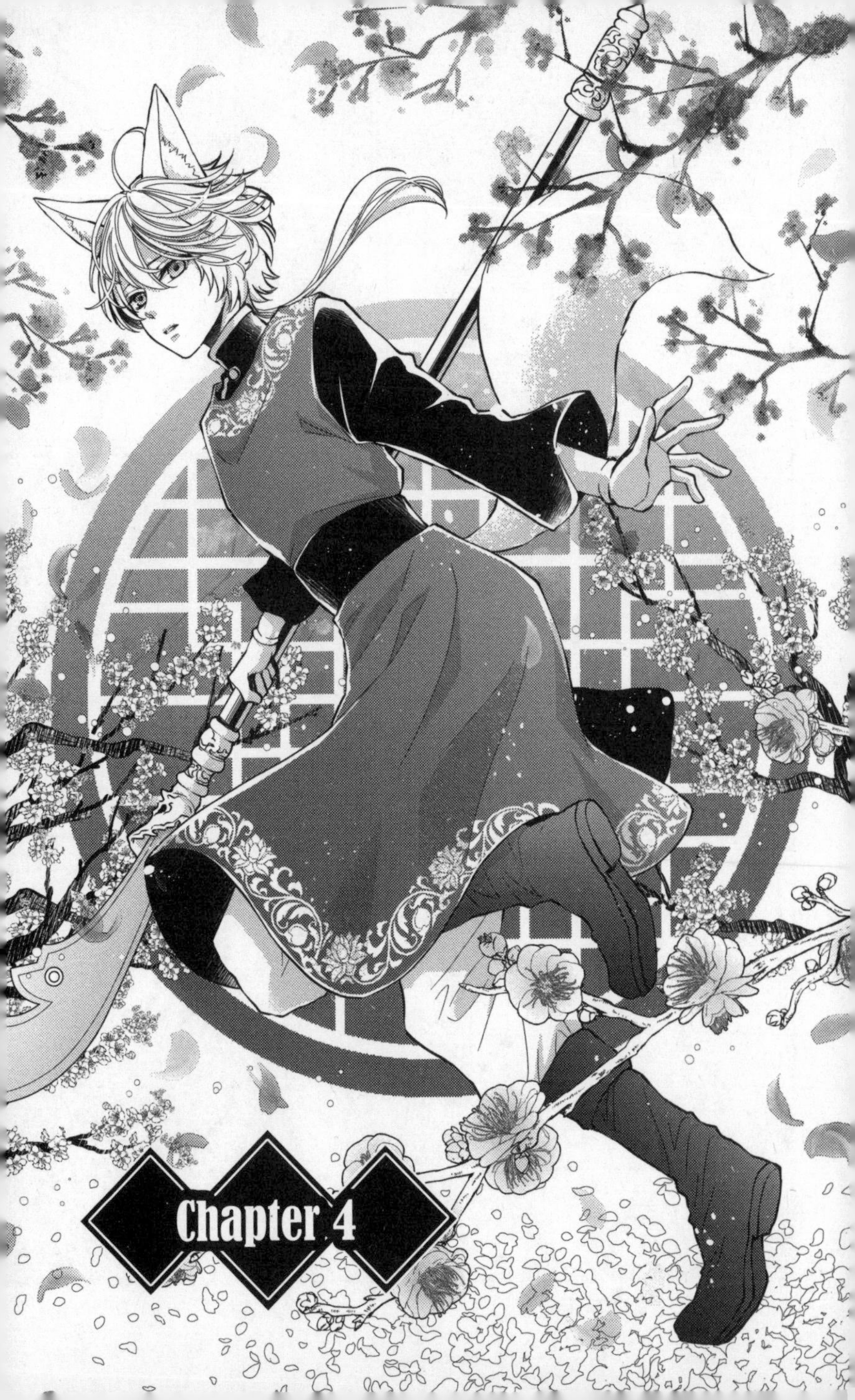
Chapter 4

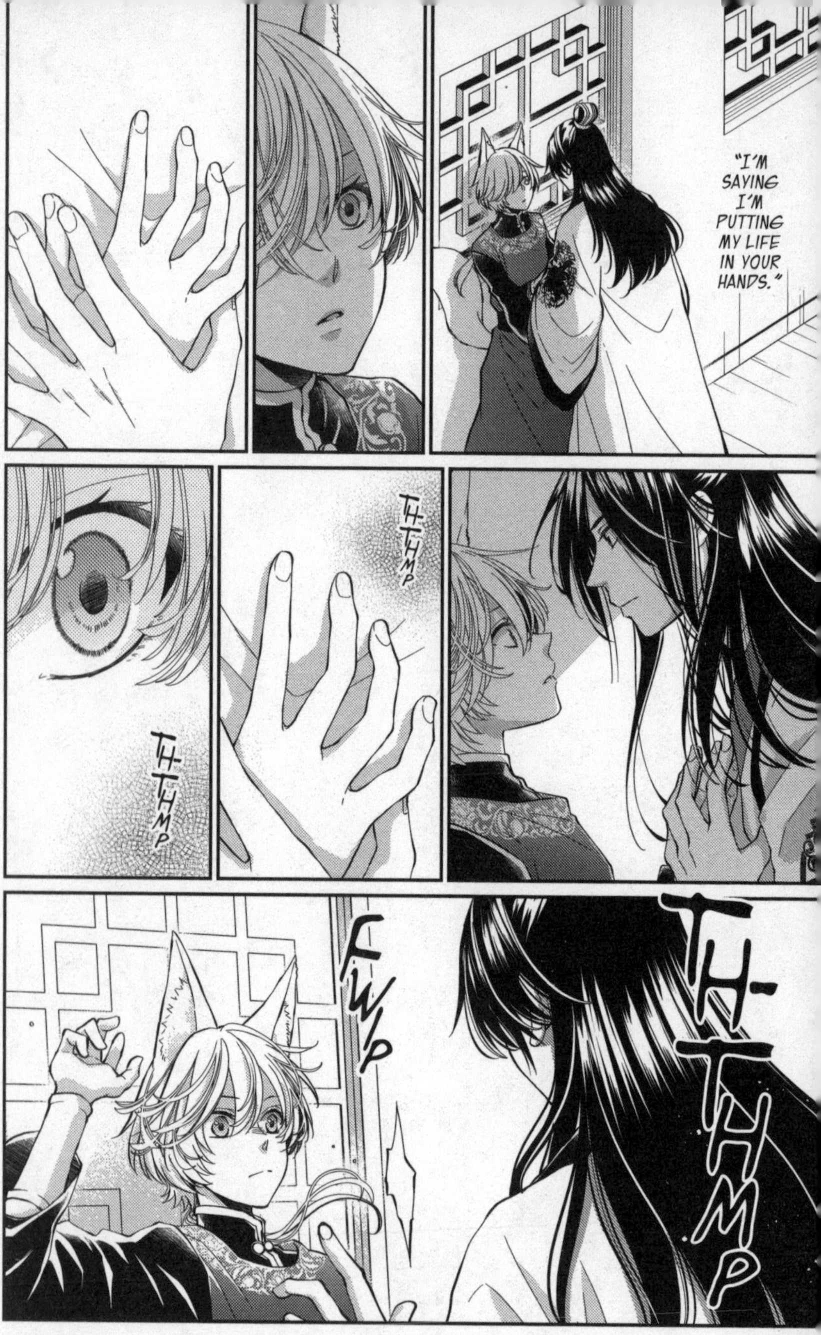
"I'M SAYING I'M PUTTING MY LIFE IN YOUR HANDS."
TH-THMP
TH-THMP
TH-THMP
FWIP

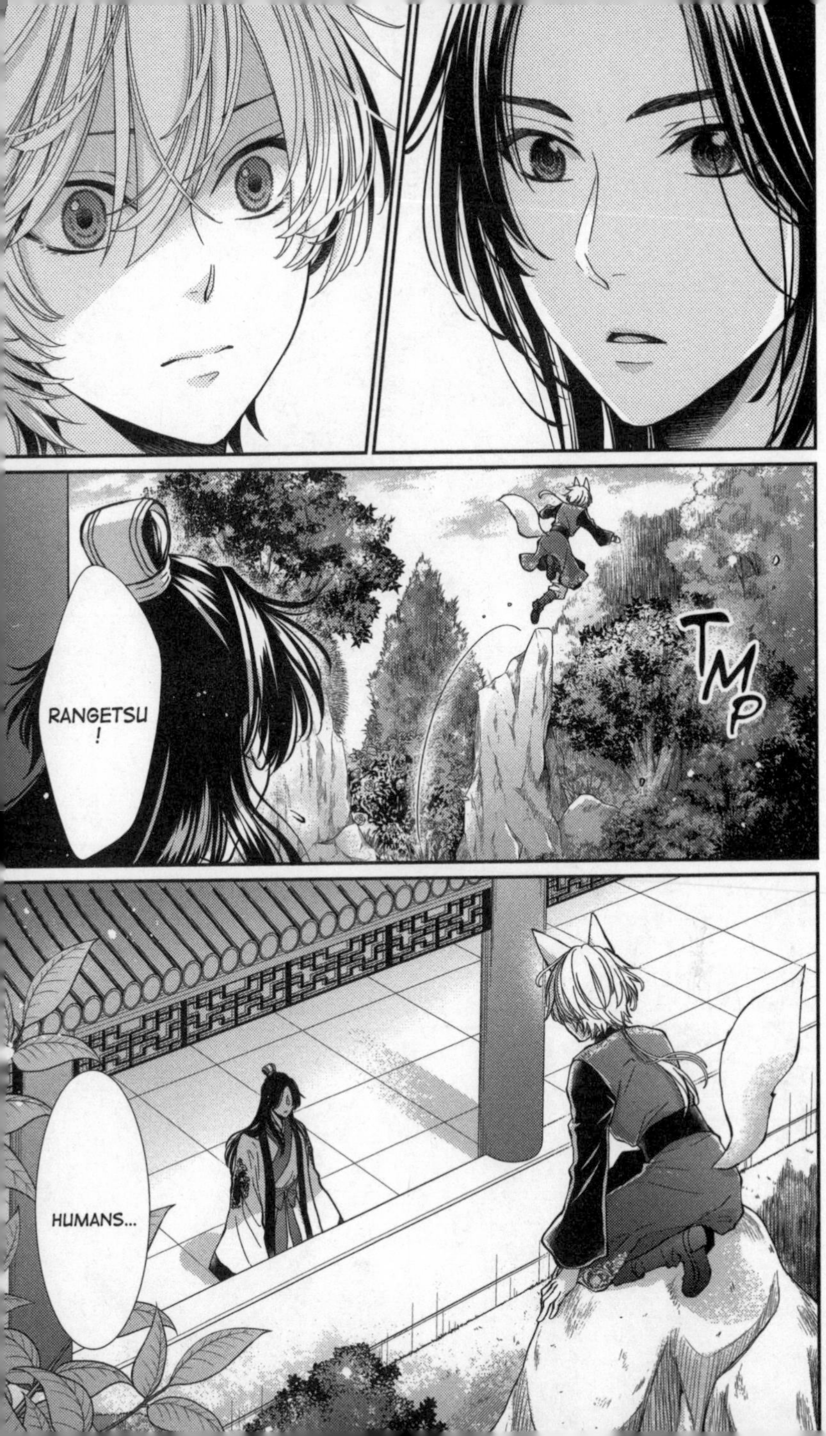
TMP
RANGETSU!
HUMANS...

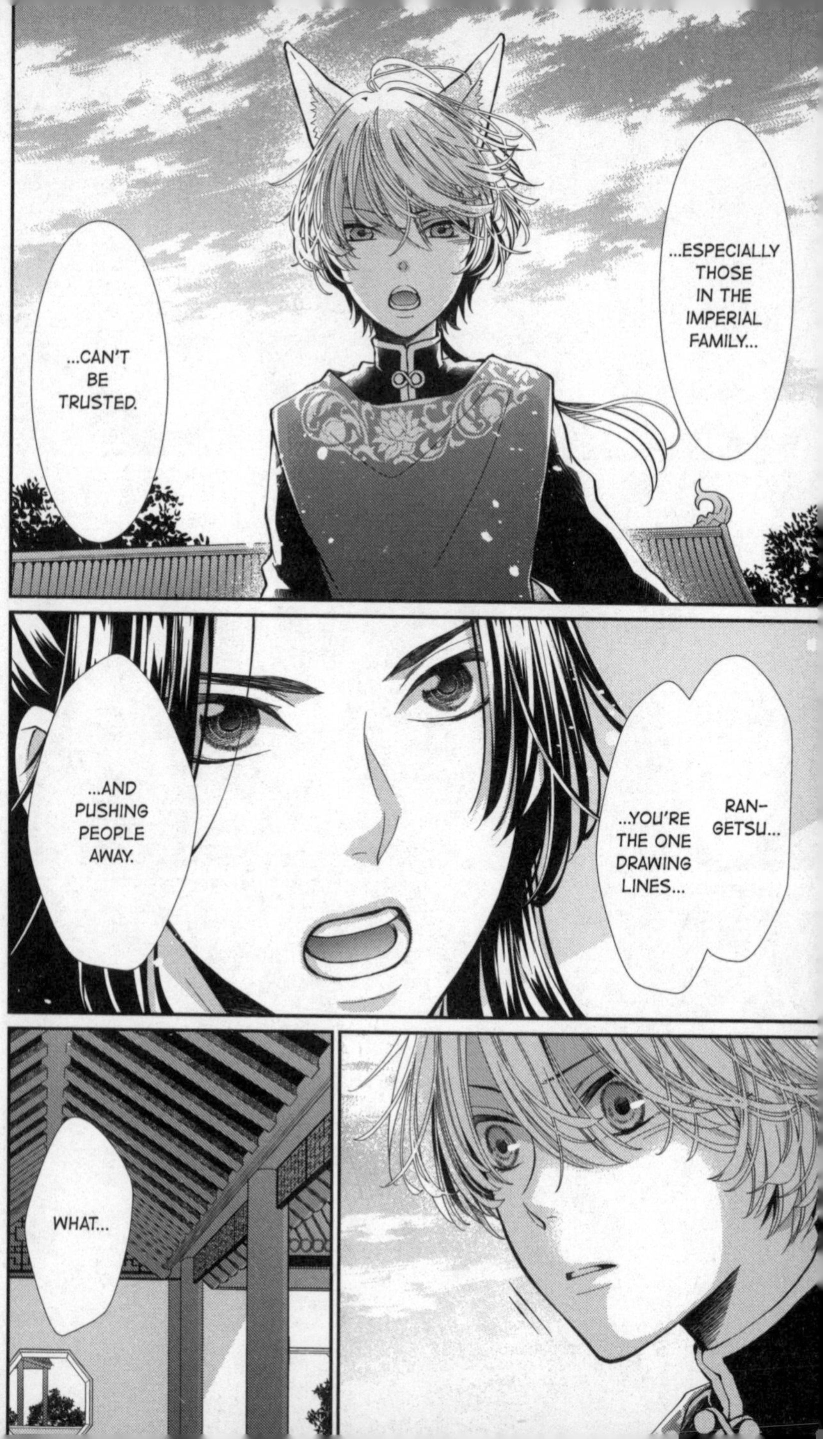
...ESPECIALLY THOSE IN THE IMPERIAL FAMILY...
...CAN'T BE TRUSTED.
RAN-GETSU...
...YOU'RE THE ONE DRAWING LINES...
...AND PUSHING PEOPLE AWAY.
WHAT...

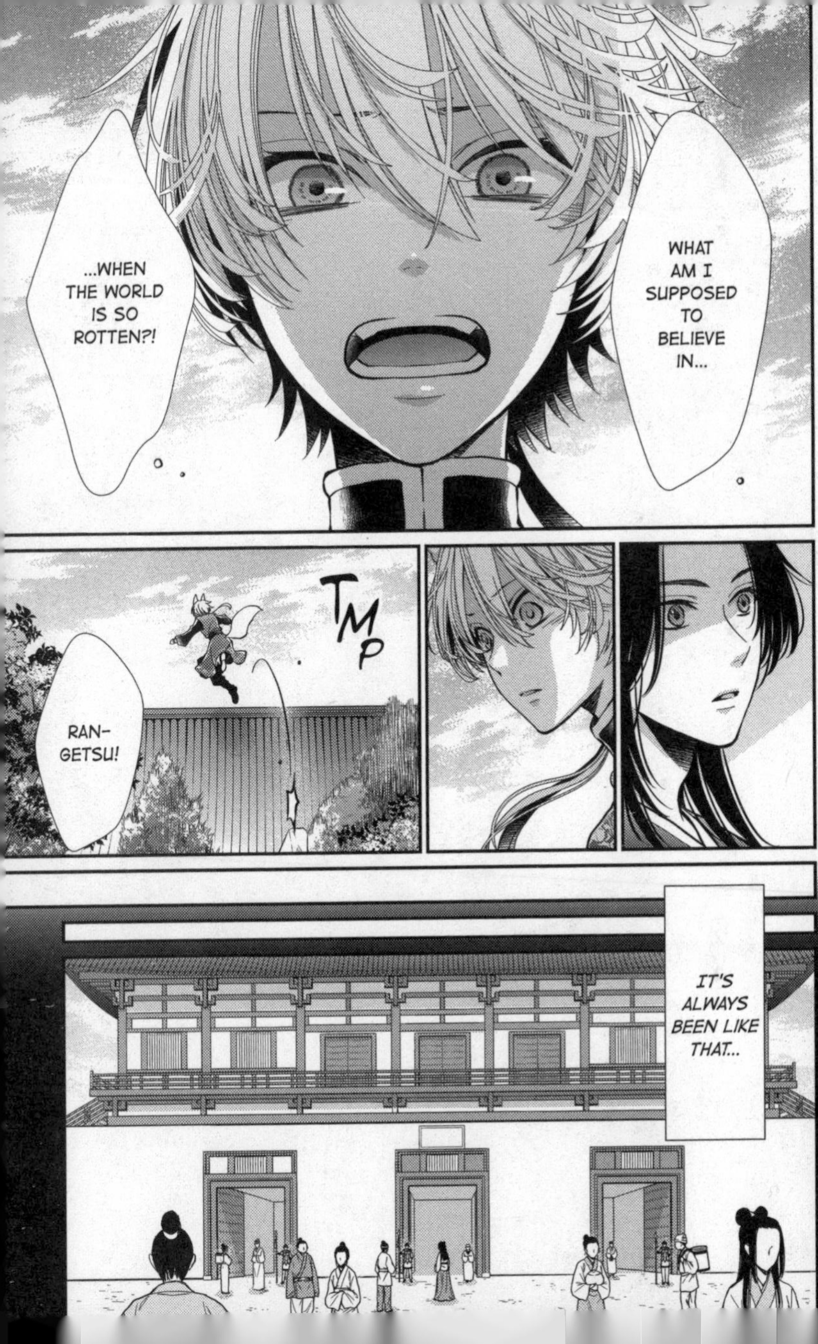
WHAT AM I SUPPOSED TO BELIEVE IN...
...WHEN THE WORLD IS SO ROTTEN?!
TMP
RAN-GETSU!
IT'S ALWAYS BEEN LIKE THAT...

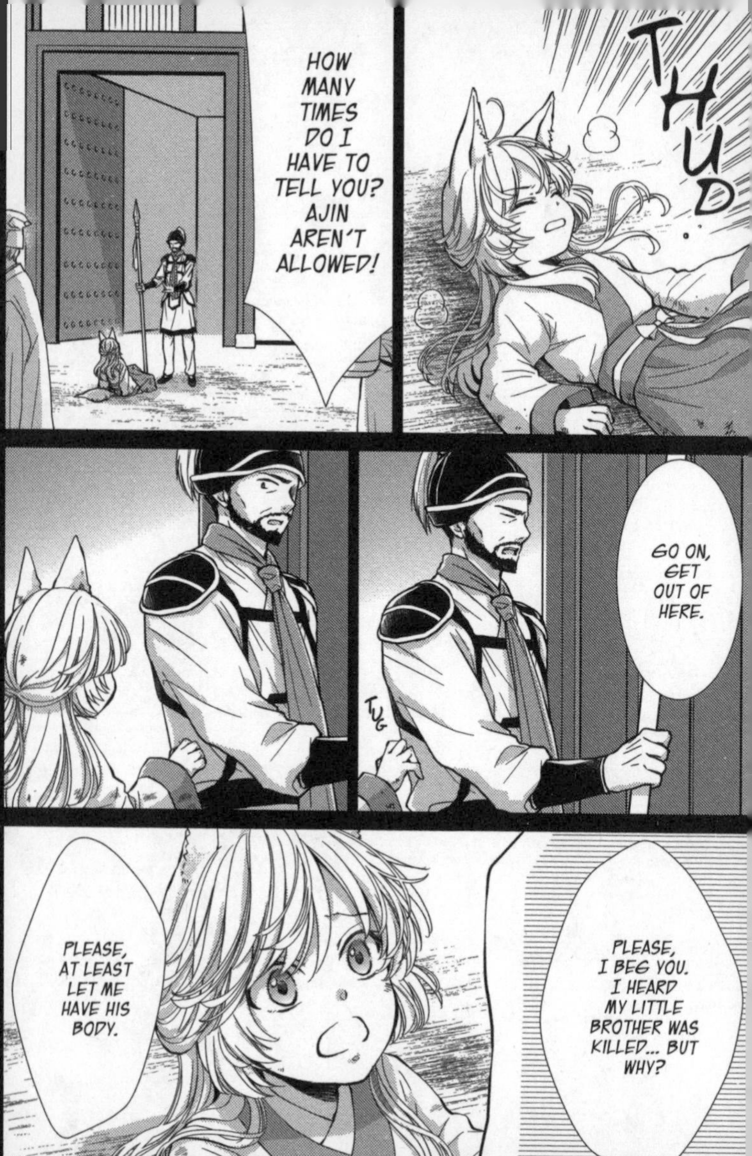
THUD
HOW MANY TIMES DO I HAVE TO TELL YOU? AJIN AREN'T ALLOWED!
GO ON, GET OUT OF HERE.
TUG
PLEASE, I BEG YOU. I HEARD MY LITTLE BROTHER WAS KILLED... BUT WHY?
PLEASE, AT LEAST LET ME HAVE HIS BODY.

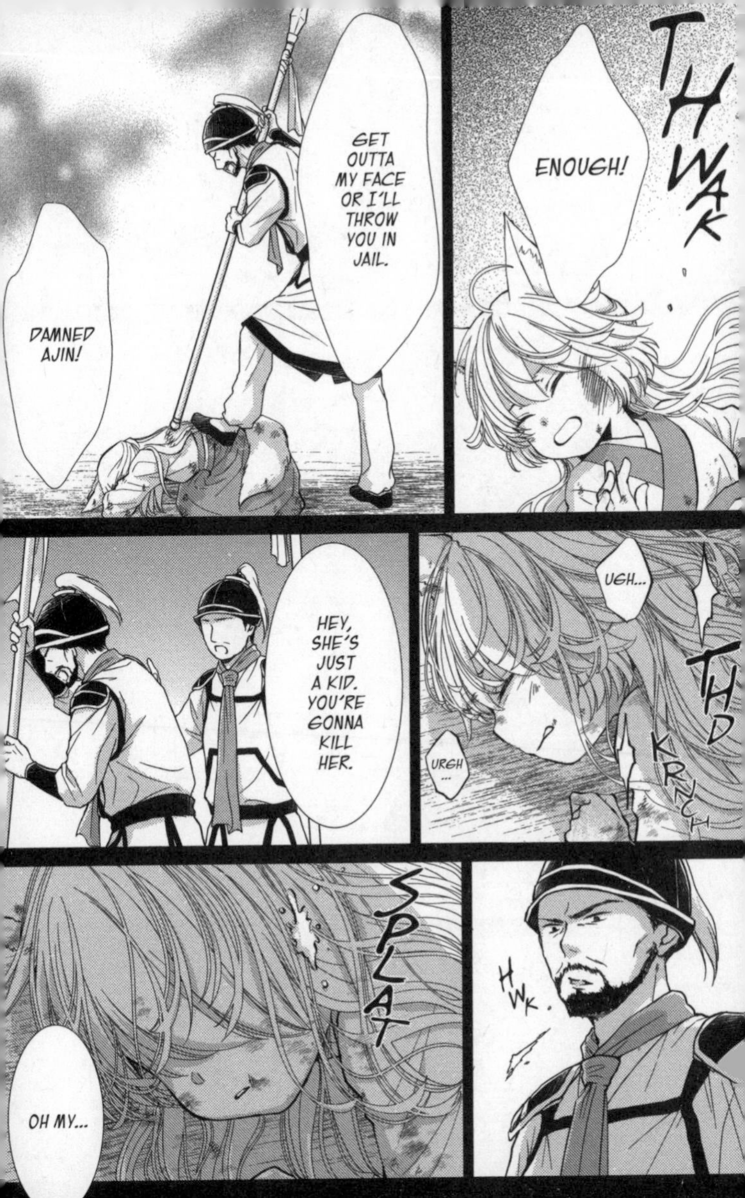
THWAK
ENOUGH!
GET OUTTA MY FACE OR I'LL THROW YOU IN JAIL.
DAMNED AJIN!
UGH...
THD
KRNCH
URGH...
HEY, SHE'S JUST A KID. YOU'RE GONNA KILL HER.
HWK.
SPLAT
OH MY...

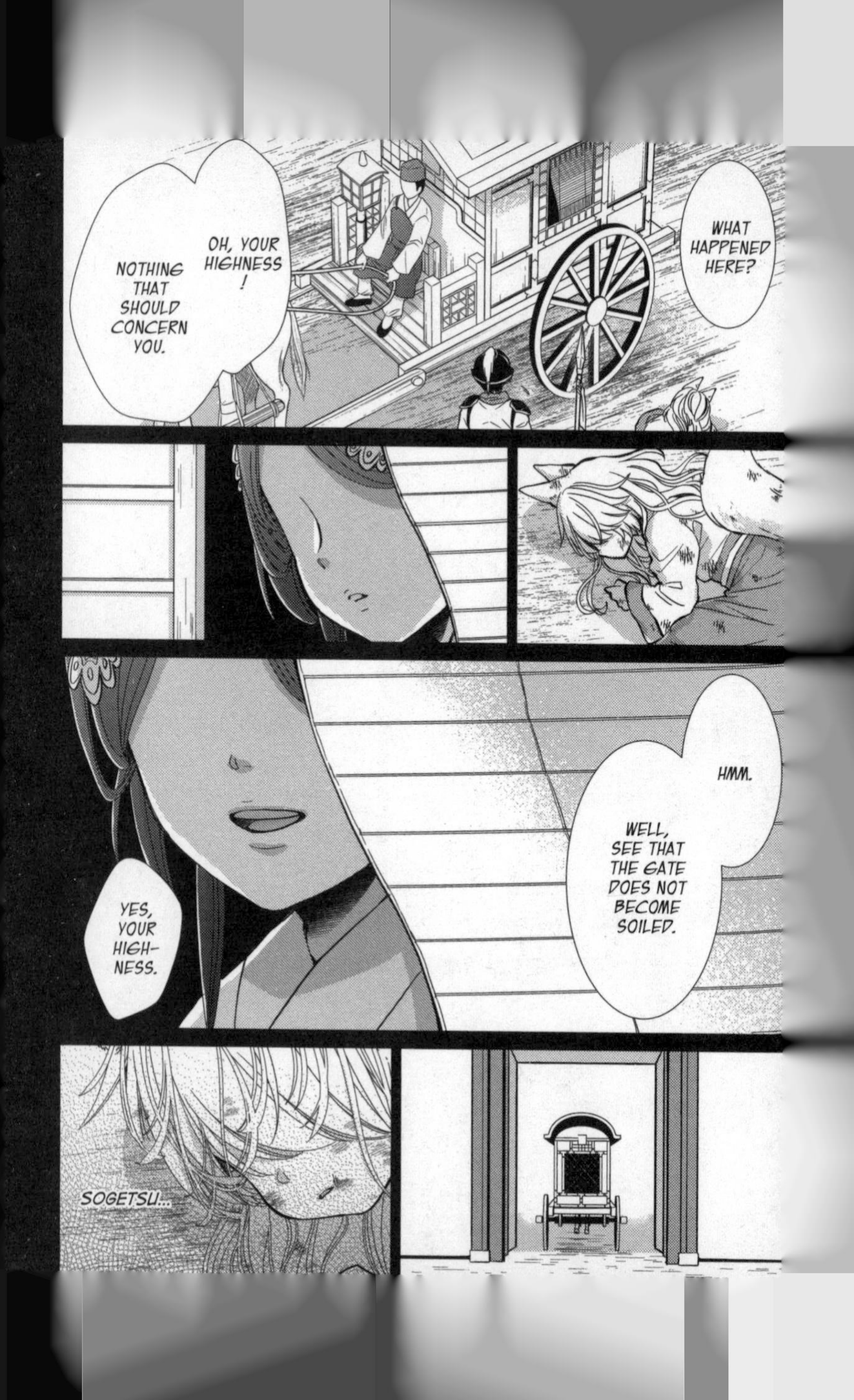
WHAT HAPPENED HERE?
OH, YOUR HIGHNESS!
NOTHING THAT SHOULD CONCERN YOU.
HMM.
WELL, SEE THAT THE GATE DOES NOT BECOME SOILED.
YES, YOUR HIGH-NESS.
SOGETSU...

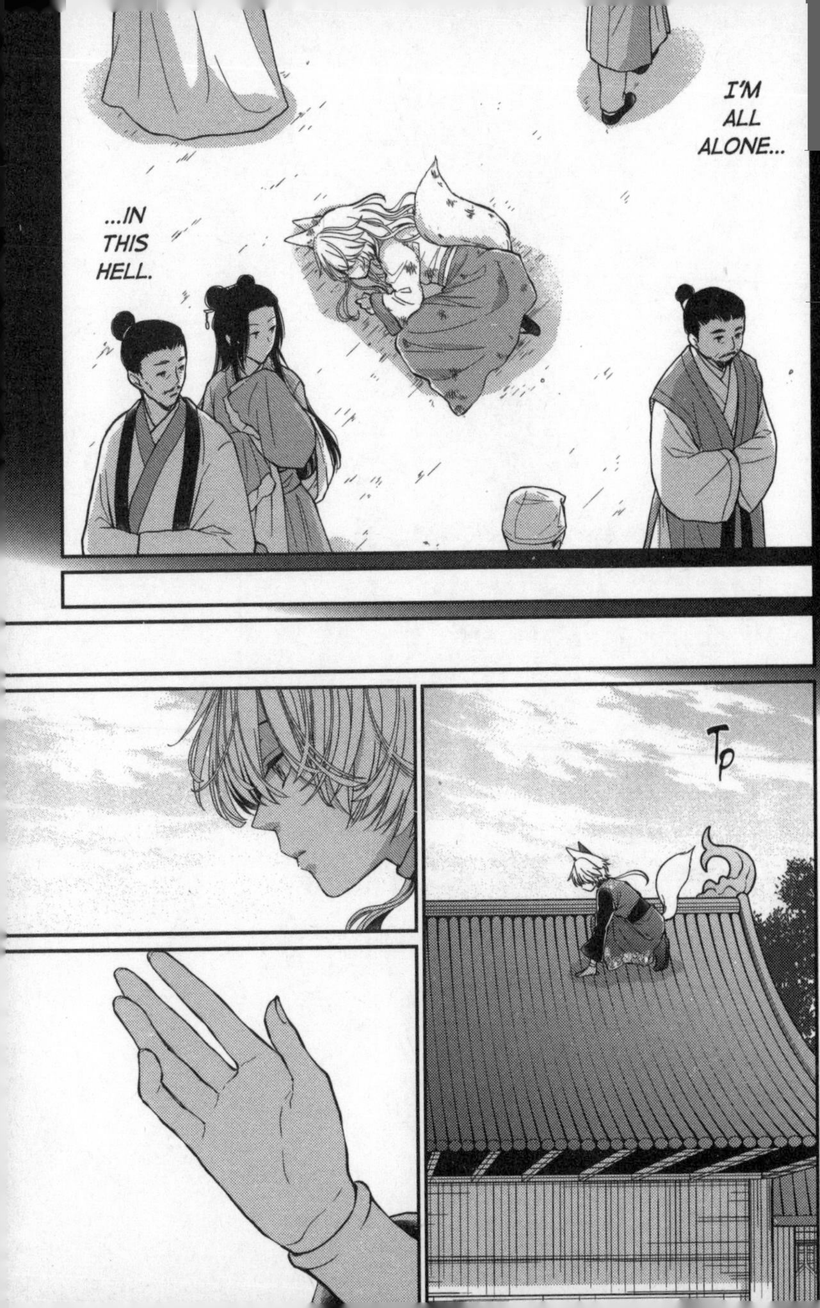
I'M ALL ALONE...
...IN THIS HELL.
Tp

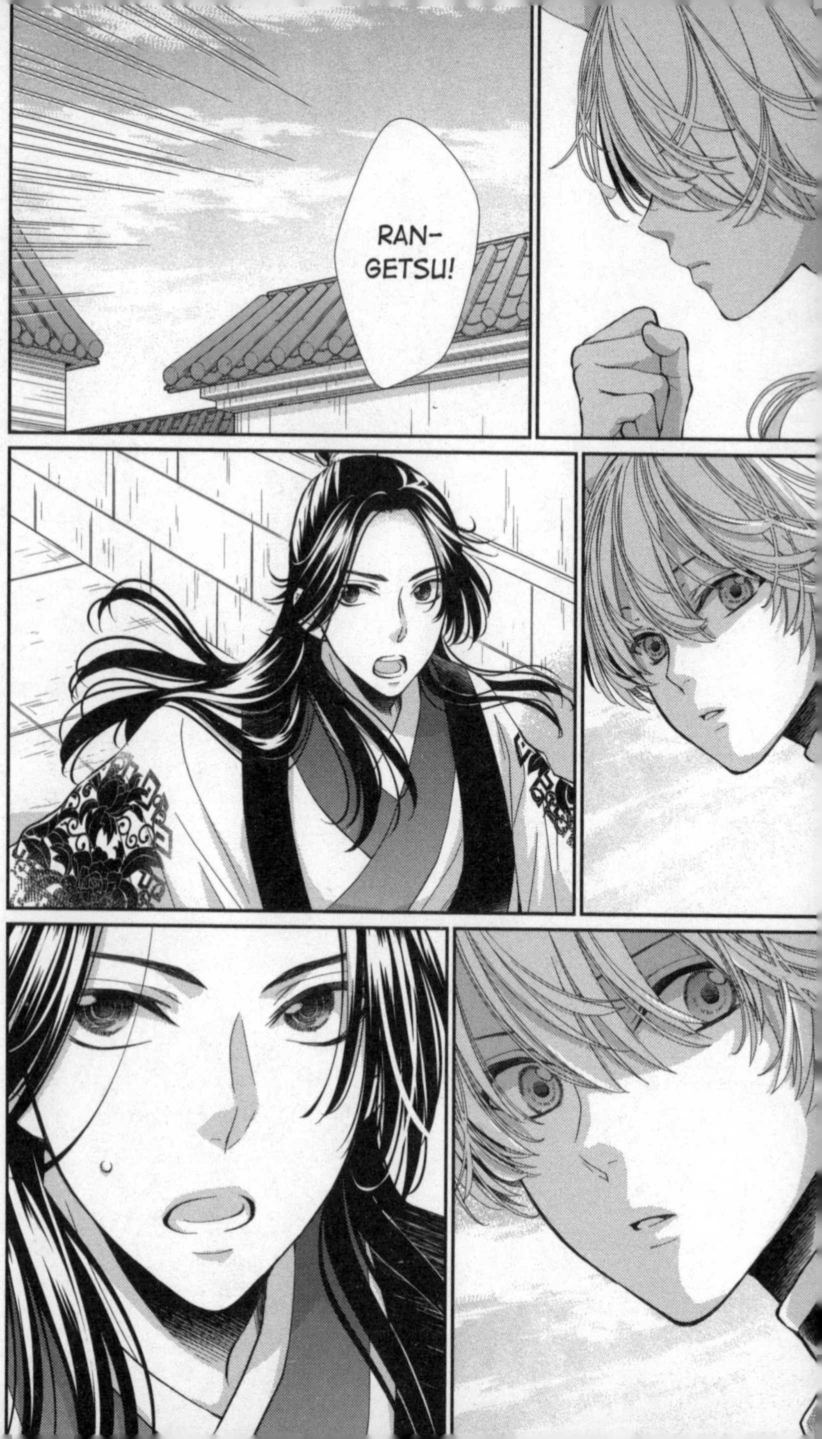
RAN-
GETSU!

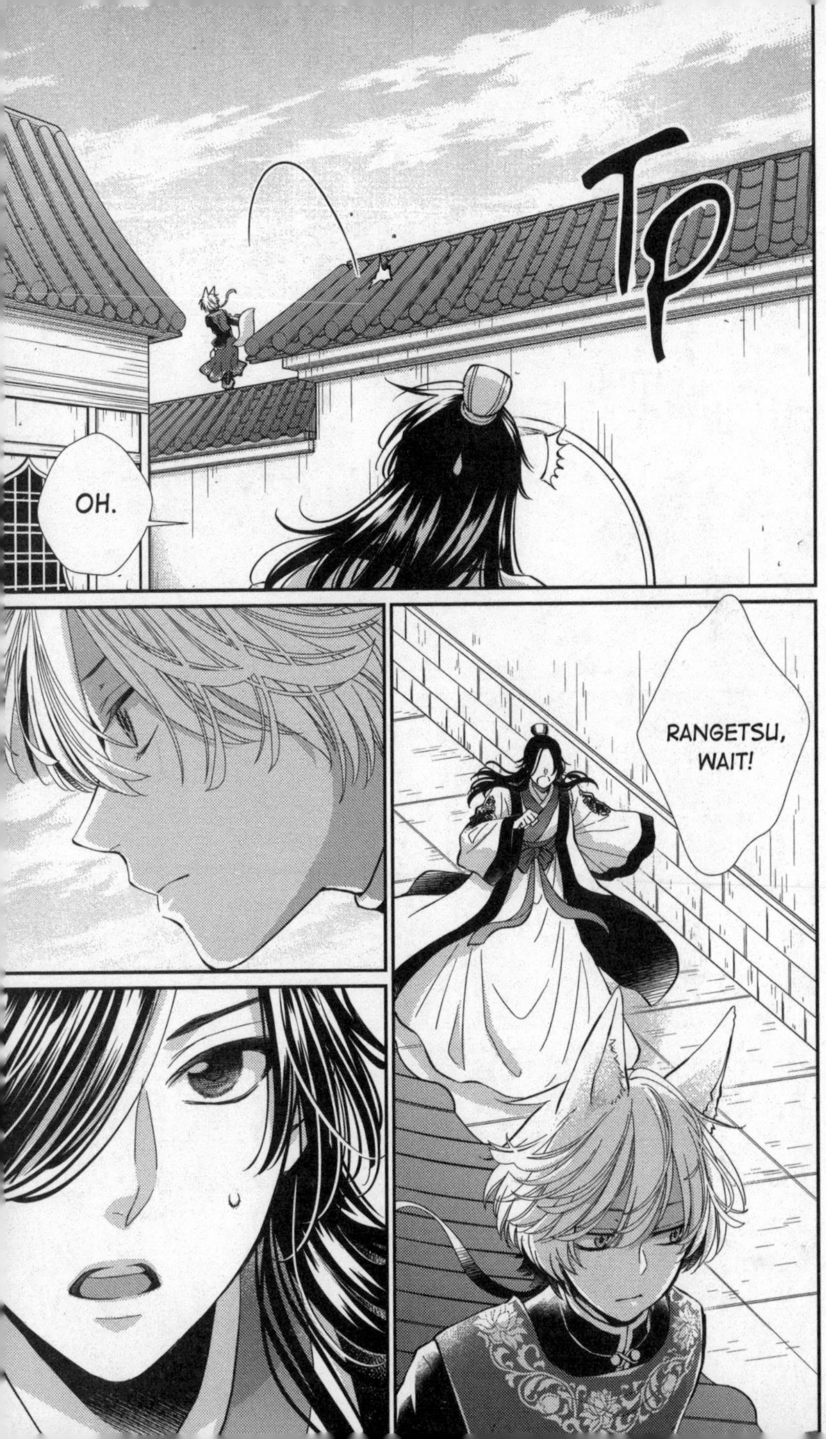
TP
OH.
RANGETSU, WAIT!

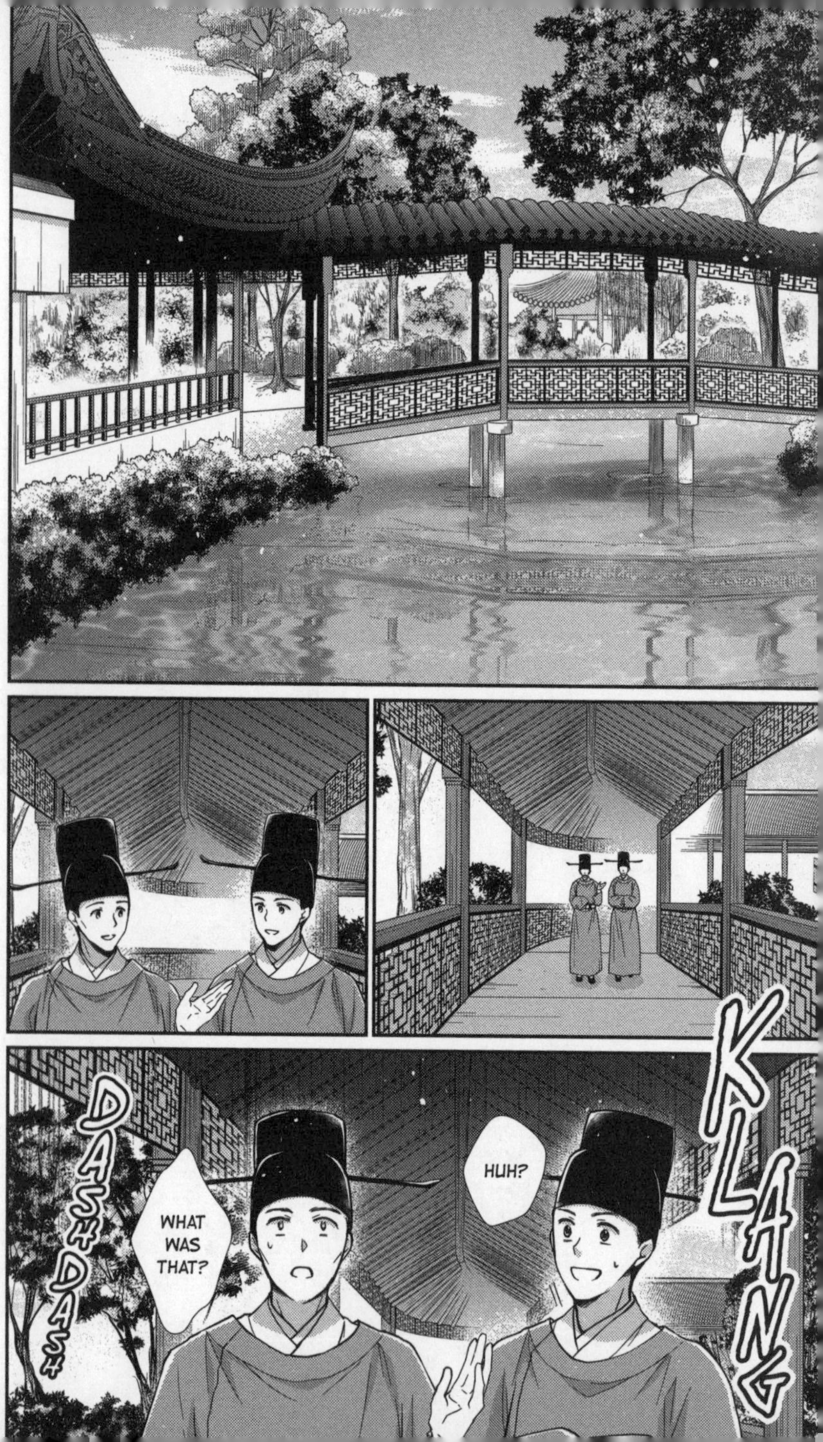
KLANG
HUH?
WHAT WAS THAT?
DASH DASH

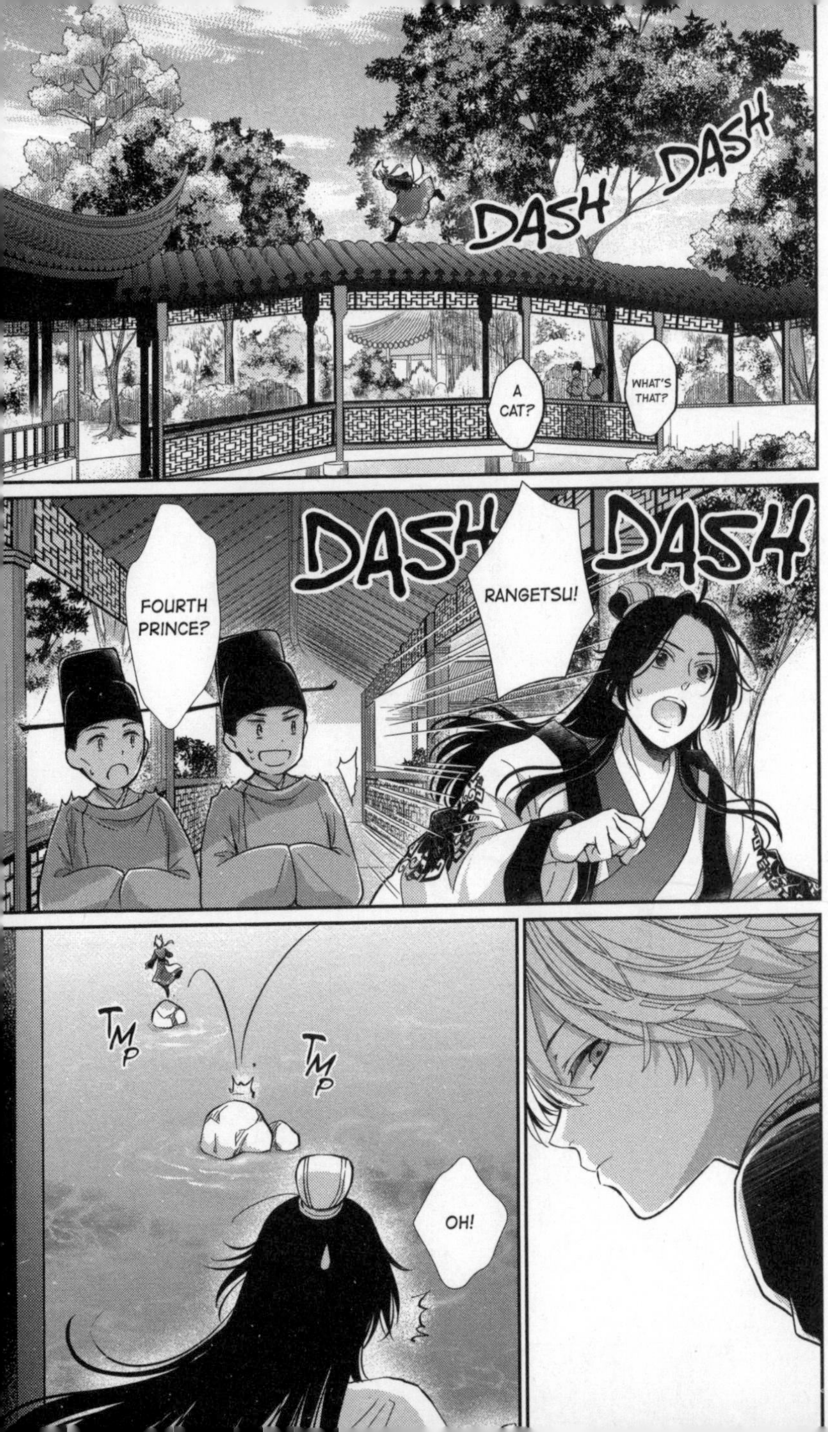
DASH
DASH
WHAT'S THAT?
A CAT?
DASH
DASH
RANGETSU!
FOURTH PRINCE?
TMP
TMP
OH!

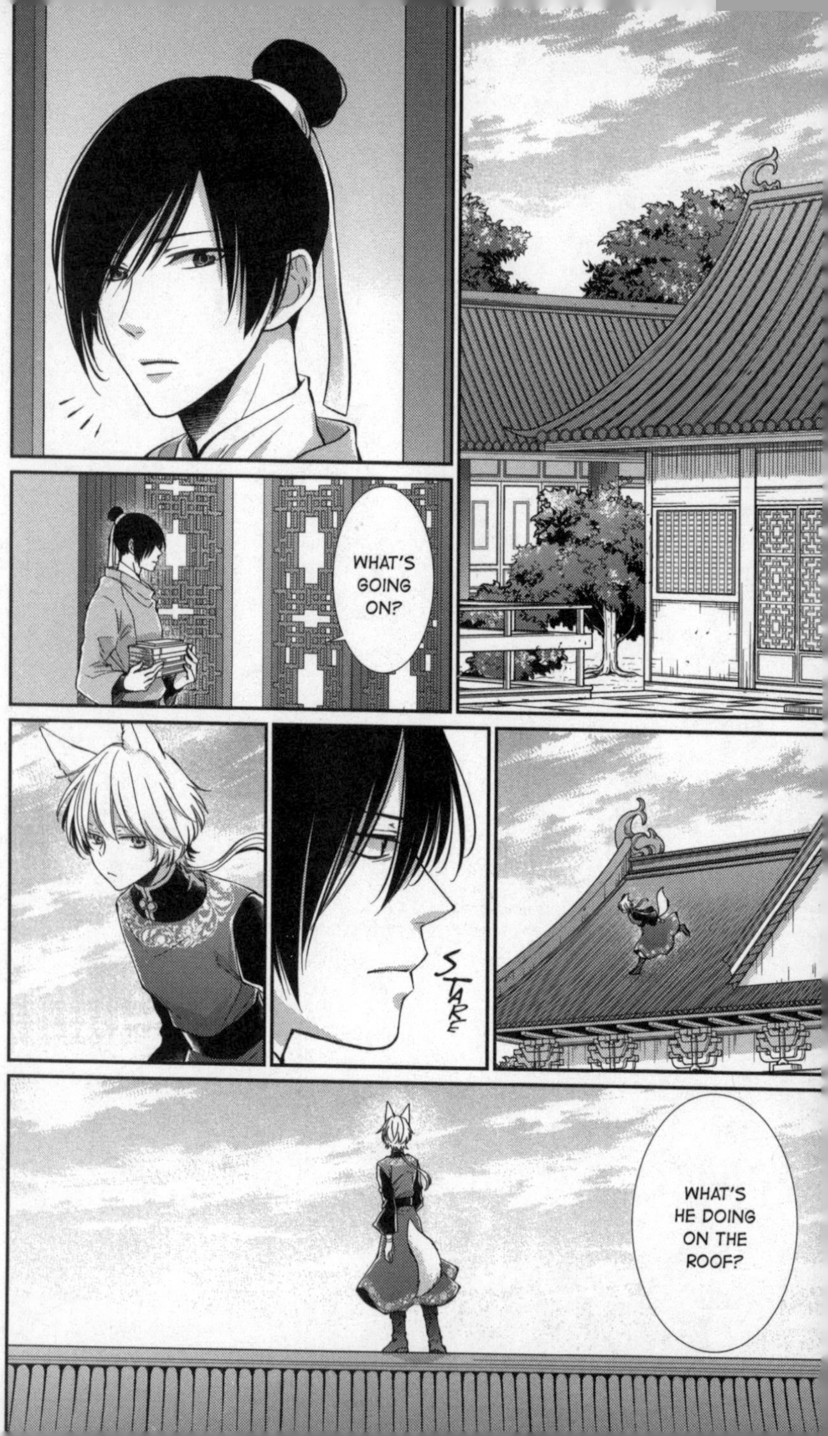
WHAT'S GOING ON?
STARE
WHAT'S HE DOING ON THE ROOF?

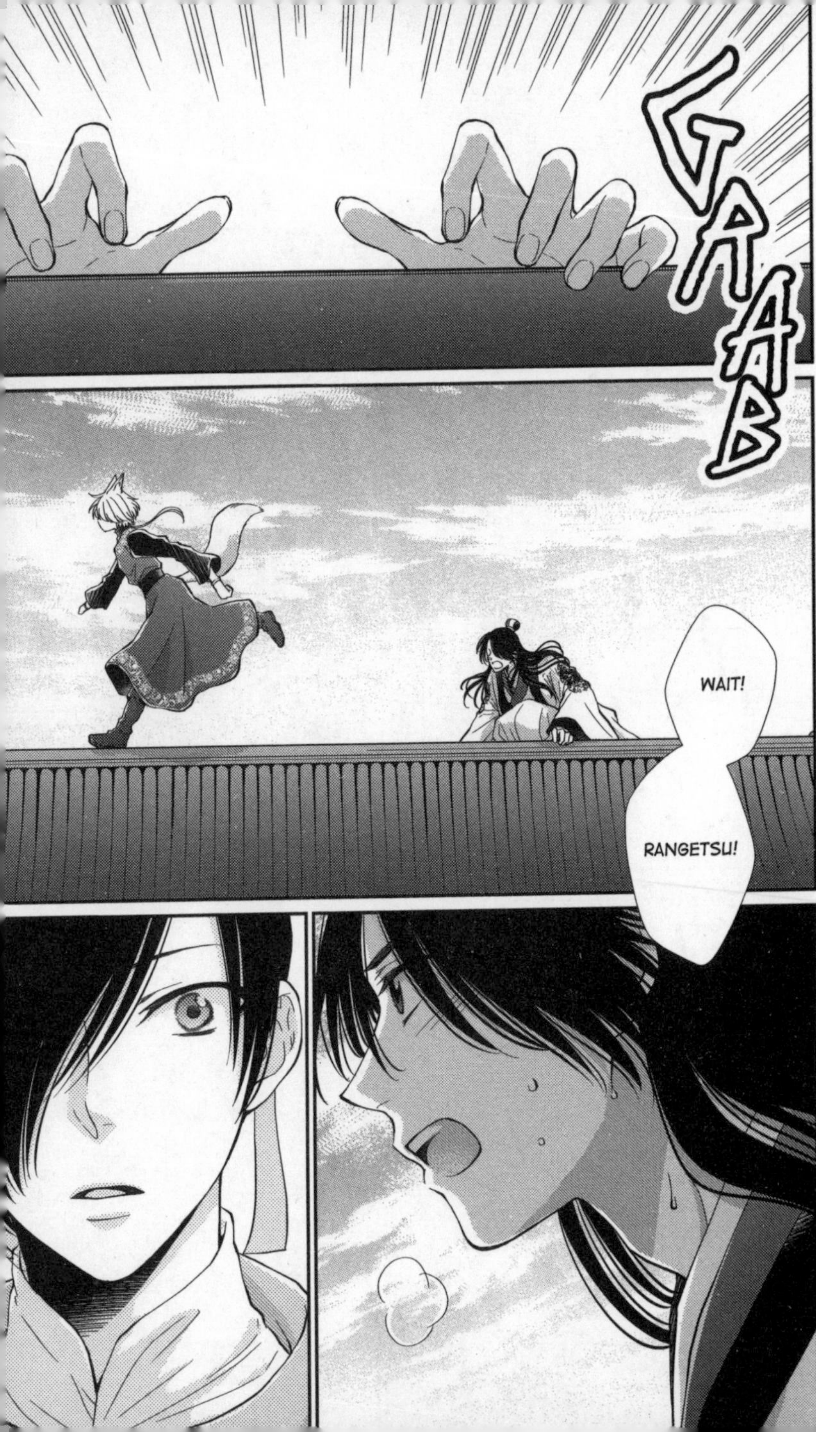
GRAAB
WAIT!
RANGETSU!

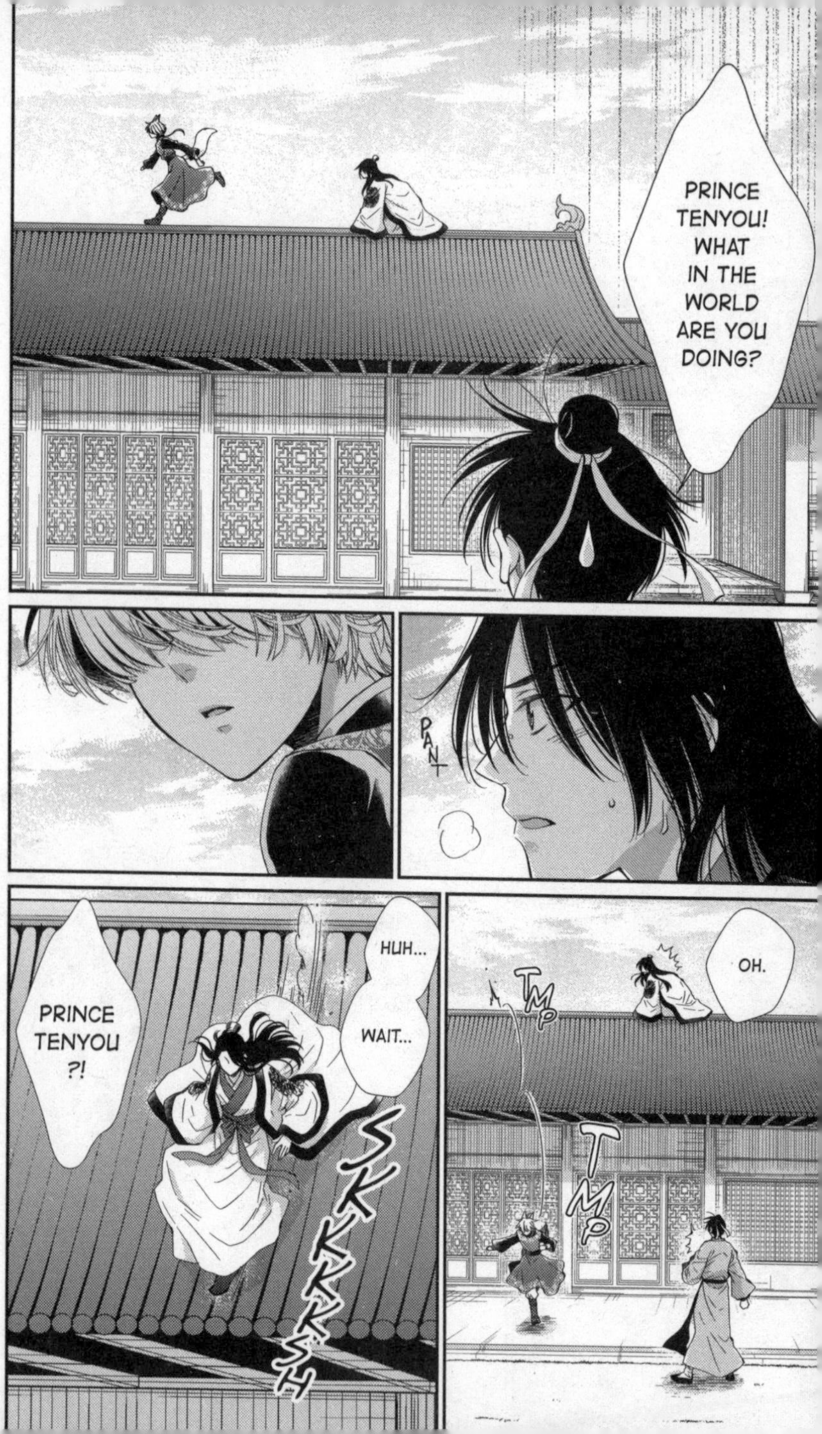
PRINCE TENYOU! WHAT IN THE WORLD ARE YOU DOING?
PANT
OH.
TMP
TMP
HUH...
WAIT...
PRINCE TENYOU ?!
SKKKKKSH

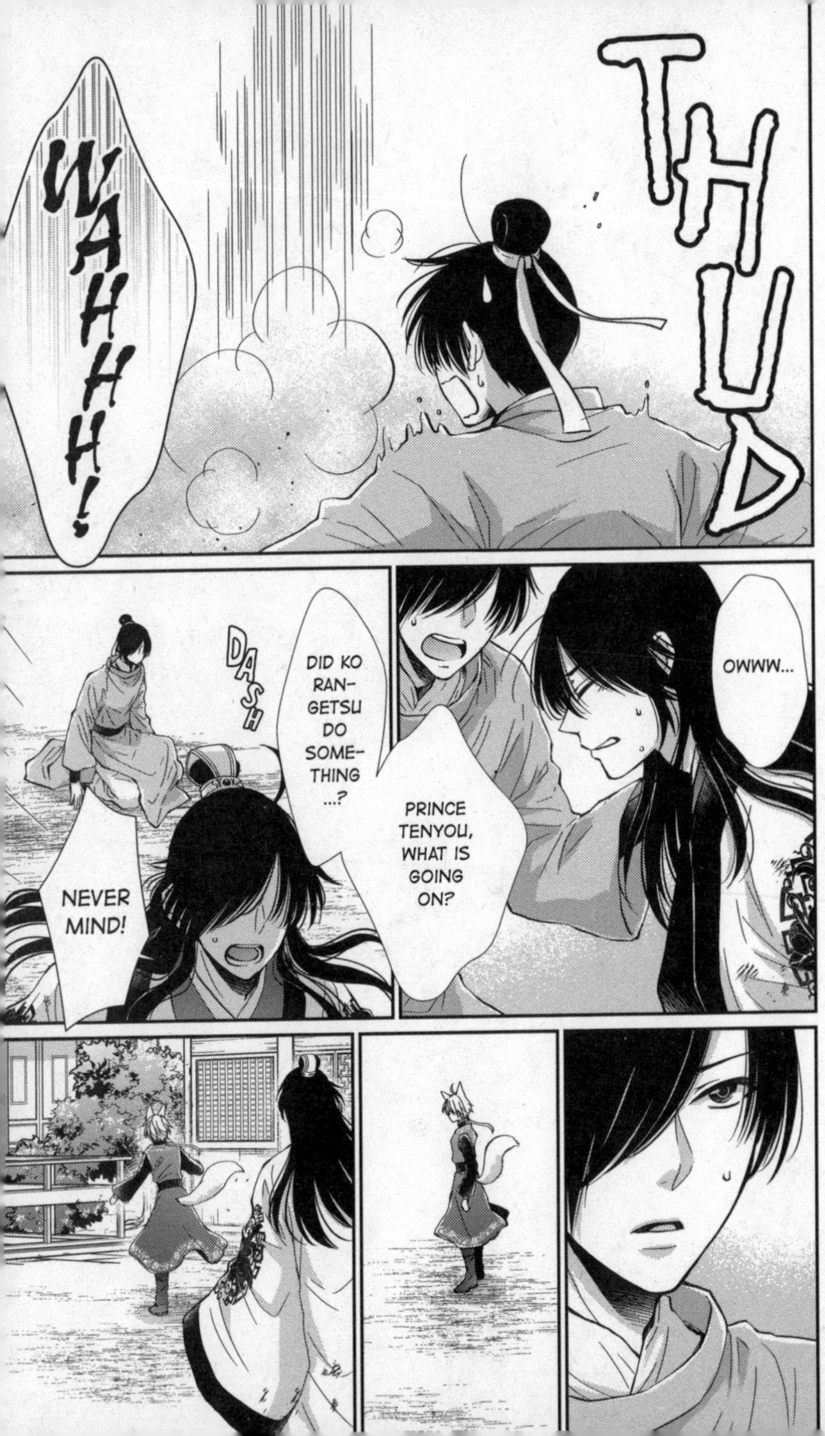
THUD
WAHHHH!
OWWW...
PRINCE TENYOU, WHAT IS GOING ON?
DASH
DID KO RANGETSU DO SOMETHING ...?
NEVER MIND!

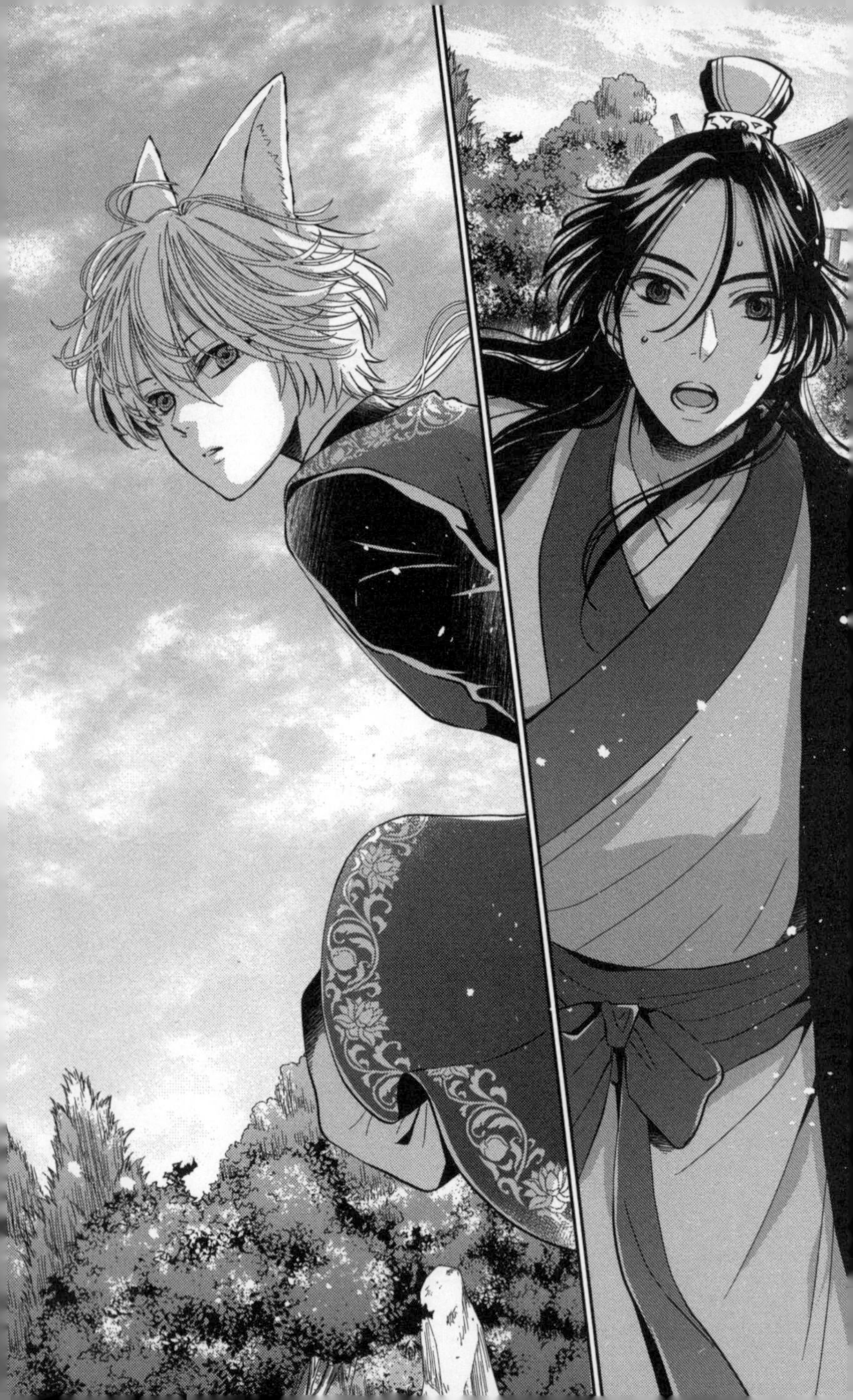

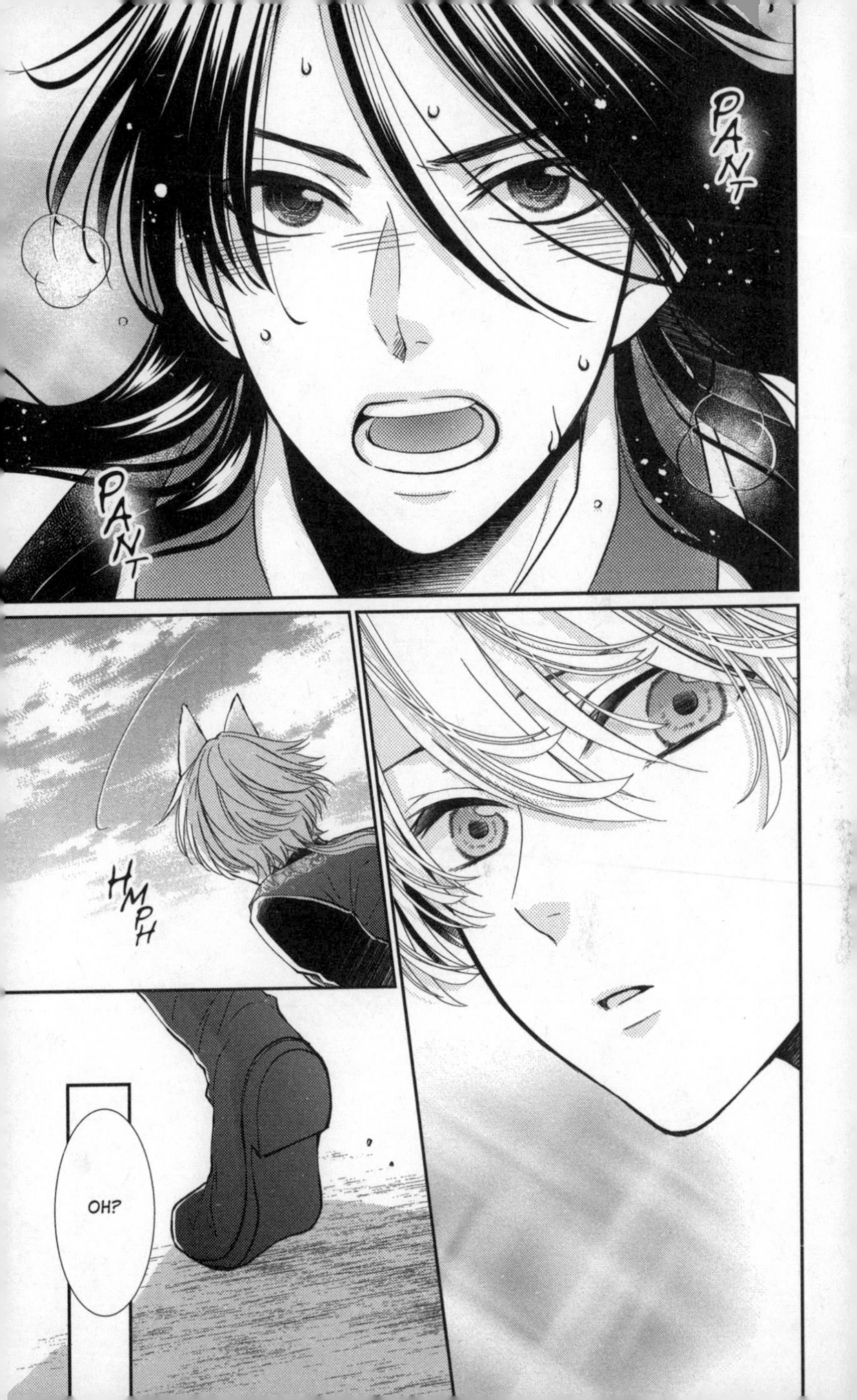
PANT
PANT
HMPH
OH?

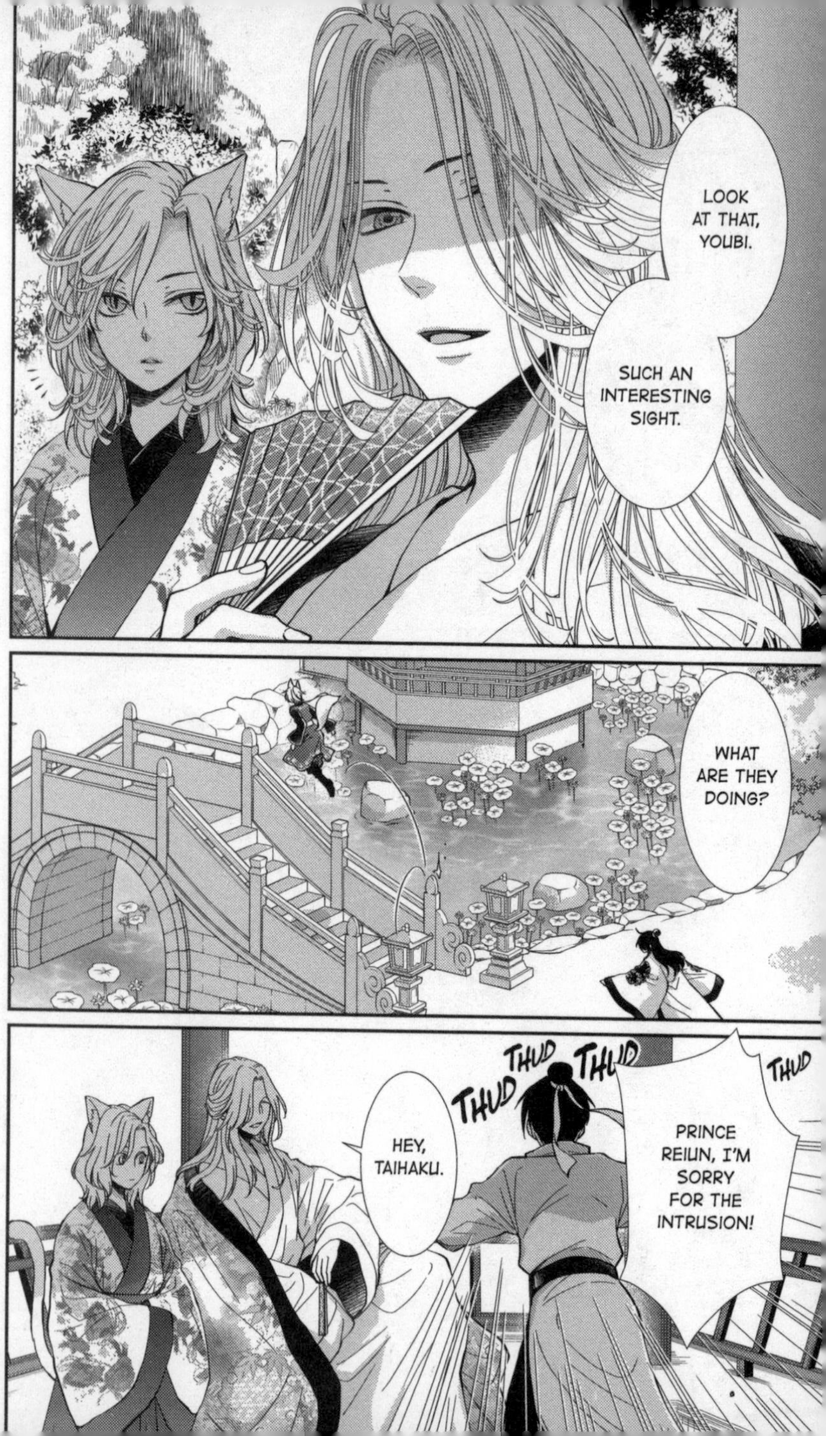
LOOK AT THAT, YOUBI.
SUCH AN INTERESTING SIGHT.
WHAT ARE THEY DOING?
THUD
THUD THUD
THUD
THUD
PRINCE REIUN, I'M SORRY FOR THE INTRUSION!
HEY, TAIHAKU.

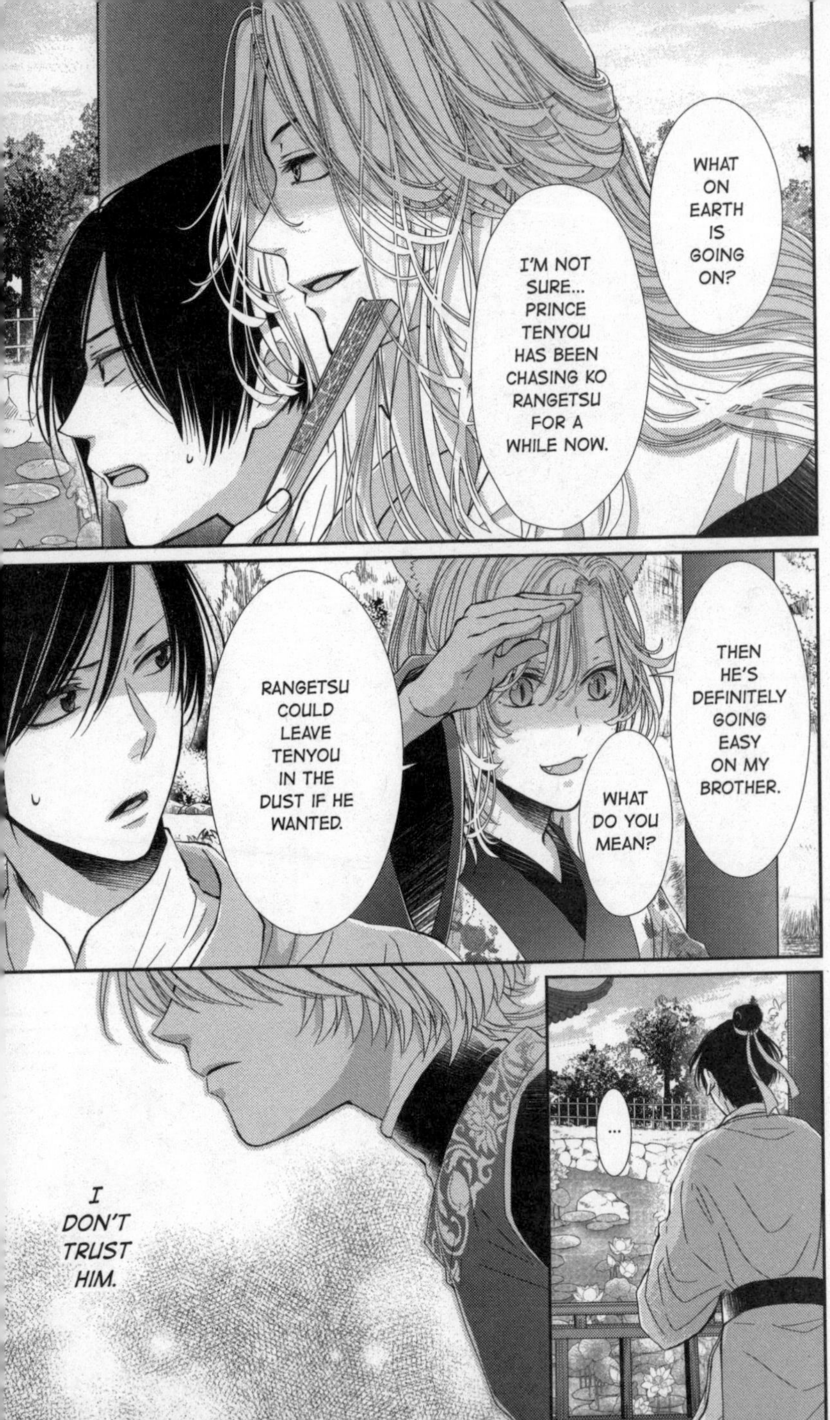
WHAT ON EARTH IS GOING ON?
I'M NOT SURE... PRINCE TENYOU HAS BEEN CHASING KO RANGETSU FOR A WHILE NOW.
THEN HE'S DEFINITELY GOING EASY ON MY BROTHER.
WHAT DO YOU MEAN?
RANGETSU COULD LEAVE TENYOU IN THE DUST IF HE WANTED.
...
I DON'T TRUST HIM.

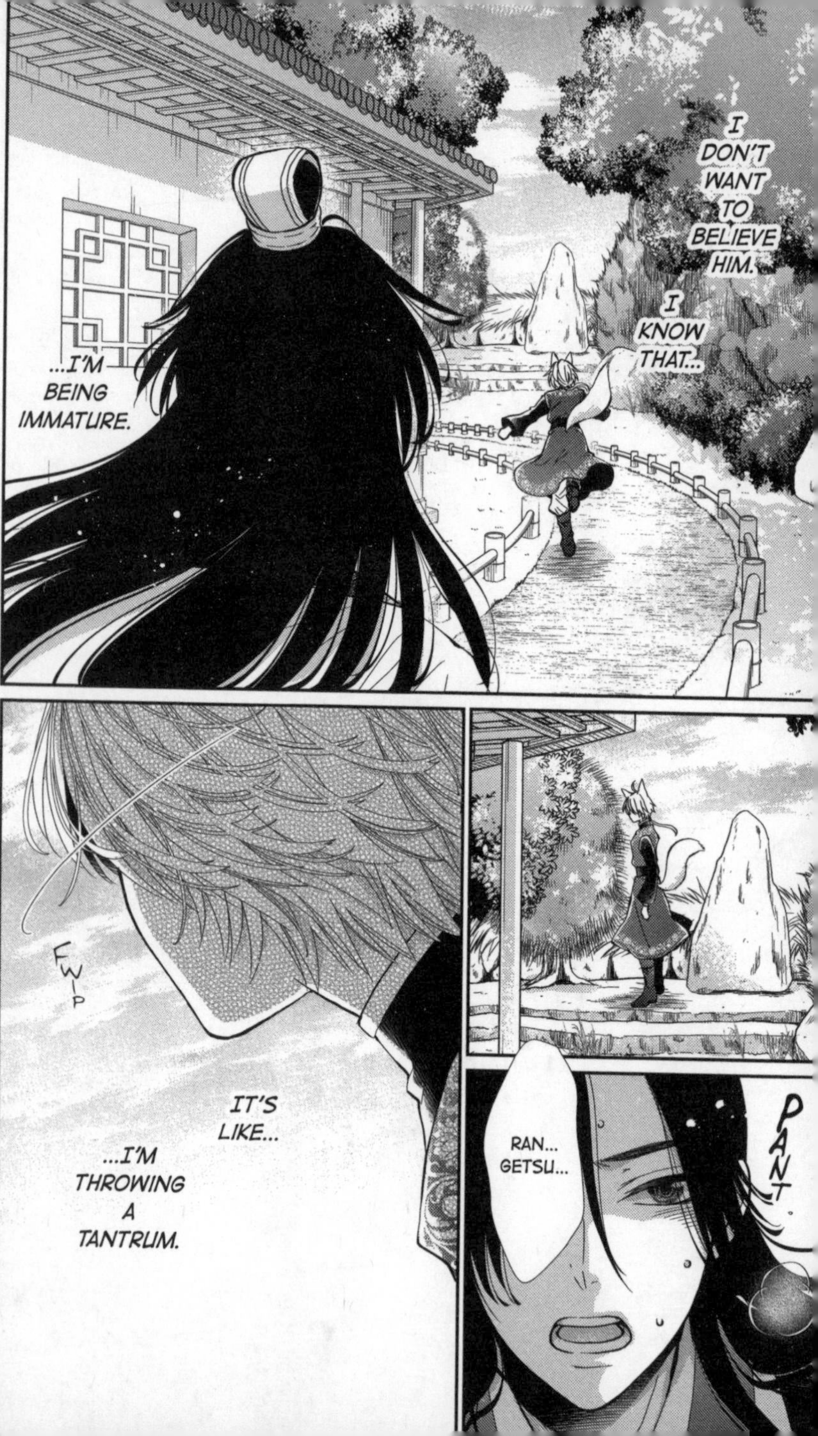
I DON'T WANT TO BELIEVE HIM.
I KNOW THAT...
...I'M BEING IMMATURE.
PANT
RAN... GETSU...
FWIP
IT'S LIKE...
...I'M THROWING A TANTRUM.

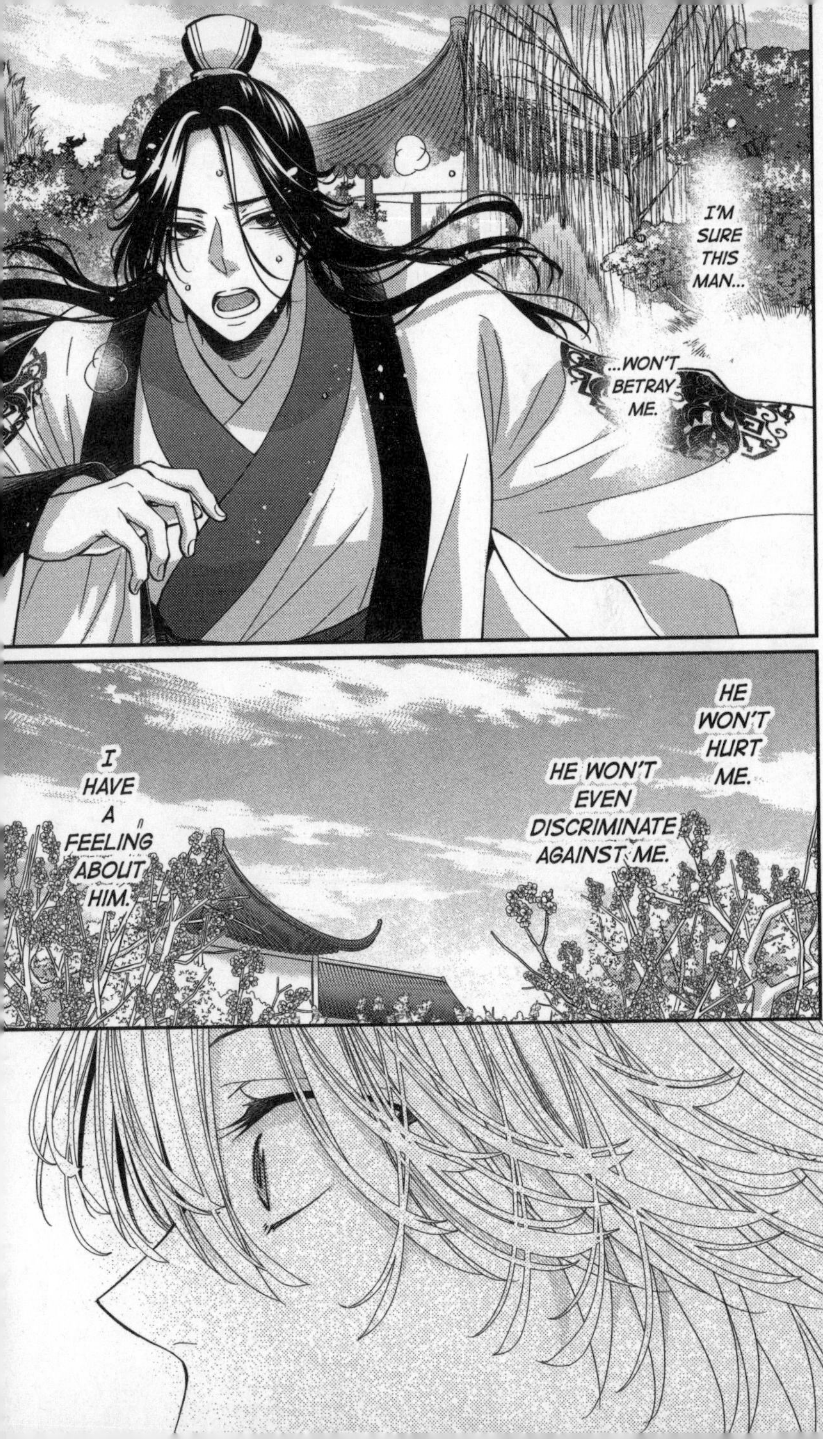
I'M SURE THIS MAN...
...WON'T BETRAY ME.
HE WON'T HURT ME.
HE WON'T EVEN DISCRIMINATE AGAINST ME.
I HAVE A FEELING ABOUT HIM.

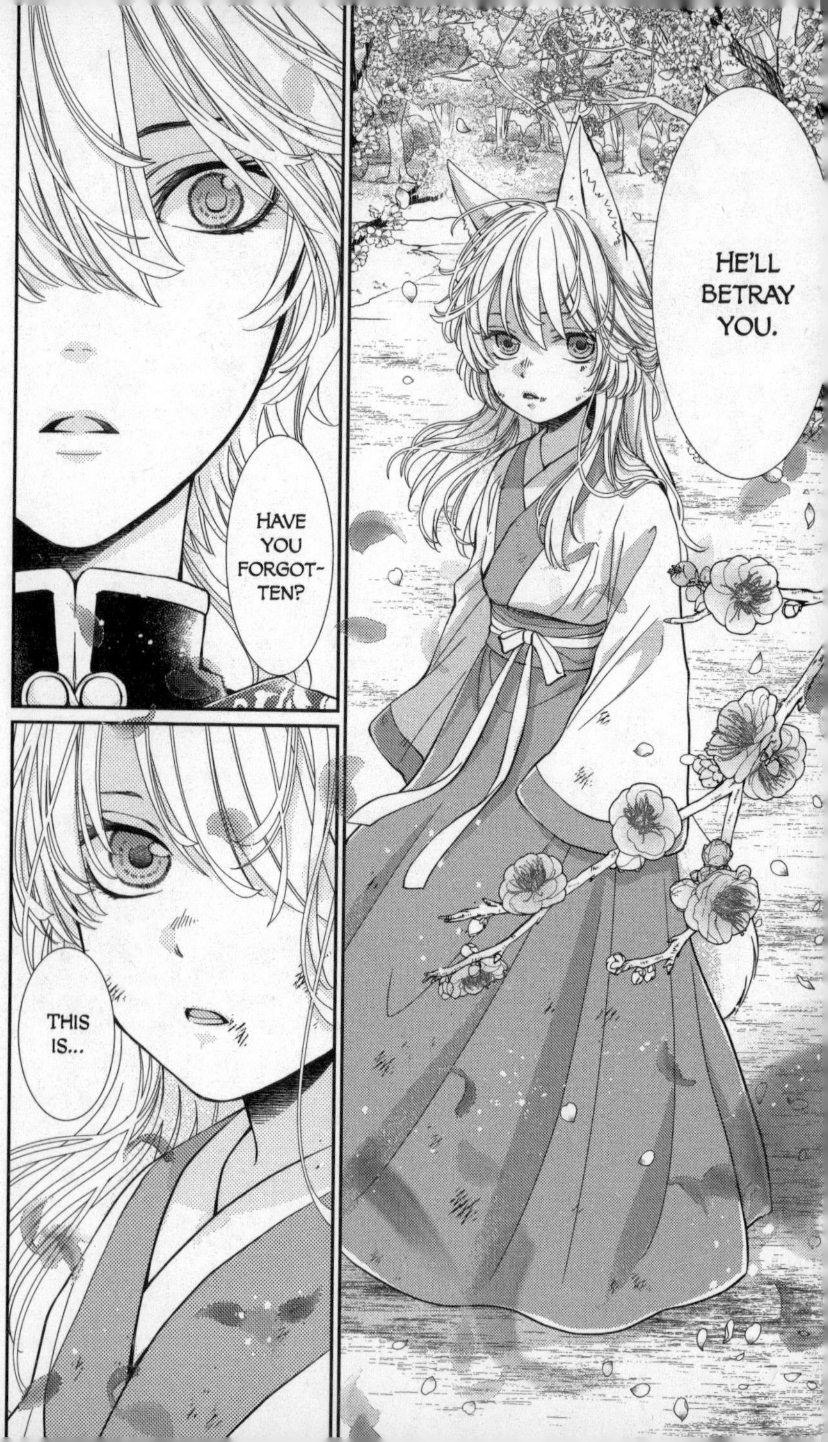
HE'LL BETRAY YOU.
HAVE YOU FORGOT-TEN?
THIS IS...

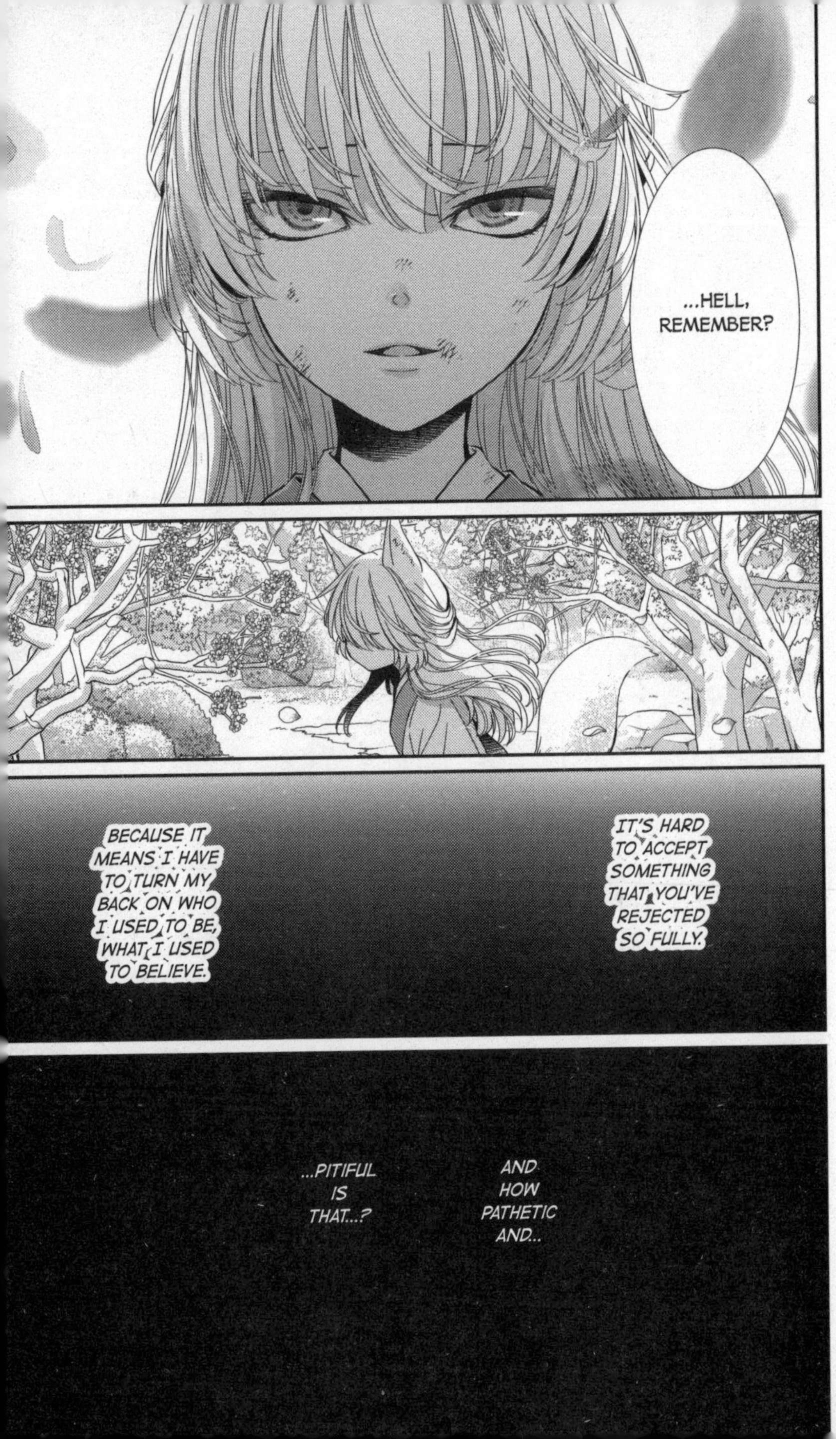
...HELL, REMEMBER?
IT'S HARD TO ACCEPT SOMETHING THAT YOU'VE REJECTED SO FULLY.
BECAUSE IT MEANS I HAVE TO TURN MY BACK ON WHO I USED TO BE, WHAT I USED TO BELIEVE.
AND HOW PATHETIC AND...
...PITIFUL IS THAT...?

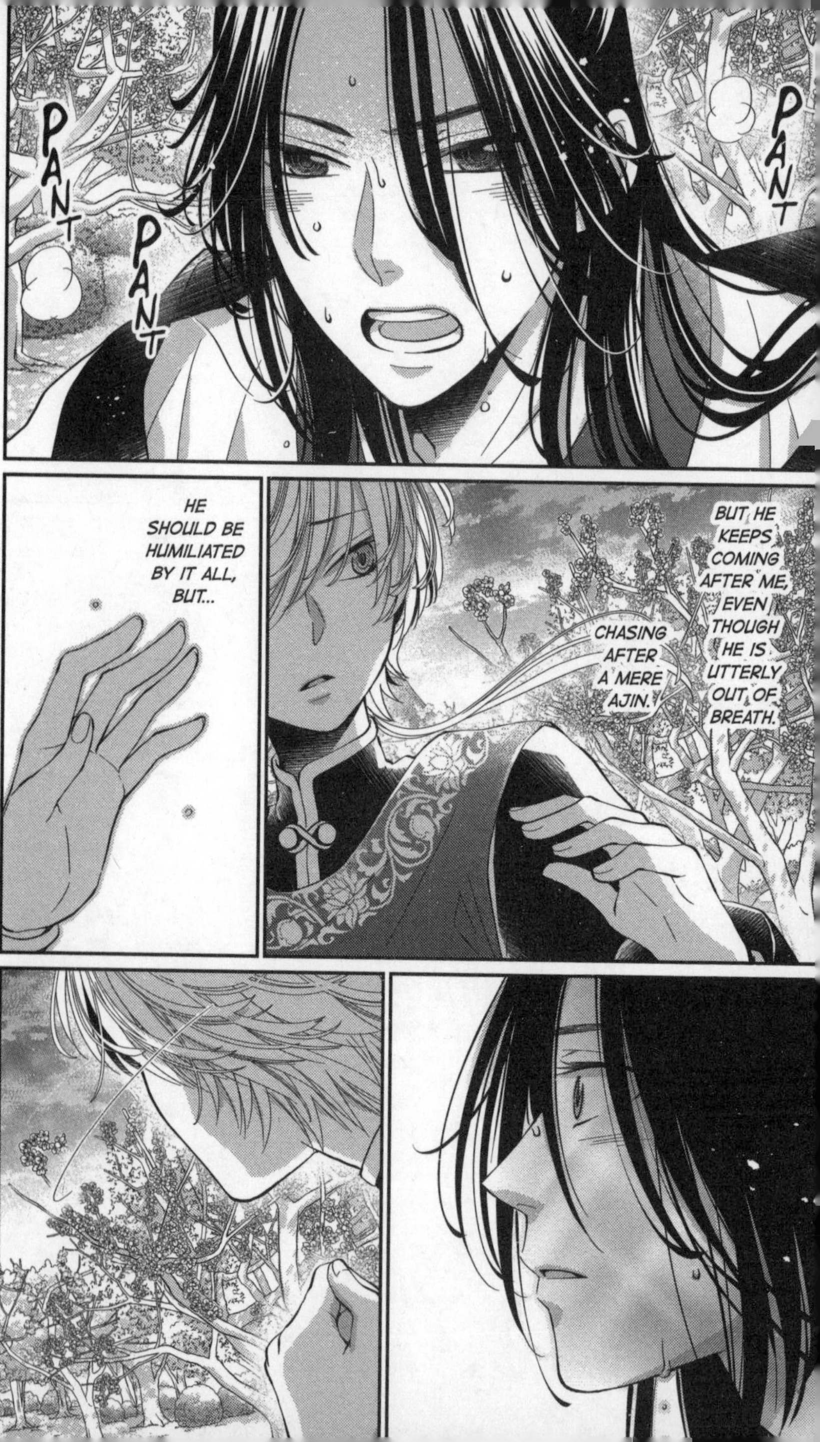
PANT
PANT
PANT PANT
BUT HE KEEPS COMING AFTER ME, EVEN THOUGH HE IS UTTERLY OUT OF BREATH.
CHASING AFTER A MERE AJIN.
HE SHOULD BE HUMILIATED BY IT ALL, BUT...

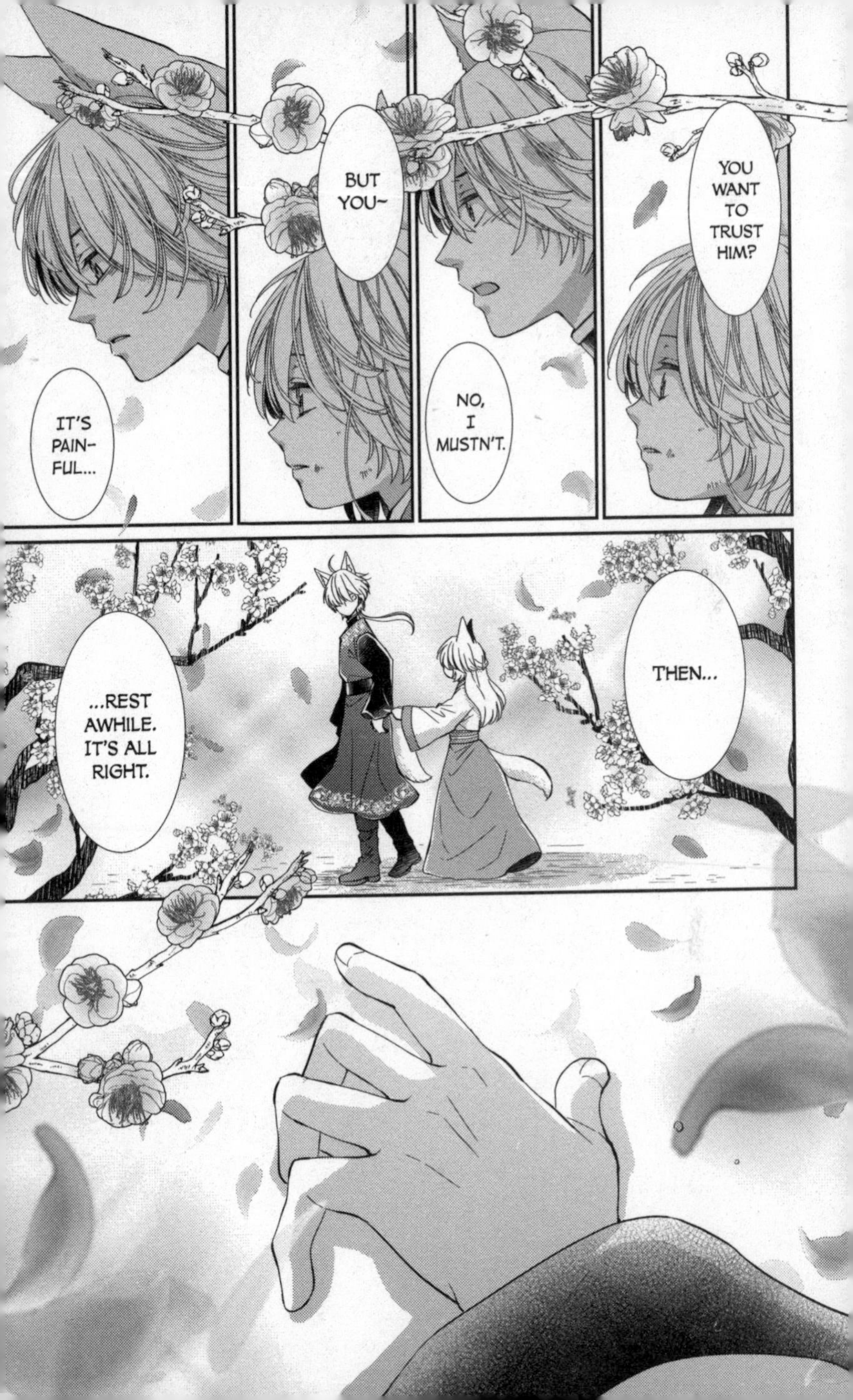
YOU WANT TO TRUST HIM?
NO, I MUSTN'T.
BUT YOU~
IT'S PAIN-FUL...
THEN...
...REST AWHILE. IT'S ALL RIGHT.

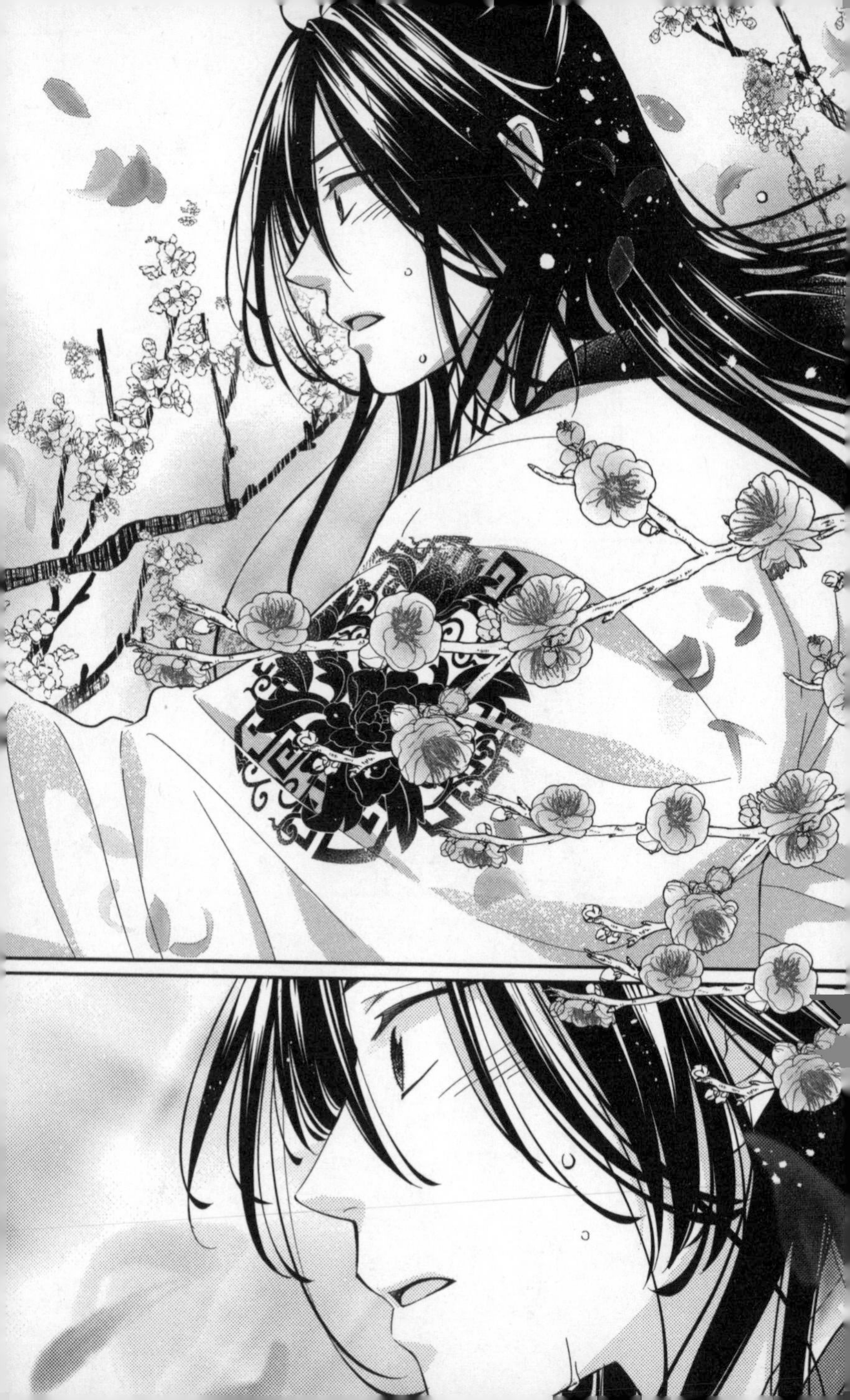

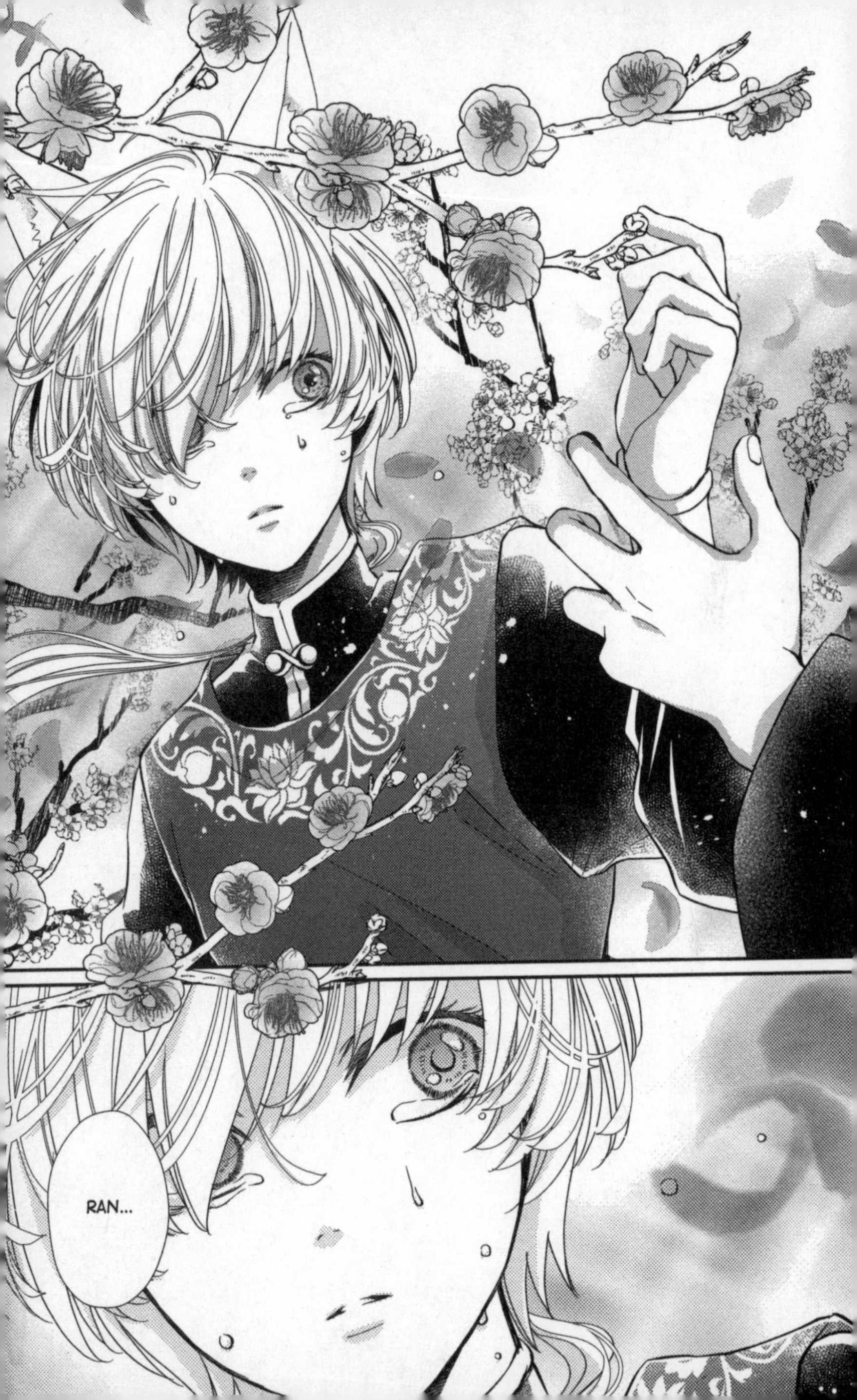
RAN...

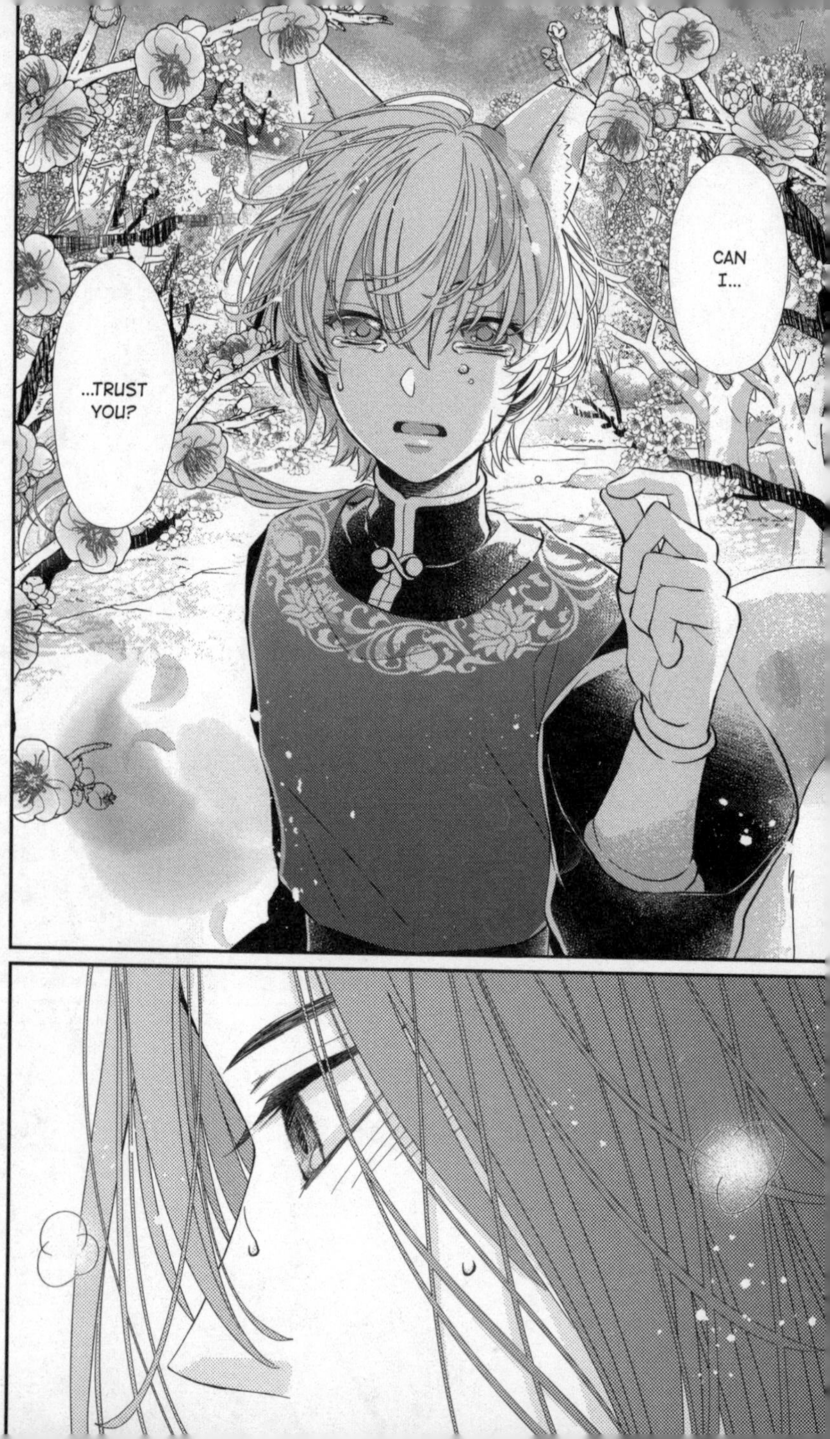
CAN I...
...TRUST YOU?

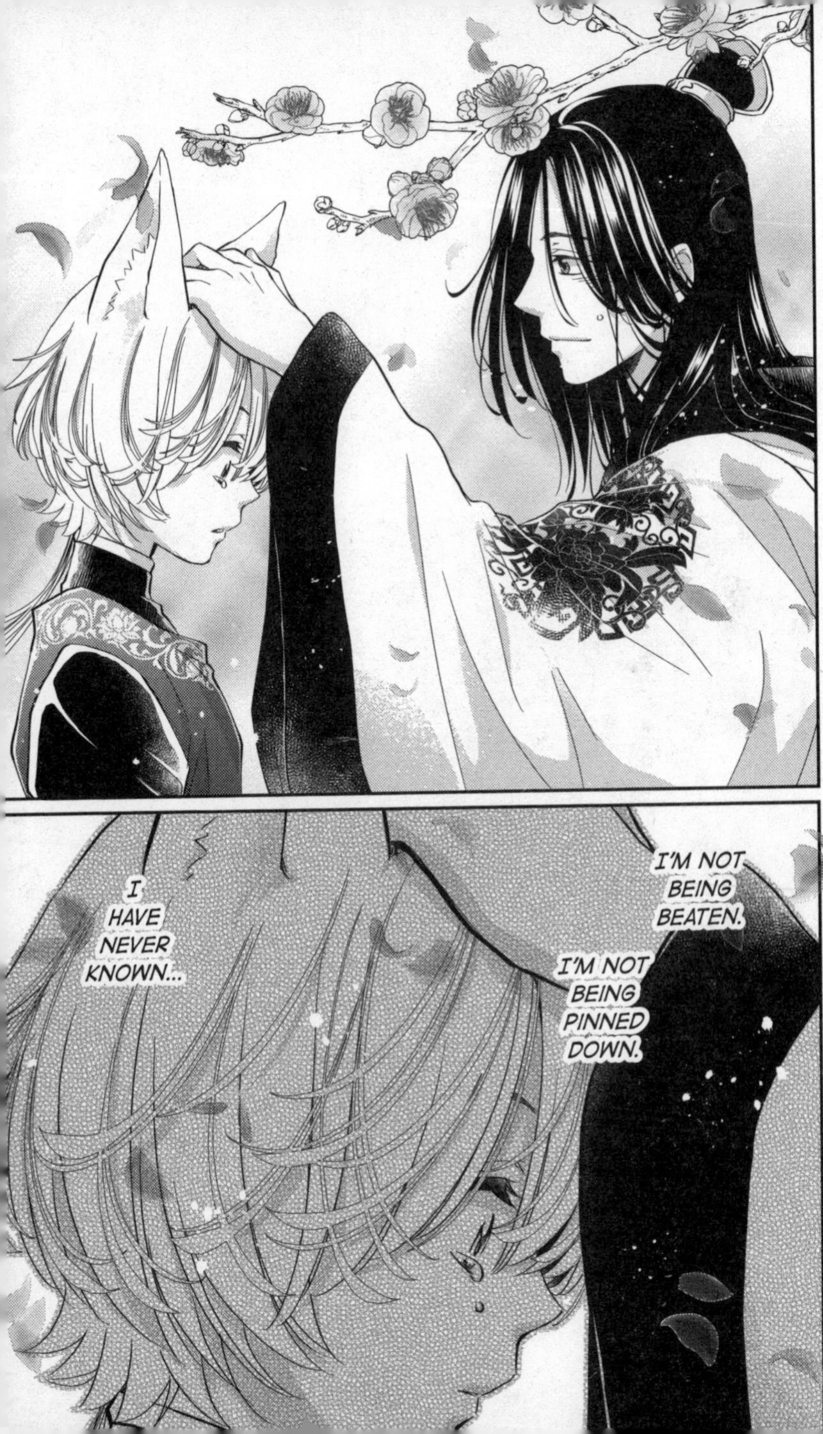
I'M NOT BEING BEATEN.
I'M NOT BEING PINNED DOWN.
I HAVE NEVER KNOWN...

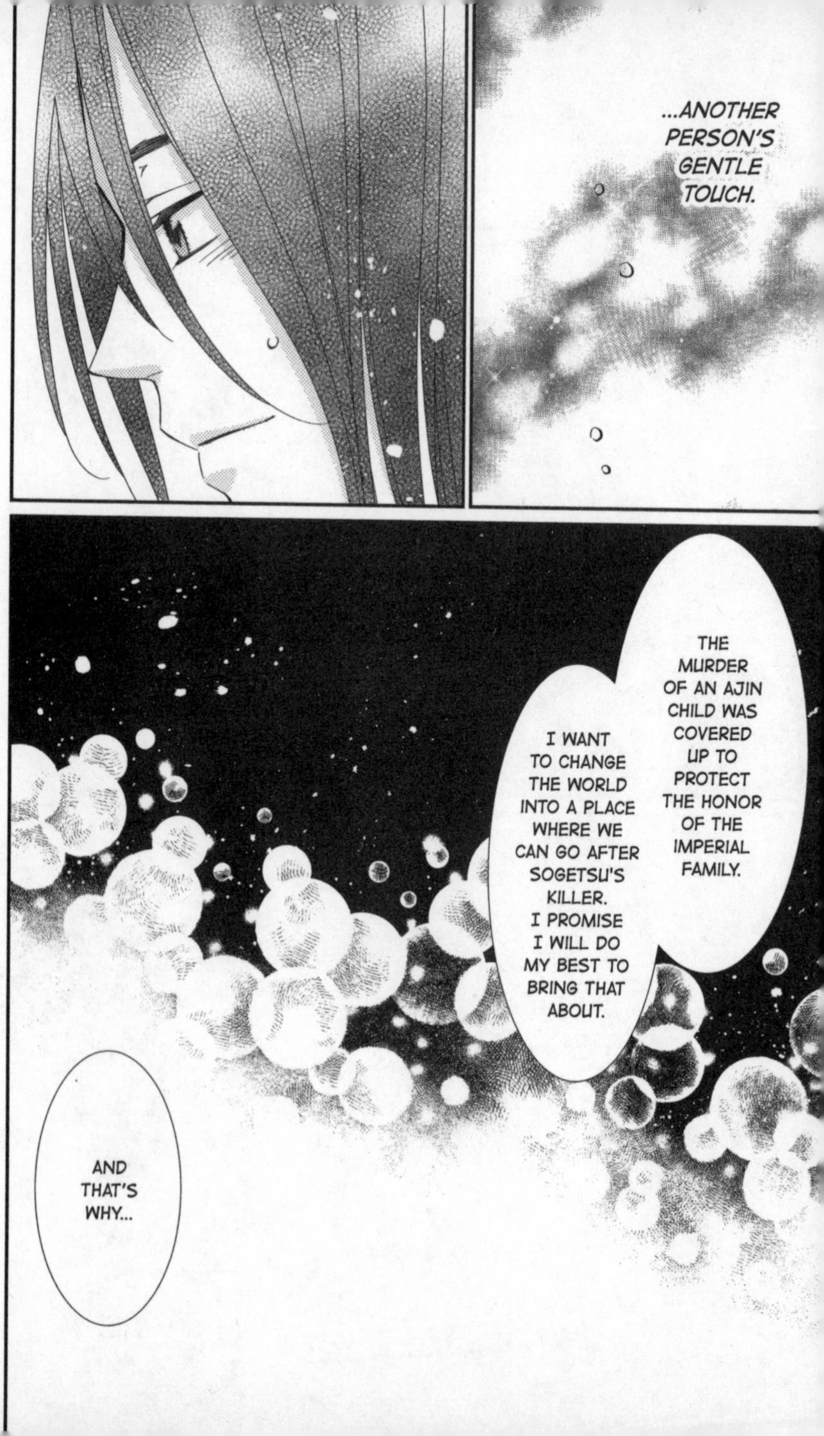
...ANOTHER PERSON'S GENTLE TOUCH.
THE MURDER OF AN AJIN CHILD WAS COVERED UP TO PROTECT THE HONOR OF THE IMPERIAL FAMILY.
I WANT TO CHANGE THE WORLD INTO A PLACE WHERE WE CAN GO AFTER SOGETSU'S KILLER. I PROMISE I WILL DO MY BEST TO BRING THAT ABOUT.
AND THAT'S WHY...

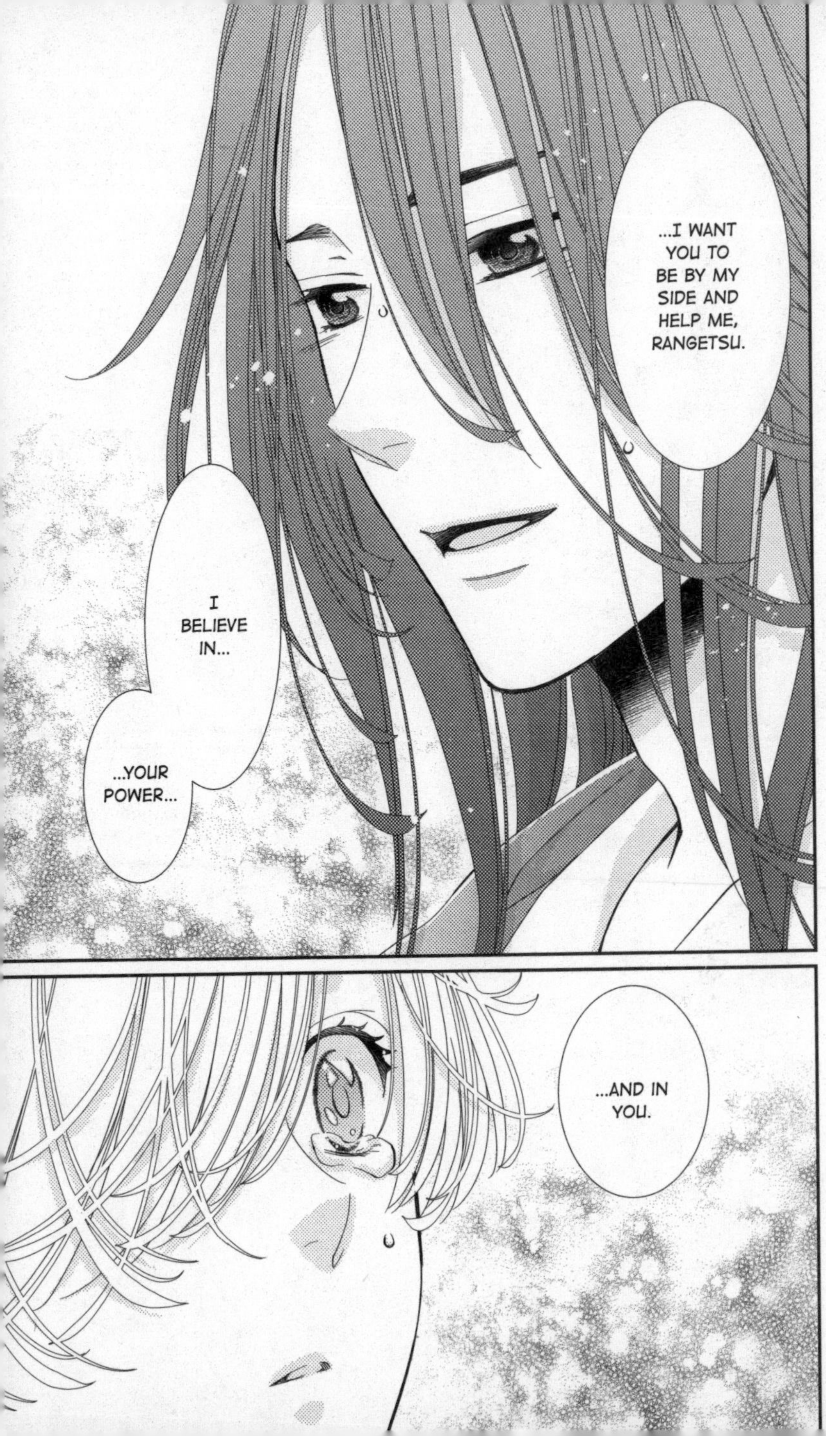
...I WANT YOU TO BE BY MY SIDE AND HELP ME, RANGETSU.
I BELIEVE IN...
...YOUR POWER...
...AND IN YOU.

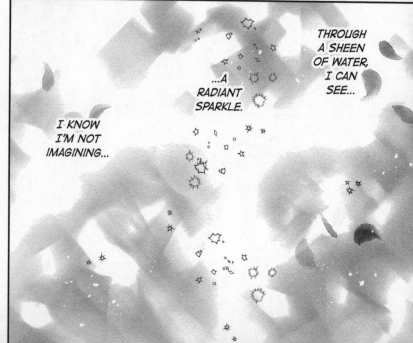

THROUGH A SHEEN OF WATER, I CAN SEE...

...A RADIANT SPARKLE.

I KNOW I'M NOT IMAGINING...

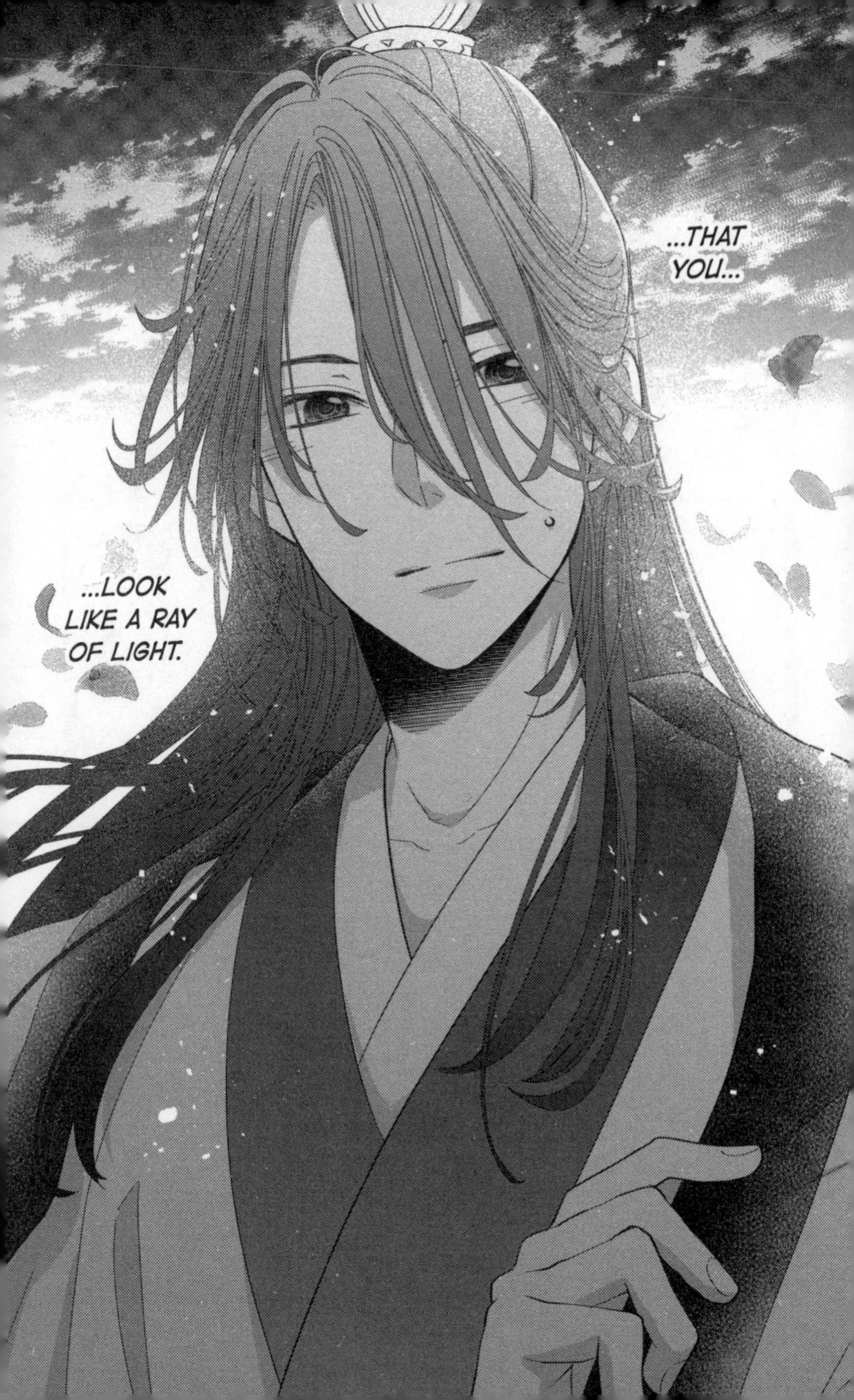
...THAT YOU...
...LOOK LIKE A RAY OF LIGHT.

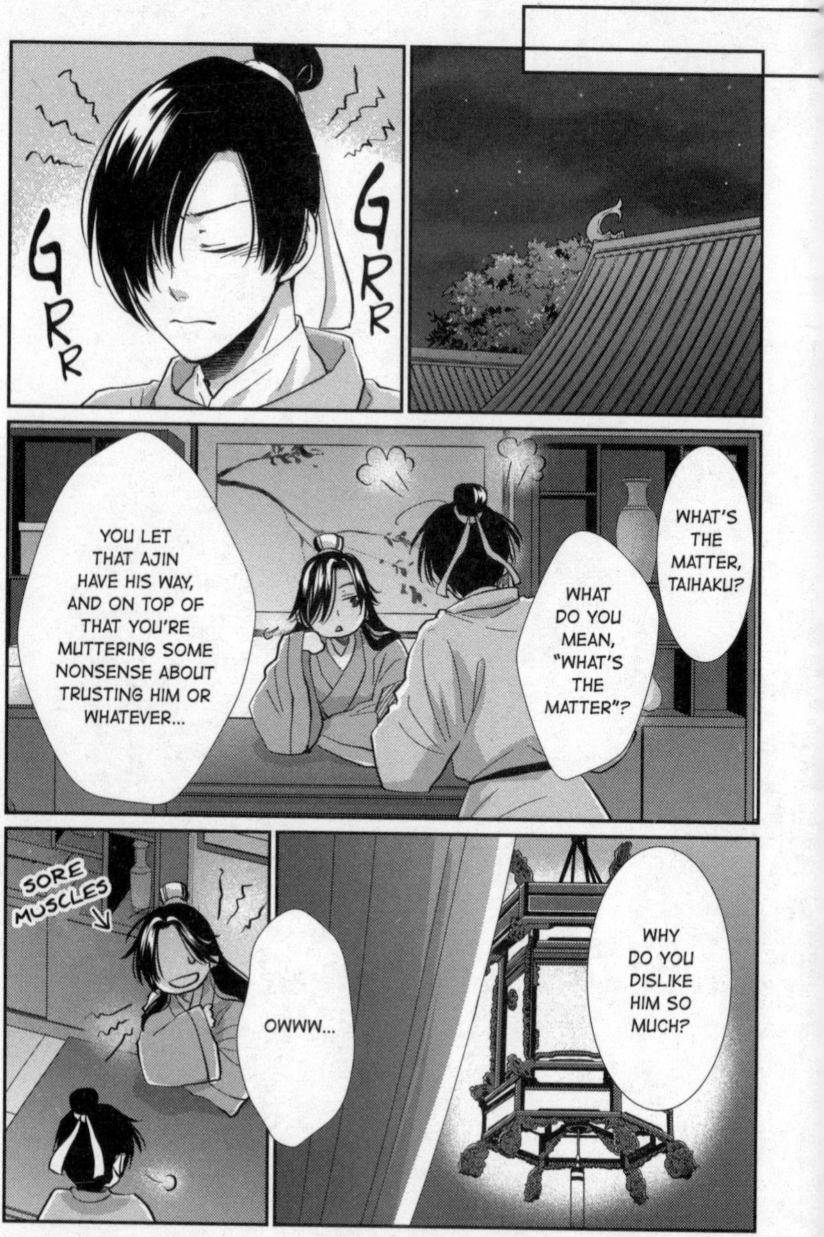
GRR
GRR
WHAT'S THE MATTER, TAIHAKU?
WHAT DO YOU MEAN, "WHAT'S THE MATTER"?
YOU LET THAT AJIN HAVE HIS WAY, AND ON TOP OF THAT YOU'RE MUTTERING SOME NONSENSE ABOUT TRUSTING HIM OR WHATEVER...
WHY DO YOU DISLIKE HIM SO MUCH?
SORE MUSCLES
OWWW...

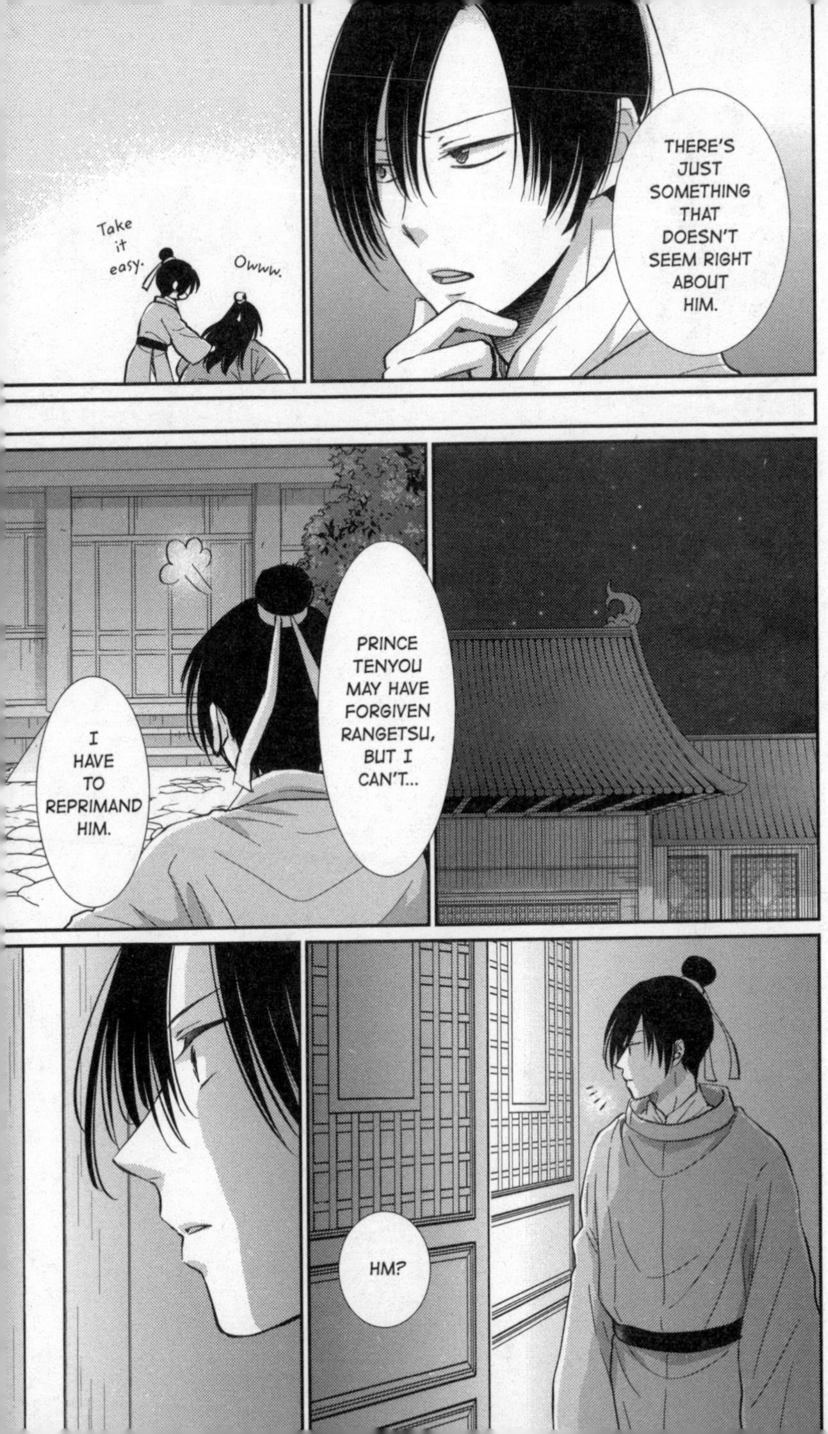
THERE'S JUST SOMETHING THAT DOESN'T SEEM RIGHT ABOUT HIM.
Take it easy.
Owww.
PRINCE TENYOU MAY HAVE FORGIVEN RANGETSU, BUT I CAN'T...
I HAVE TO REPRIMAND HIM.
HM?

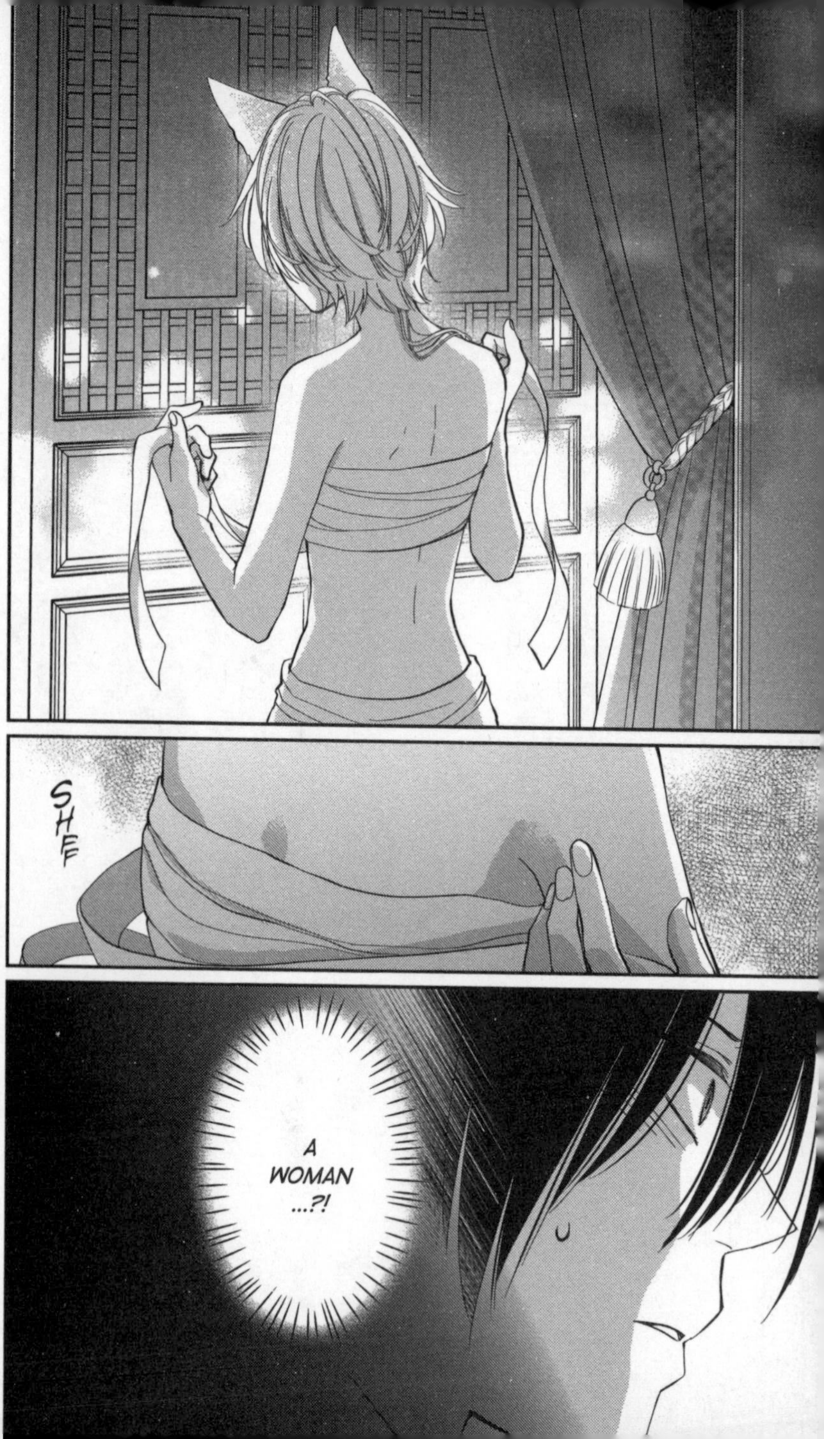
SHFF
A WOMAN ...?!

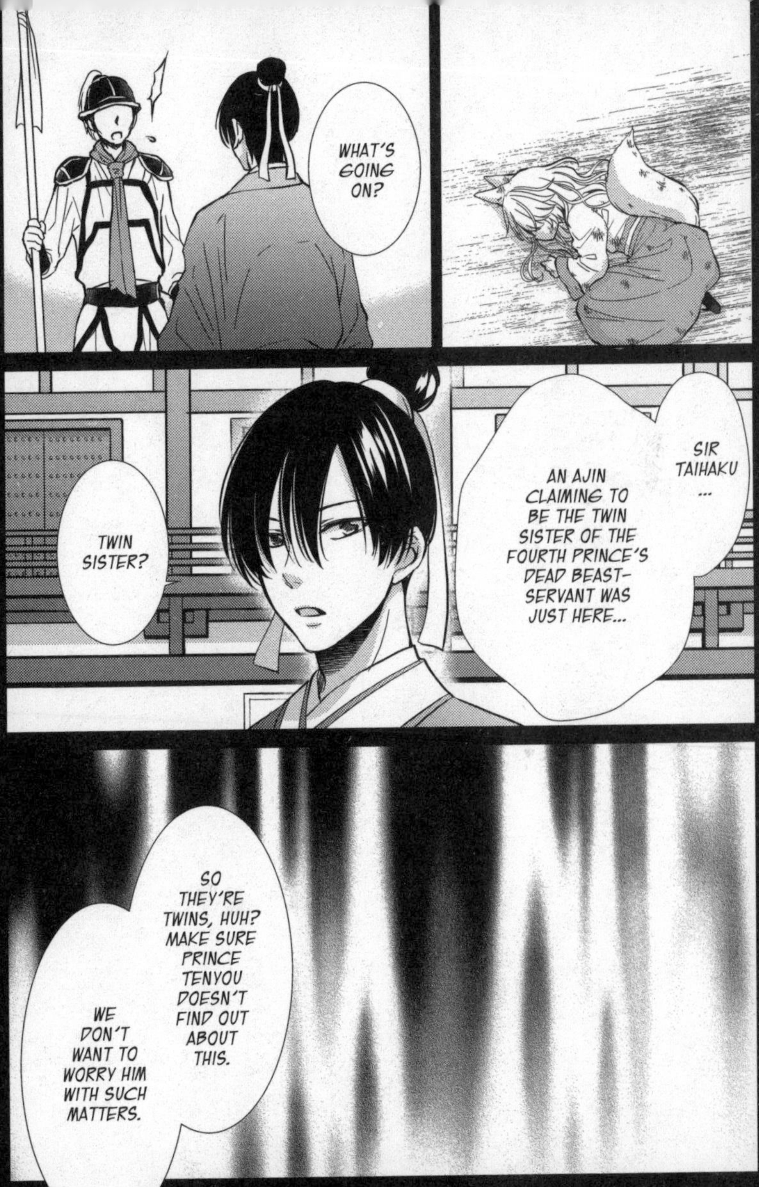
WHAT'S GOING ON?
SIR TAIHAKU ...
AN AJIN CLAIMING TO BE THE TWIN SISTER OF THE FOURTH PRINCE'S DEAD BEAST-SERVANT WAS JUST HERE...
TWIN SISTER?
SO THEY'RE TWINS, HUH? MAKE SURE PRINCE TENYOU DOESN'T FIND OUT ABOUT THIS.
WE DON'T WANT TO WORRY HIM WITH SUCH MATTERS.

THE
KING'S
Beast

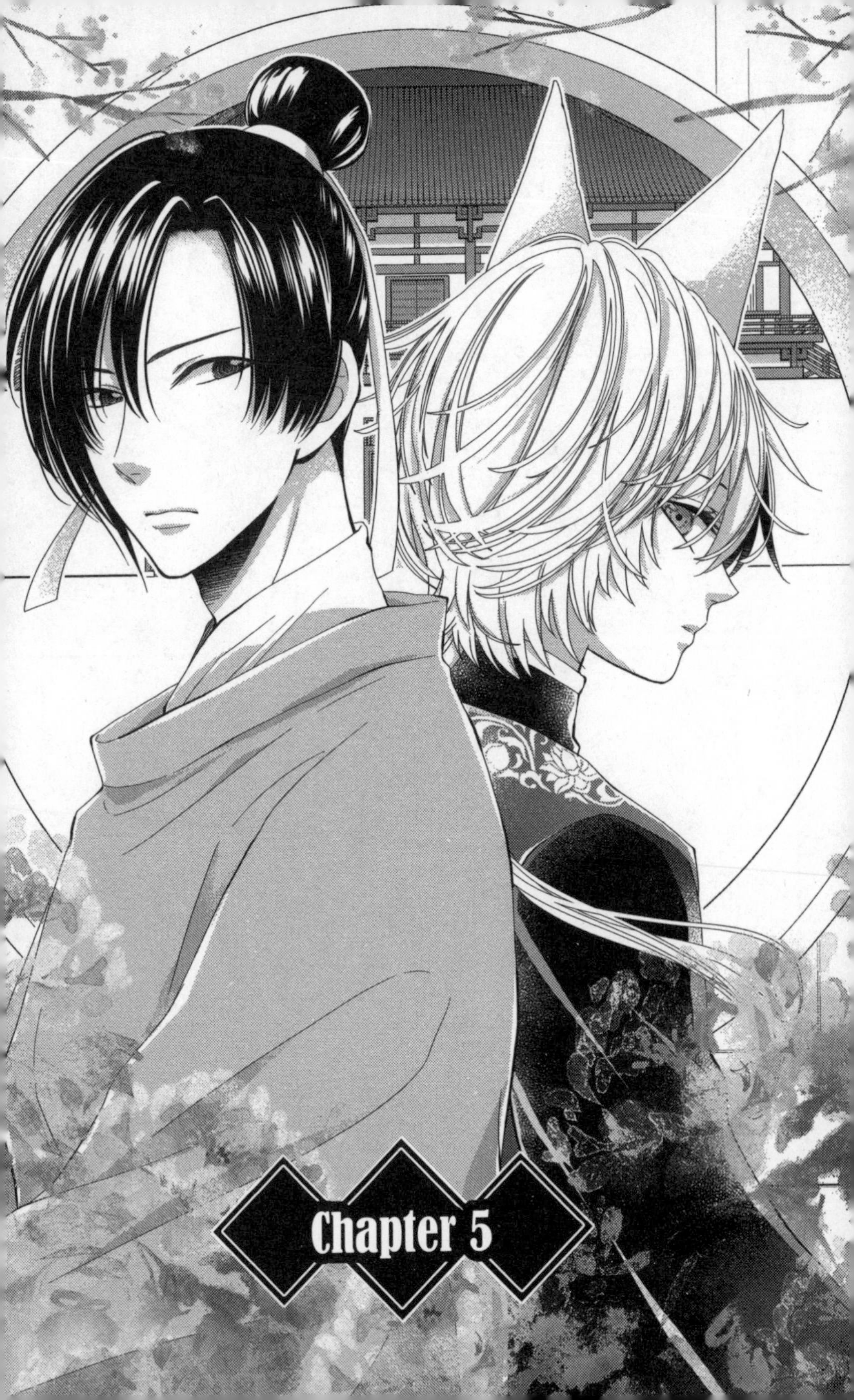
Chapter 5

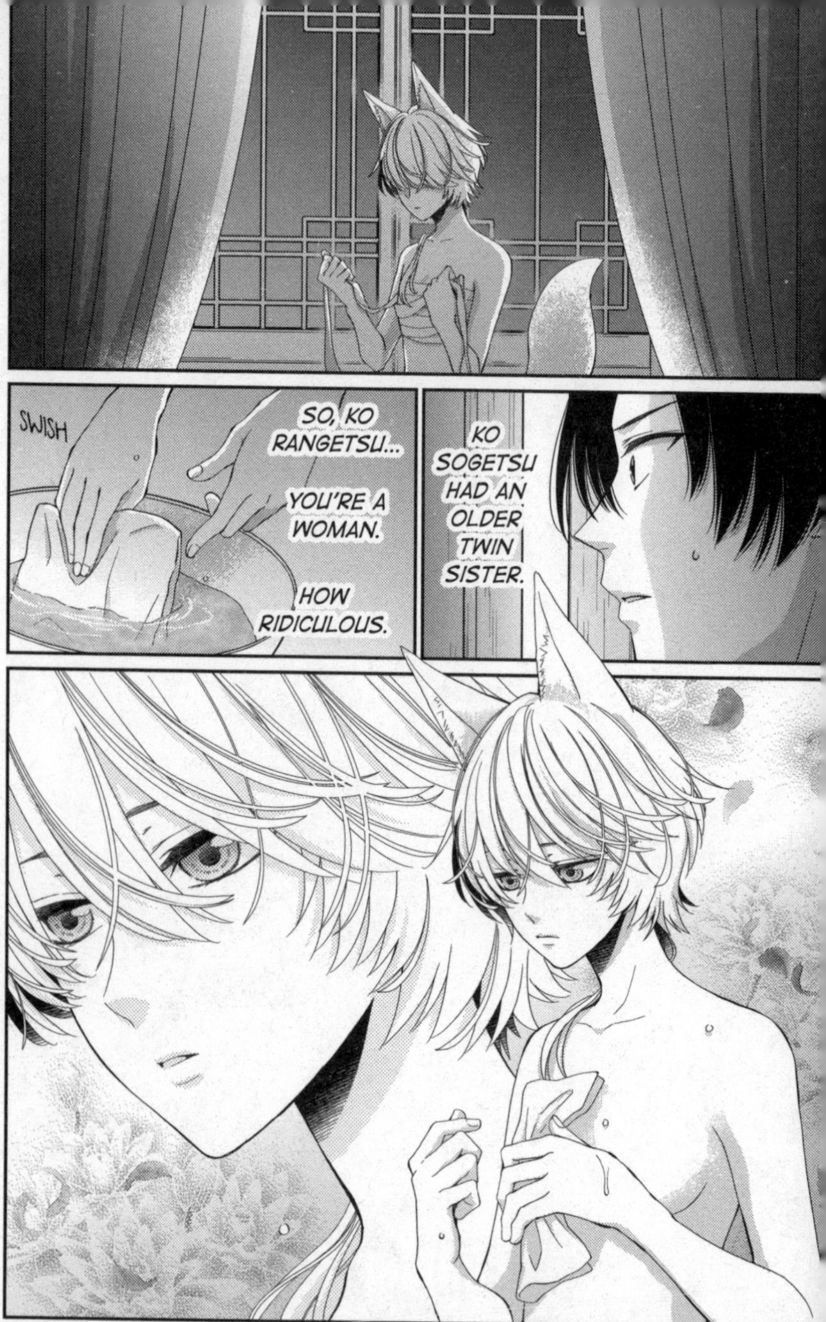
KO SOGETSU HAD AN OLDER TWIN SISTER.
SO, KO RANGETSU...
SWISH
YOU'RE A WOMAN.
HOW RIDICULOUS.

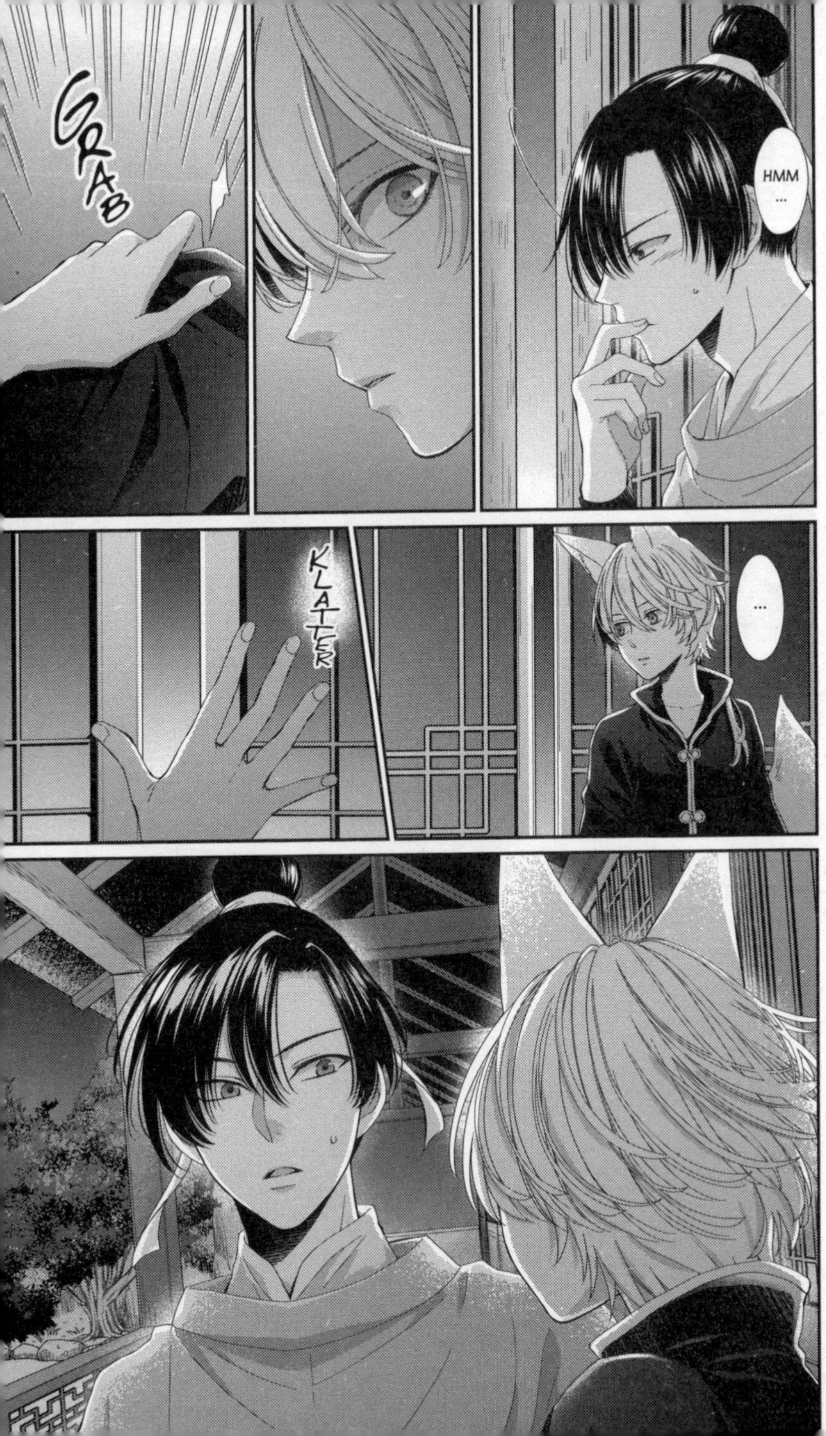
HMM ...
GRAB
...
KLATTER

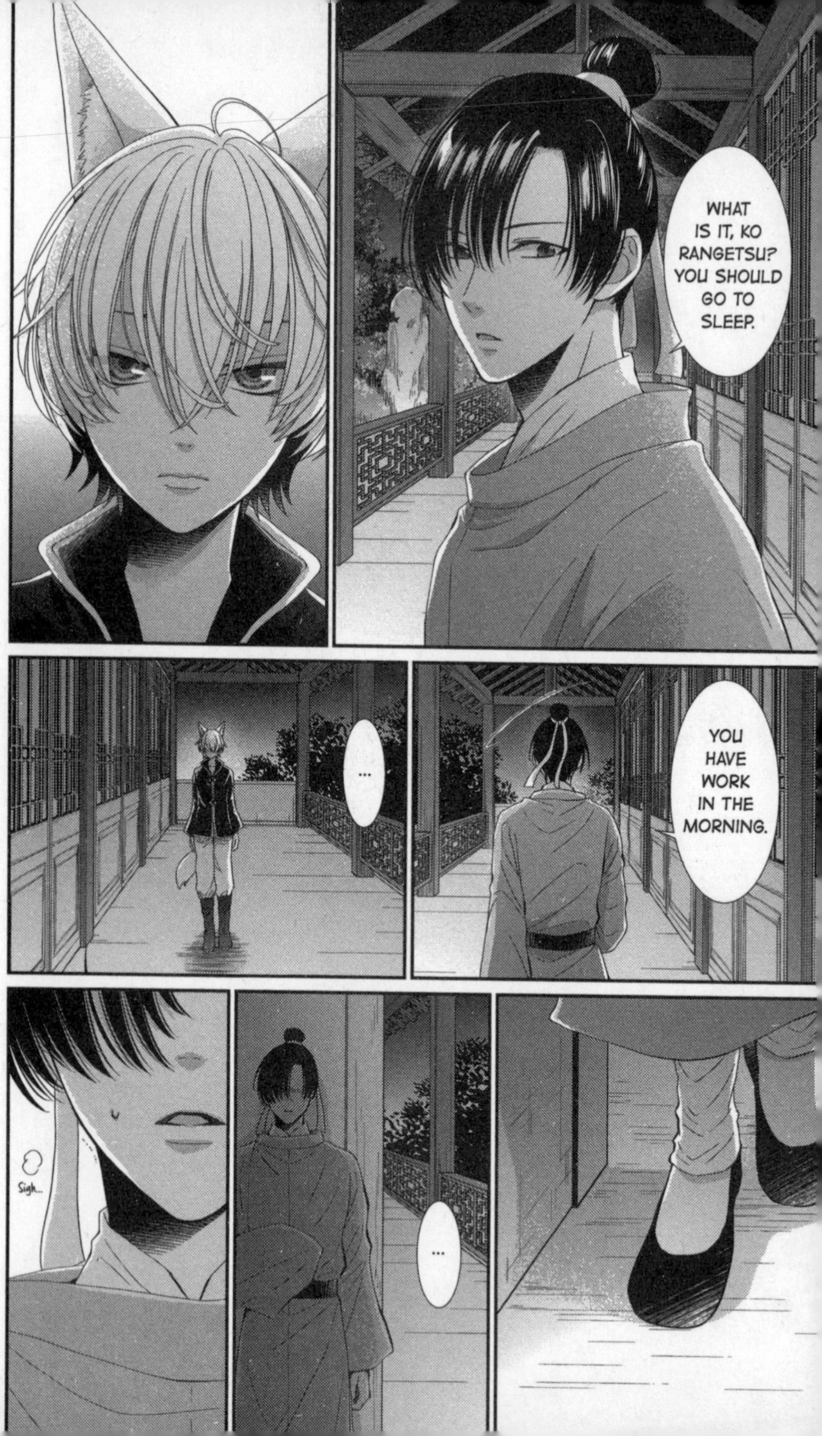
WHAT IS IT, KO RANGETSU? YOU SHOULD GO TO SLEEP.
YOU HAVE WORK IN THE MORNING.
...
...
Sigh...

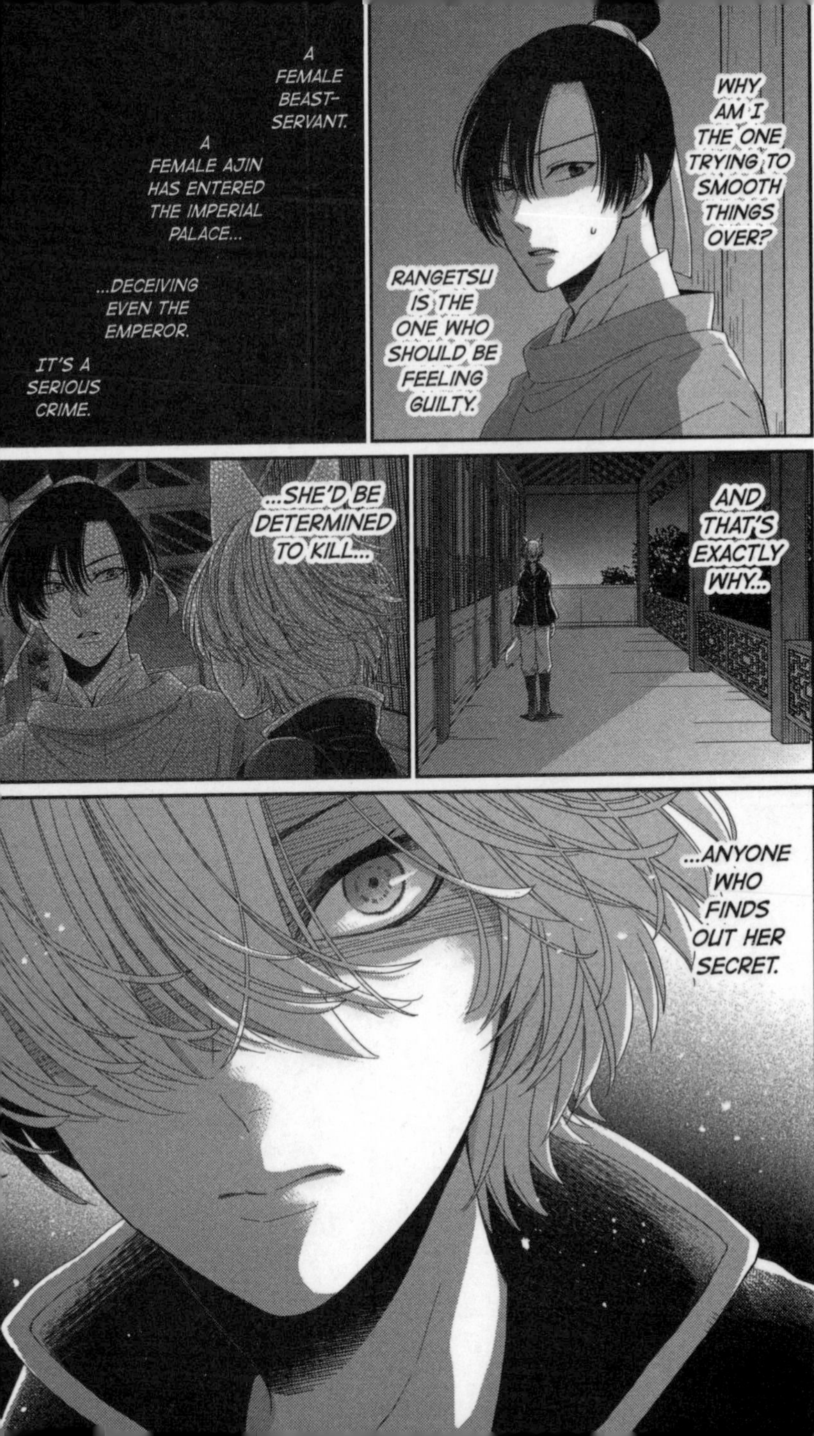
WHY AM I THE ONE TRYING TO SMOOTH THINGS OVER?
RANGETSU IS THE ONE WHO SHOULD BE FEELING GUILTY.
A FEMALE BEAST-SERVANT.
A FEMALE AJIN HAS ENTERED THE IMPERIAL PALACE...
...DECEIVING EVEN THE EMPEROR.
IT'S A SERIOUS CRIME.
AND THAT'S EXACTLY WHY...
...SHE'D BE DETERMINED TO KILL...
...ANYONE WHO FINDS OUT HER SECRET.

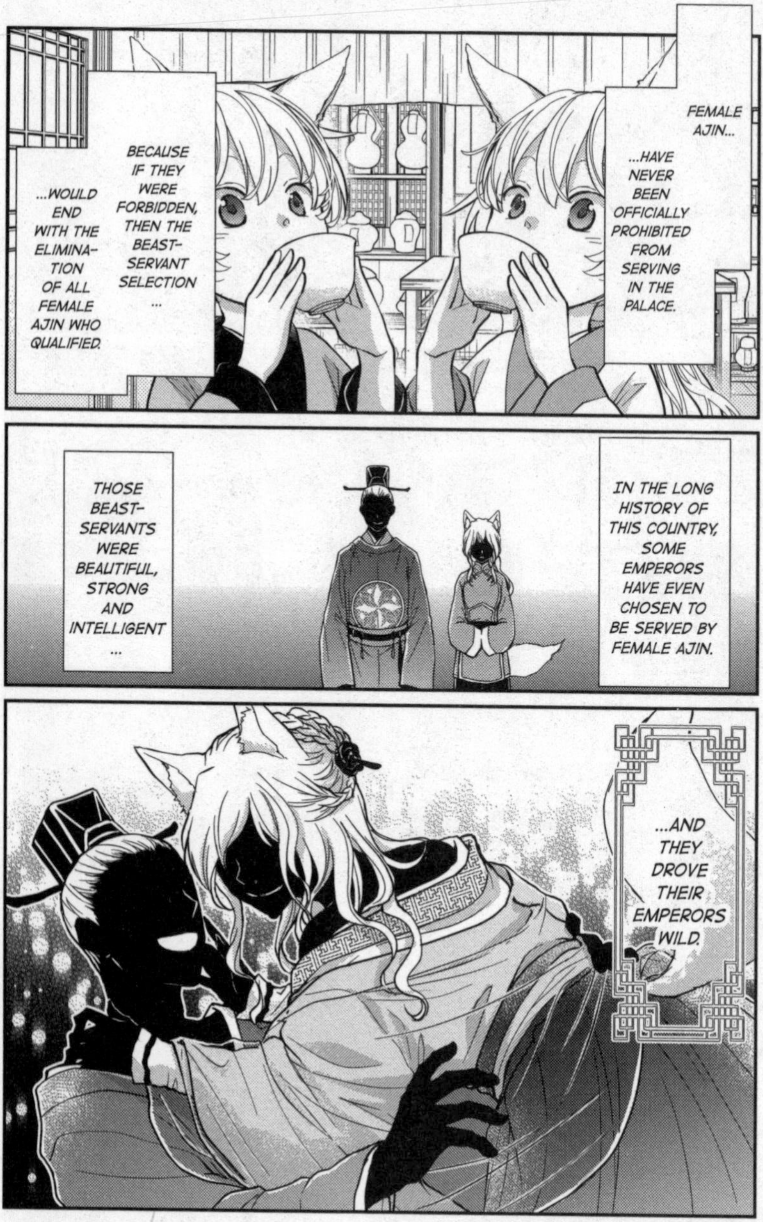
FEMALE AJIN...
...HAVE NEVER BEEN OFFICIALLY PROHIBITED FROM SERVING IN THE PALACE.
BECAUSE IF THEY WERE FORBIDDEN, THEN THE BEAST-SERVANT SELECTION ...
...WOULD END WITH THE ELIMINATION OF ALL FEMALE AJIN WHO QUALIFIED.
IN THE LONG HISTORY OF THIS COUNTRY, SOME EMPERORS HAVE EVEN CHOSEN TO BE SERVED BY FEMALE AJIN.
THOSE BEAST-SERVANTS WERE BEAUTIFUL, STRONG AND INTELLIGENT ...
...AND THEY DROVE THEIR EMPERORS WILD.

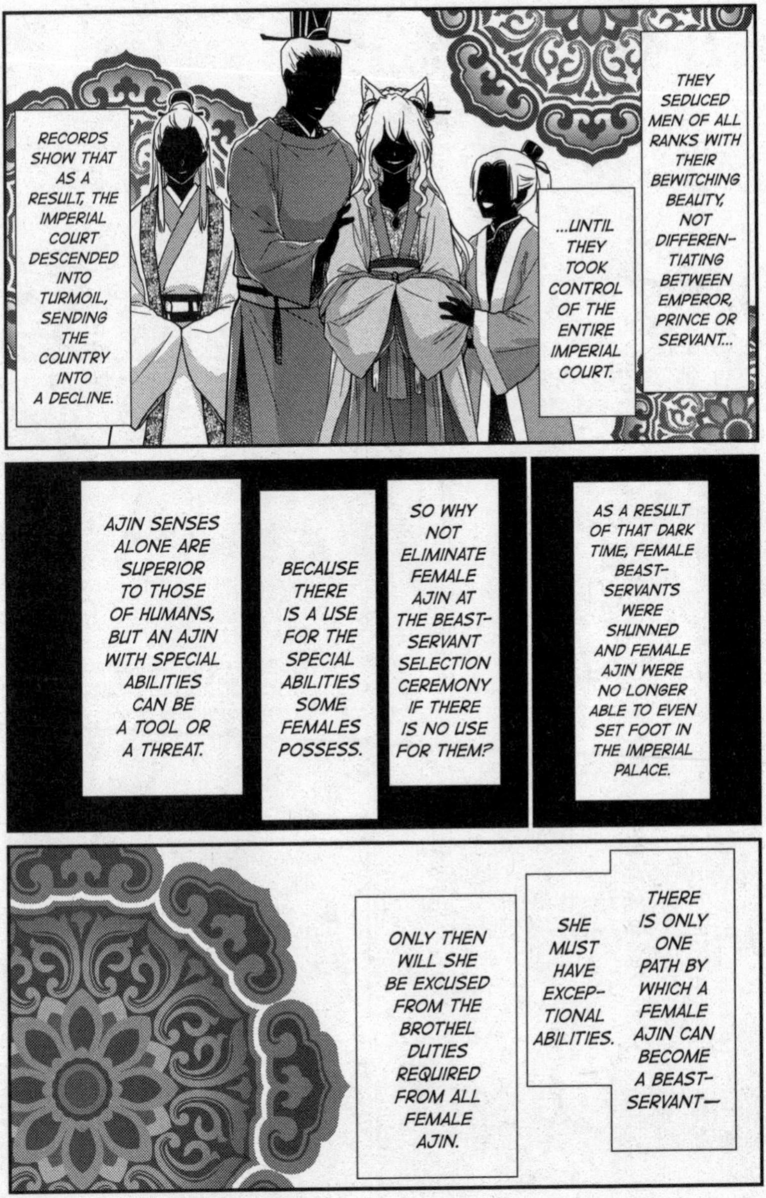
THEY SEDUCED MEN OF ALL RANKS WITH THEIR BEWITCHING BEAUTY, NOT DIFFEREN-TIATING BETWEEN EMPEROR, PRINCE OR SERVANT...
...UNTIL THEY TOOK CONTROL OF THE ENTIRE IMPERIAL COURT.
RECORDS SHOW THAT AS A RESULT, THE IMPERIAL COURT DESCENDED INTO TURMOIL, SENDING THE COUNTRY INTO A DECLINE.
AS A RESULT OF THAT DARK TIME, FEMALE BEAST-SERVANTS WERE SHUNNED AND FEMALE AJIN WERE NO LONGER ABLE TO EVEN SET FOOT IN THE IMPERIAL PALACE.
SO WHY NOT ELIMINATE FEMALE AJIN AT THE BEAST-SERVANT SELECTION CEREMONY IF THERE IS NO USE FOR THEM?
BECAUSE THERE IS A USE FOR THE SPECIAL ABILITIES SOME FEMALES POSSESS.
AJIN SENSES ALONE ARE SUPERIOR TO THOSE OF HUMANS, BUT AN AJIN WITH SPECIAL ABILITIES CAN BE A TOOL OR A THREAT.
THERE IS ONLY ONE PATH BY WHICH A FEMALE AJIN CAN BECOME A BEAST-SERVANT—
SHE MUST HAVE EXCEP-TIONAL ABILITIES.
ONLY THEN WILL SHE BE EXCUSED FROM THE BROTHEL DUTIES REQUIRED FROM ALL FEMALE AJIN.

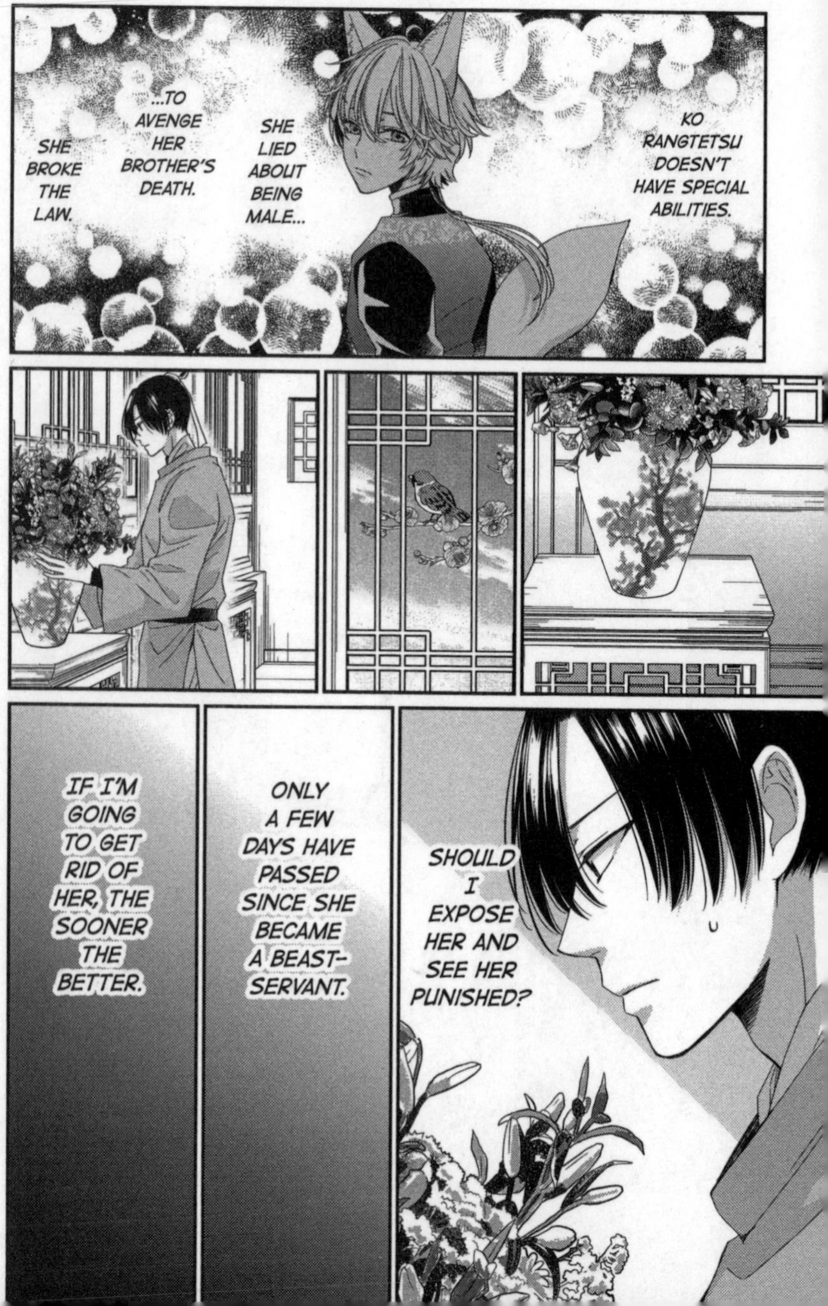
KO RANGTETSU DOESN'T HAVE SPECIAL ABILITIES.
SHE LIED ABOUT BEING MALE...
...TO AVENGE HER BROTHER'S DEATH.
SHE BROKE THE LAW.
SHOULD I EXPOSE HER AND SEE HER PUNISHED?
ONLY A FEW DAYS HAVE PASSED SINCE SHE BECAME A BEAST-SERVANT.
IF I'M GOING TO GET RID OF HER, THE SOONER THE BETTER.

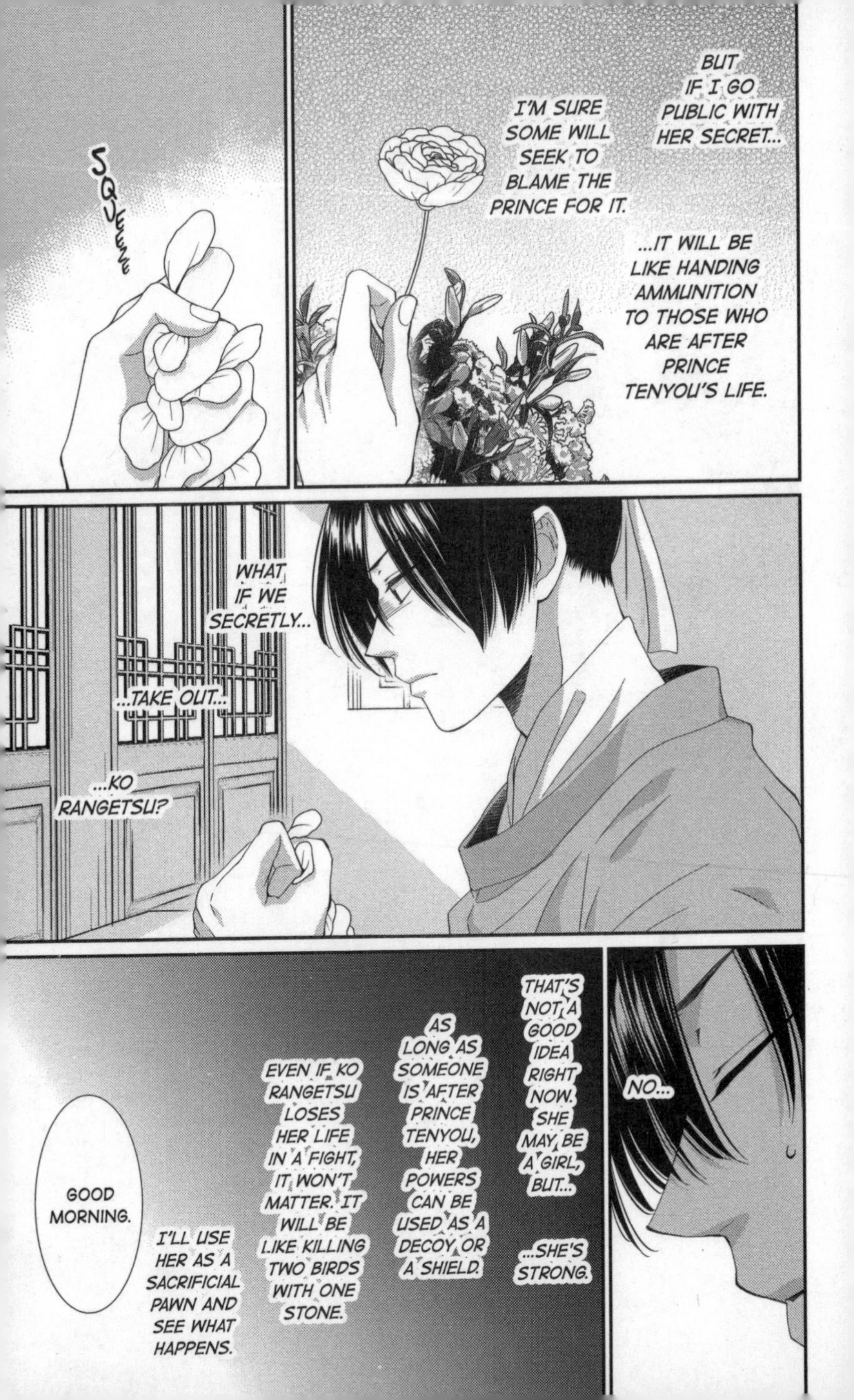

BUT IF I GO PUBLIC WITH HER SECRET...
I'M SURE SOME WILL SEEK TO BLAME THE PRINCE FOR IT.
...IT WILL BE LIKE HANDING AMMUNITION TO THOSE WHO ARE AFTER PRINCE TENYOU'S LIFE.
SQUEEZE
WHAT IF WE SECRETLY...
...TAKE OUT...
...KO RANGETSU?
NO...
THAT'S NOT A GOOD IDEA RIGHT NOW. SHE MAY BE A GIRL, BUT...
...SHE'S STRONG.
AS LONG AS SOMEONE IS AFTER PRINCE TENYOU, HER POWERS CAN BE USED AS A DECOY OR A SHIELD.
EVEN IF KO RANGETSU LOSES HER LIFE IN A FIGHT, IT WON'T MATTER. IT WILL BE LIKE KILLING TWO BIRDS WITH ONE STONE.
I'LL USE HER AS A SACRIFICIAL PAWN AND SEE WHAT HAPPENS.
GOOD MORNING.

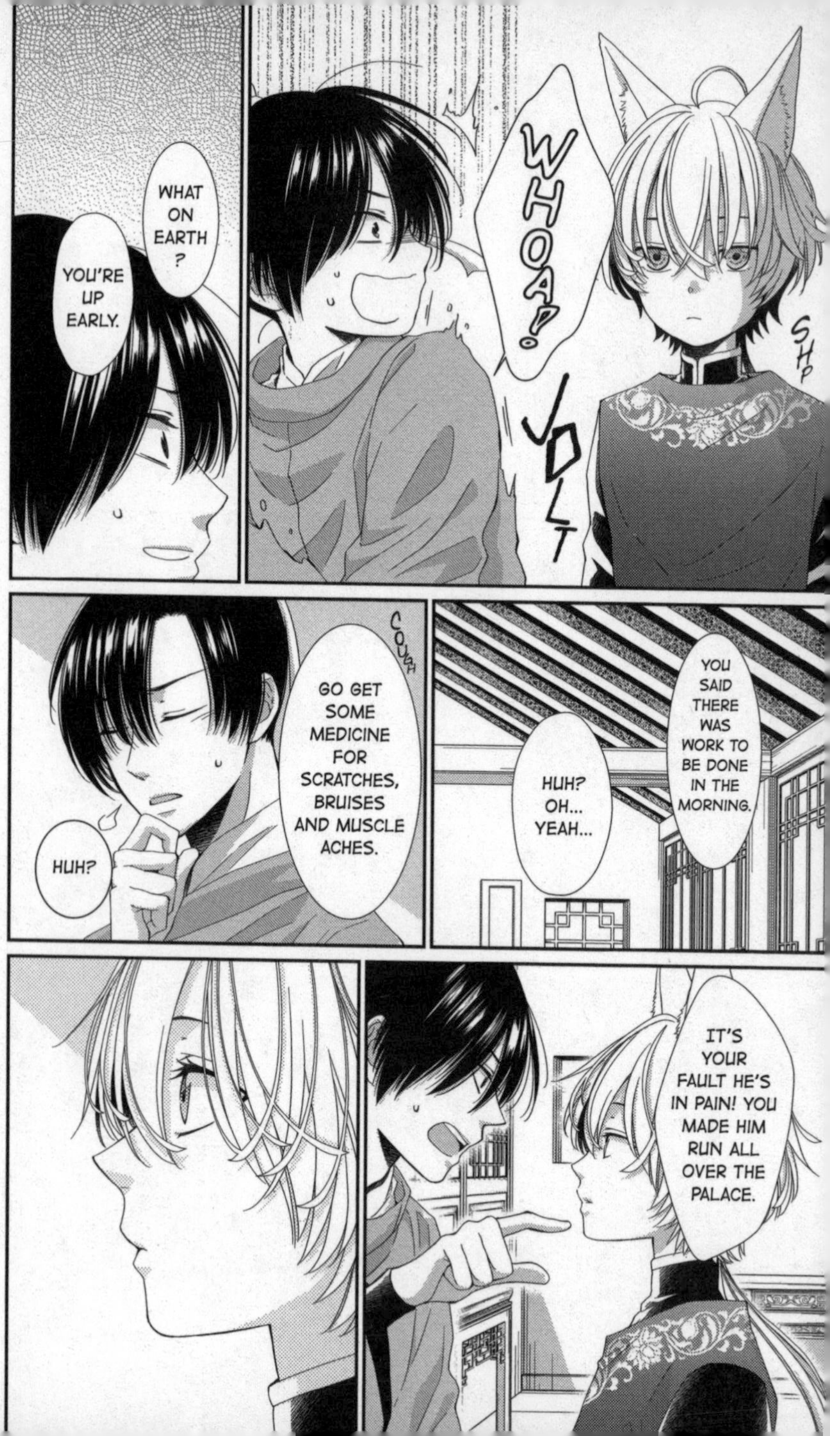
SHP
WHOA!!
JOLT
WHAT ON EARTH?
YOU'RE UP EARLY.
YOU SAID THERE WAS WORK TO BE DONE IN THE MORNING.
HUH? OH... YEAH...
COUGH
GO GET SOME MEDICINE FOR SCRATCHES, BRUISES AND MUSCLE ACHES.
HUH?
IT'S YOUR FAULT HE'S IN PAIN! YOU MADE HIM RUN ALL OVER THE PALACE.

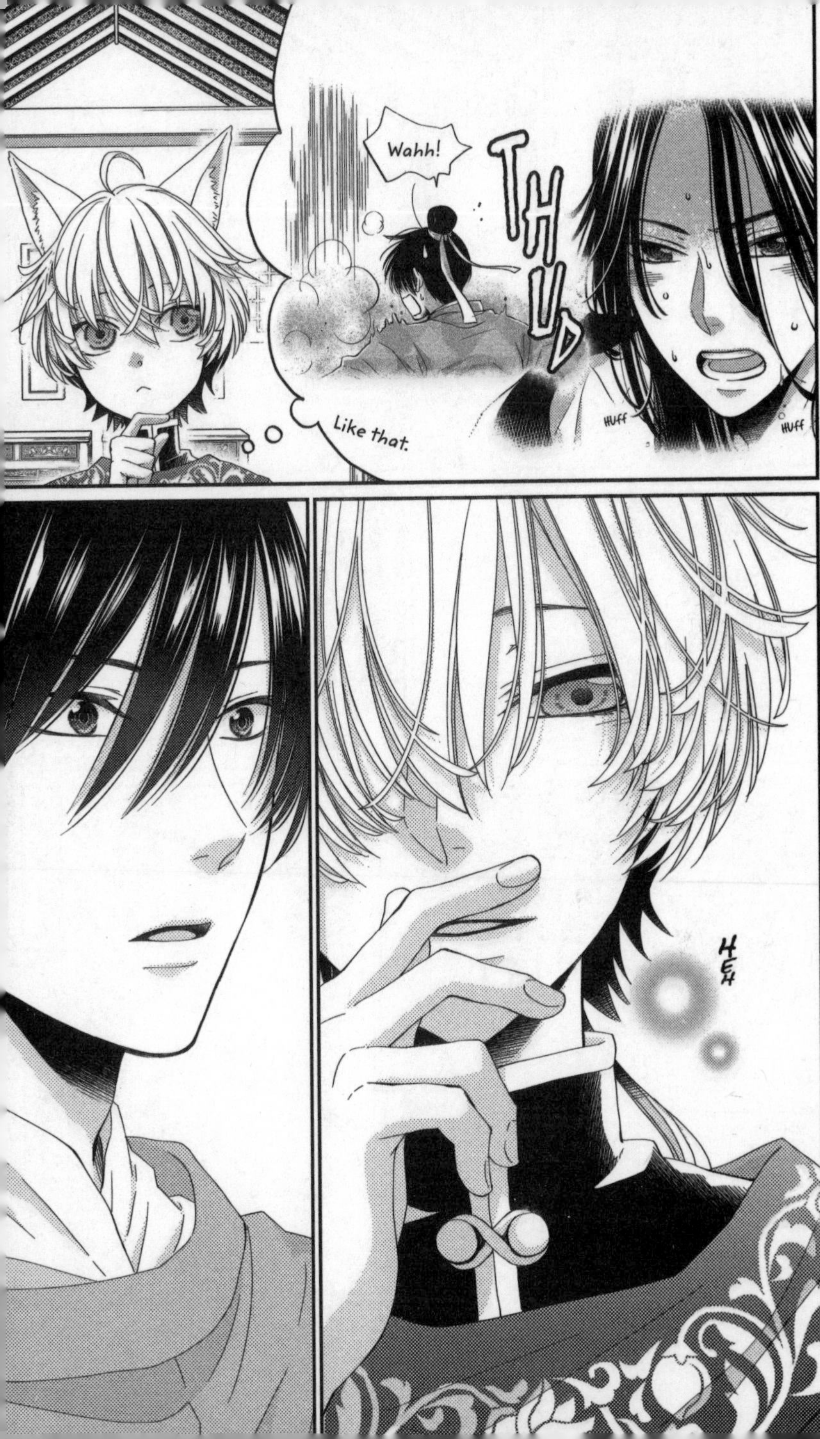
HUFF
HUFF
THUD
Wahh!
Like that.
HEH

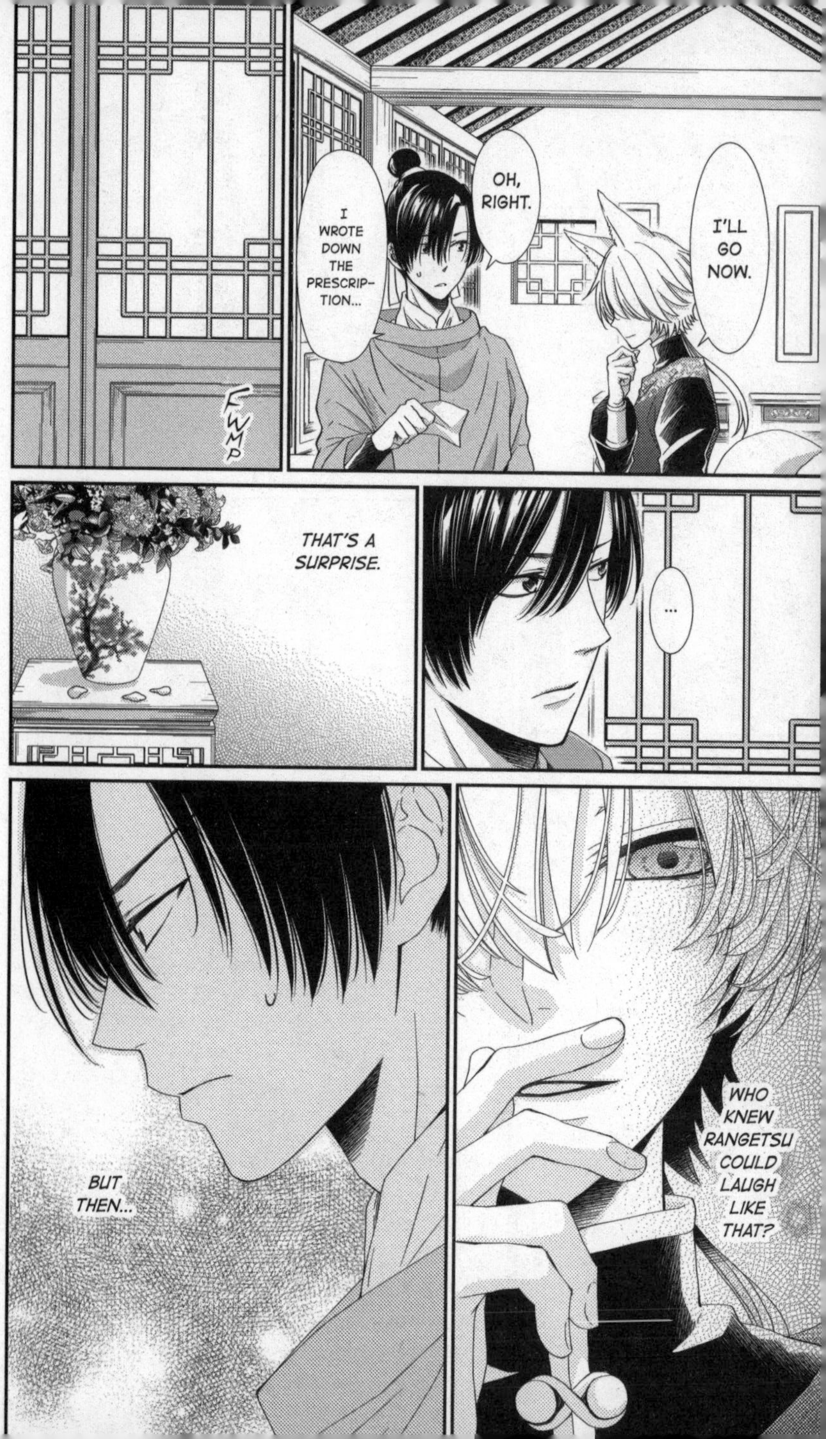
I'LL GO NOW.
OH, RIGHT.
I WROTE DOWN THE PRESCRIPTION...
FWMP
...
THAT'S A SURPRISE.
WHO KNEW RANGETSU COULD LAUGH LIKE THAT?
BUT THEN...

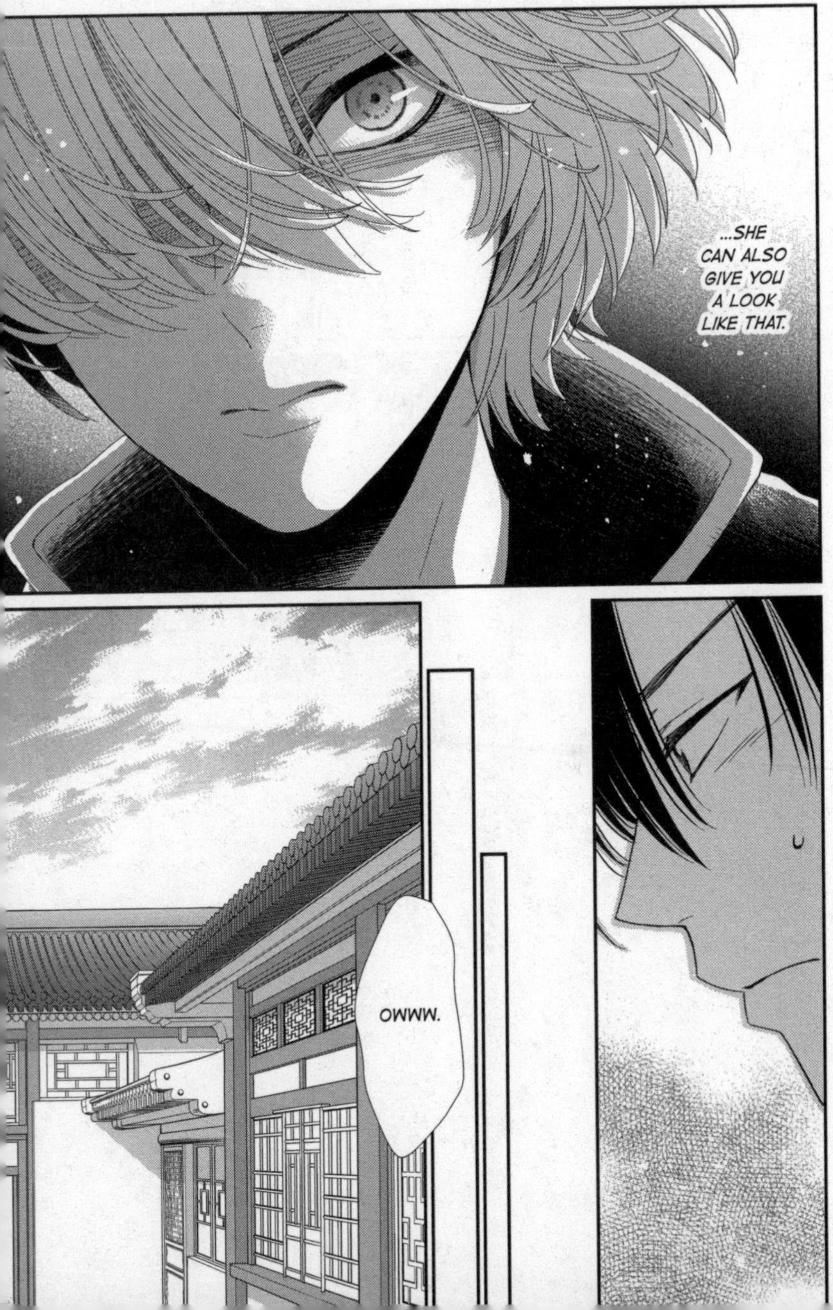
...SHE CAN ALSO GIVE YOU A LOOK LIKE THAT.
OWWW.

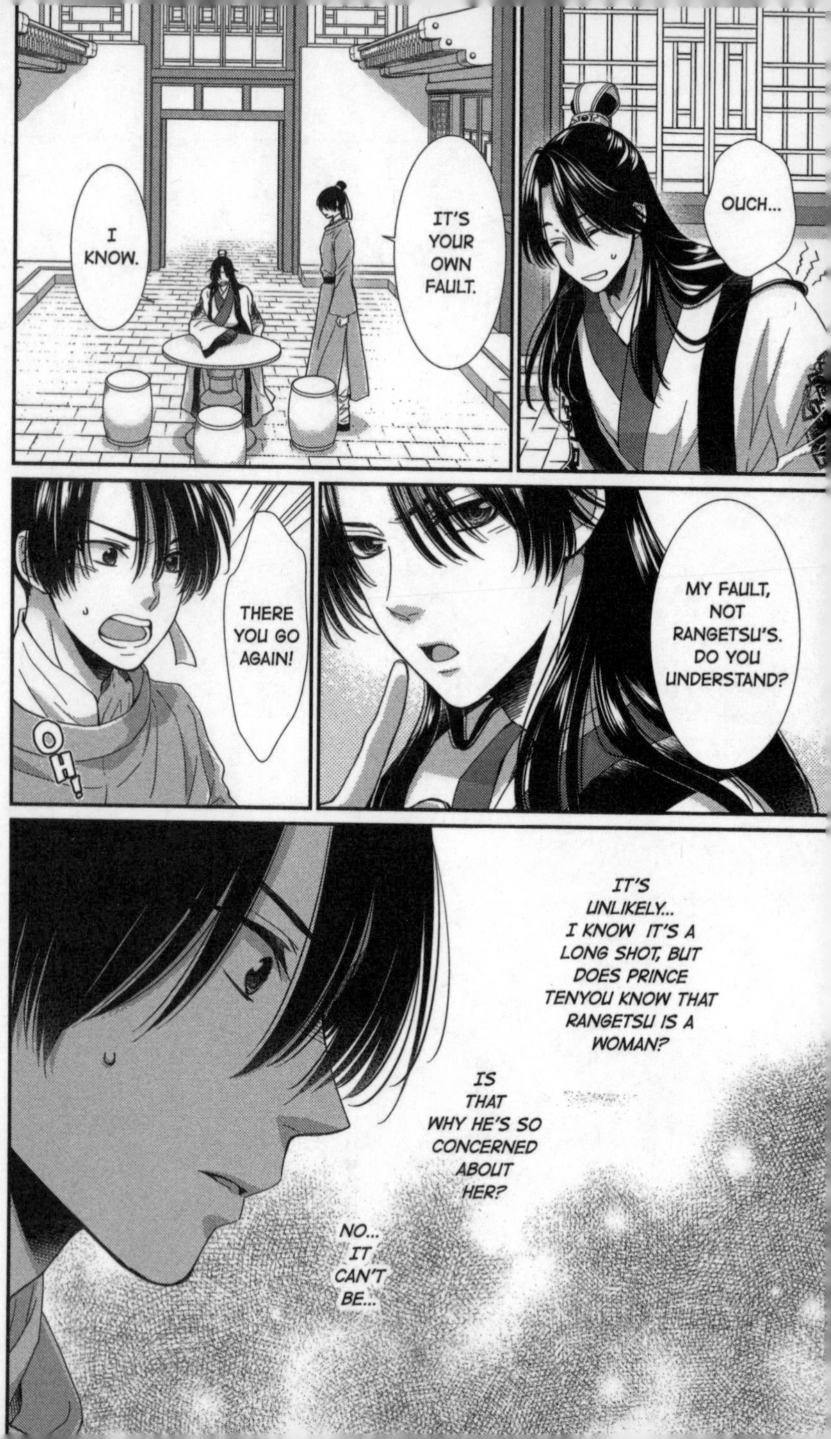
OUCH...
IT'S YOUR OWN FAULT.
I KNOW.
MY FAULT, NOT RANGETSU'S. DO YOU UNDERSTAND?
THERE YOU GO AGAIN!
OH!
IT'S UNLIKELY... I KNOW IT'S A LONG SHOT, BUT DOES PRINCE TENYOU KNOW THAT RANGETSU IS A WOMAN?
IS THAT WHY HE'S SO CONCERNED ABOUT HER?
NO... IT CAN'T BE...

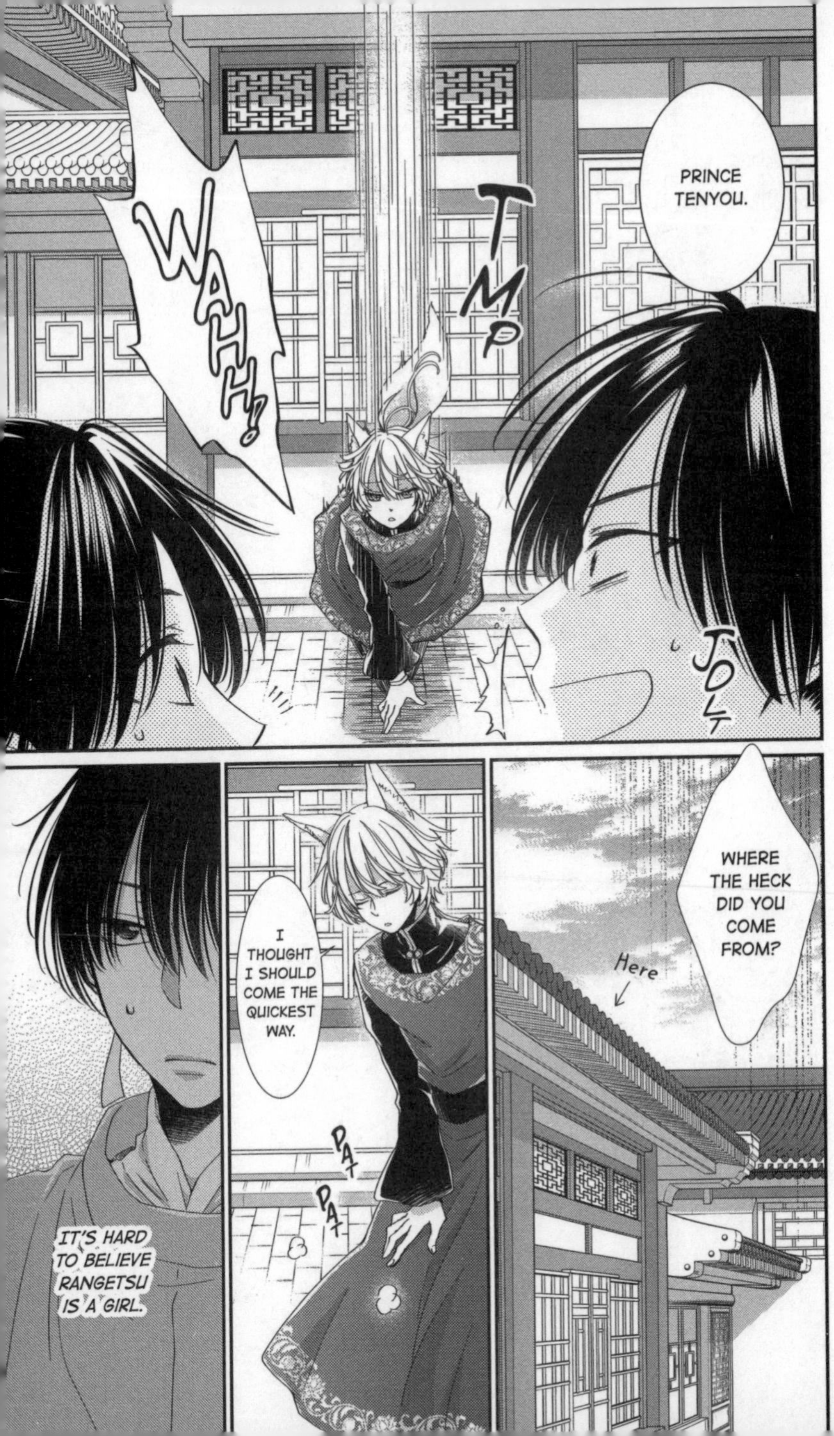
PRINCE TENYOU.
TMP
WAHH!
JOLT
WHERE THE HECK DID YOU COME FROM?
Here
I THOUGHT I SHOULD COME THE QUICKEST WAY.
PAT PAT
IT'S HARD TO BELIEVE RANGETSU IS A GIRL.

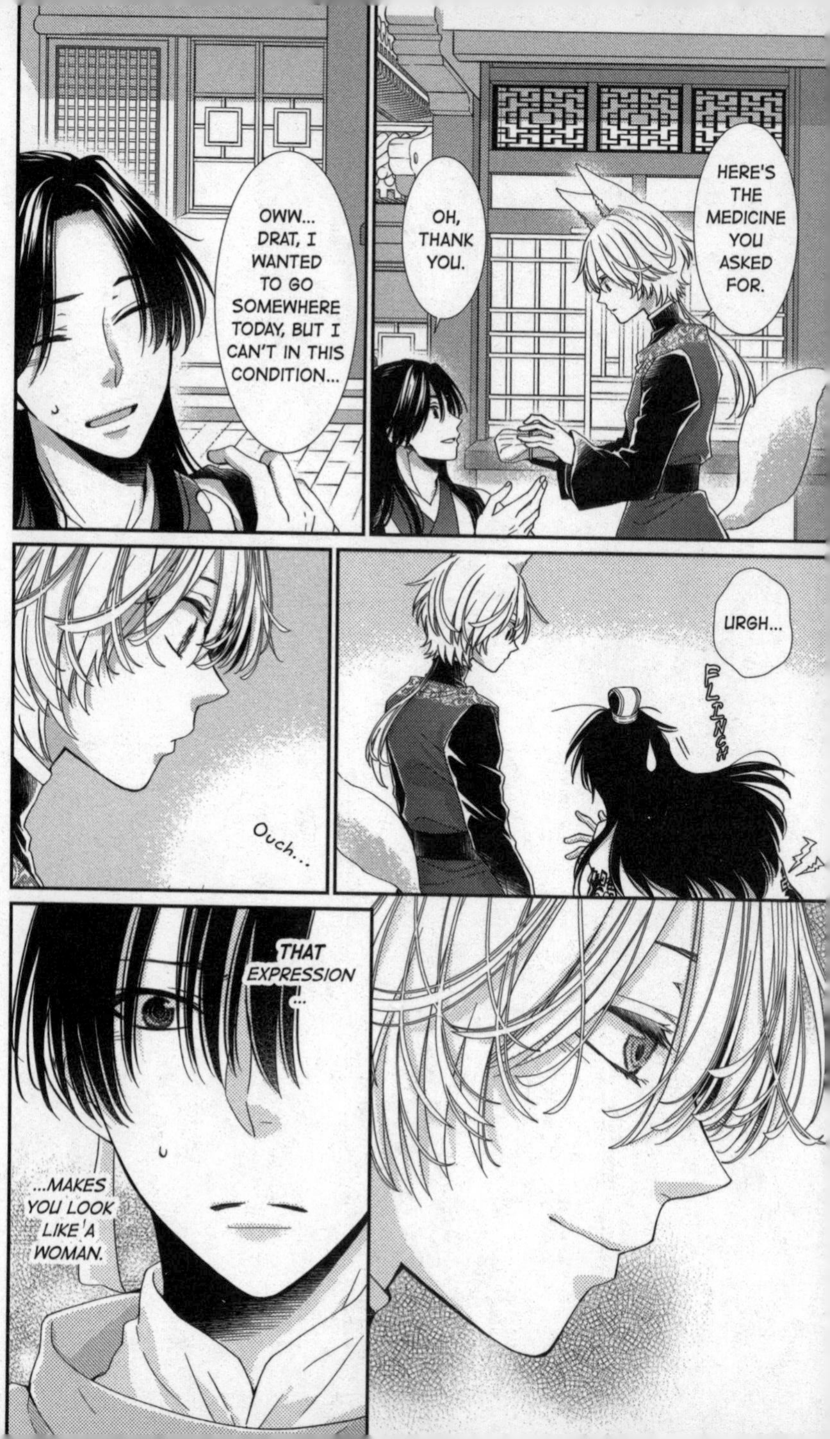
HERE'S THE MEDICINE YOU ASKED FOR.
OH, THANK YOU.
OWW... DRAT, I WANTED TO GO SOMEWHERE TODAY, BUT I CAN'T IN THIS CONDITION...
URGH...
FLINCH
Ouch...
THAT EXPRESSION...
...MAKES YOU LOOK LIKE A WOMAN.

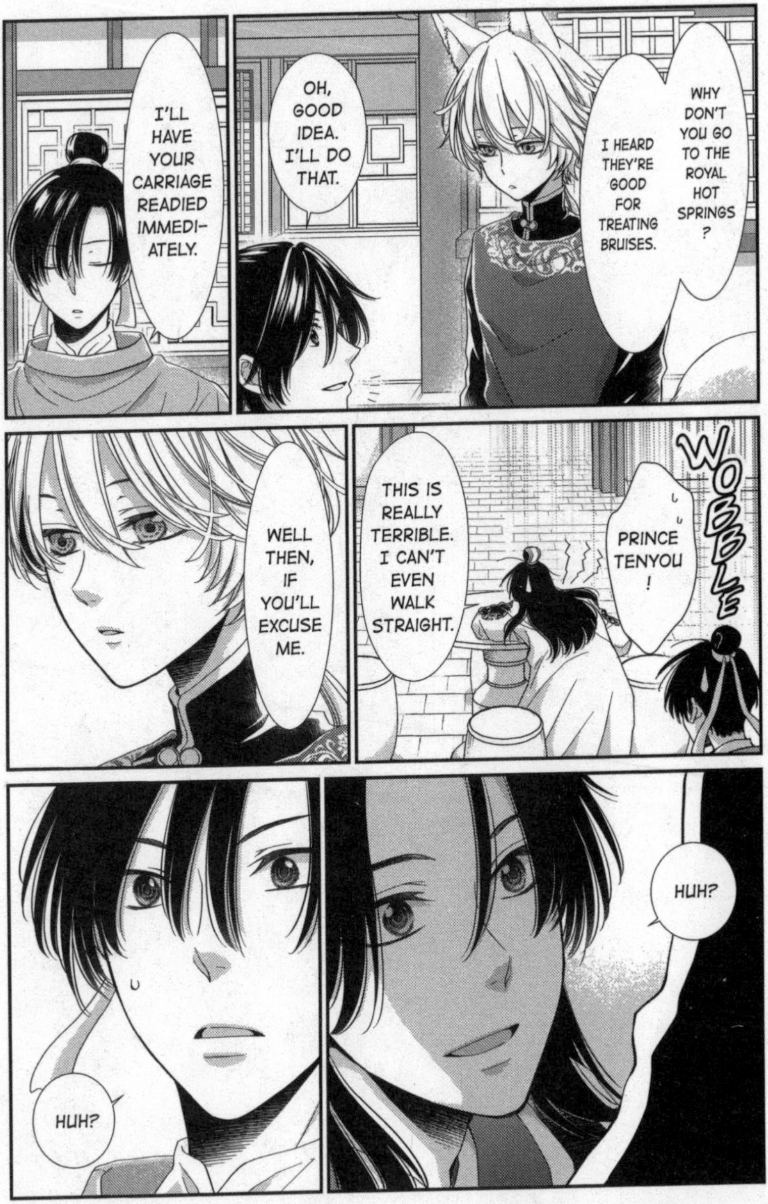
WHY DON'T YOU GO TO THE ROYAL HOT SPRINGS?
I HEARD THEY'RE GOOD FOR TREATING BRUISES.
OH, GOOD IDEA. I'LL DO THAT.
I'LL HAVE YOUR CARRIAGE READIED IMMEDIATELY.
WOBBLE
PRINCE TENYOU!
THIS IS REALLY TERRIBLE. I CAN'T EVEN WALK STRAIGHT.
WELL THEN, IF YOU'LL EXCUSE ME.
HUH?
HUH?

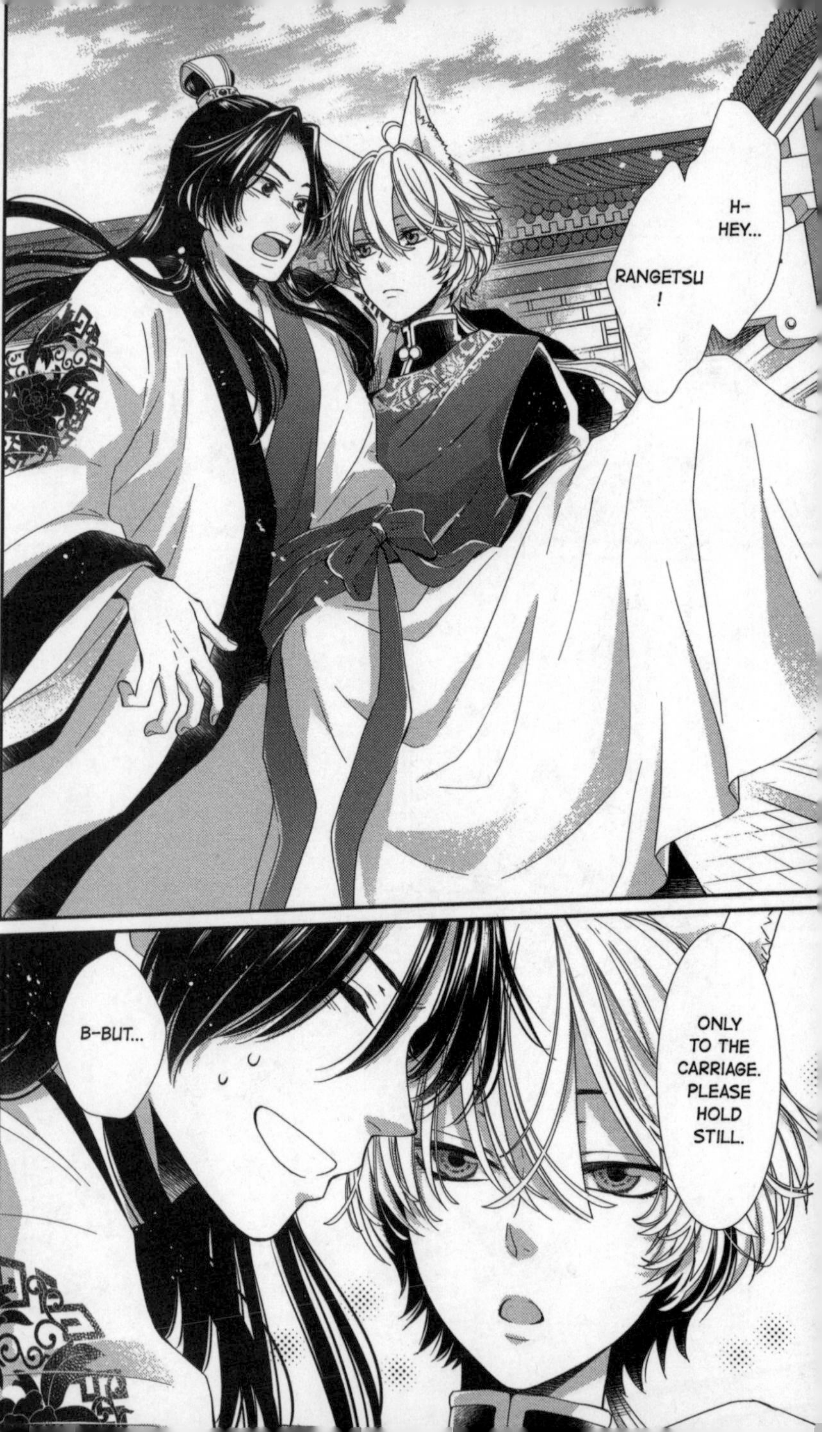
H-HEY...
RANGETSU!
ONLY TO THE CARRIAGE. PLEASE HOLD STILL.
B-BUT...

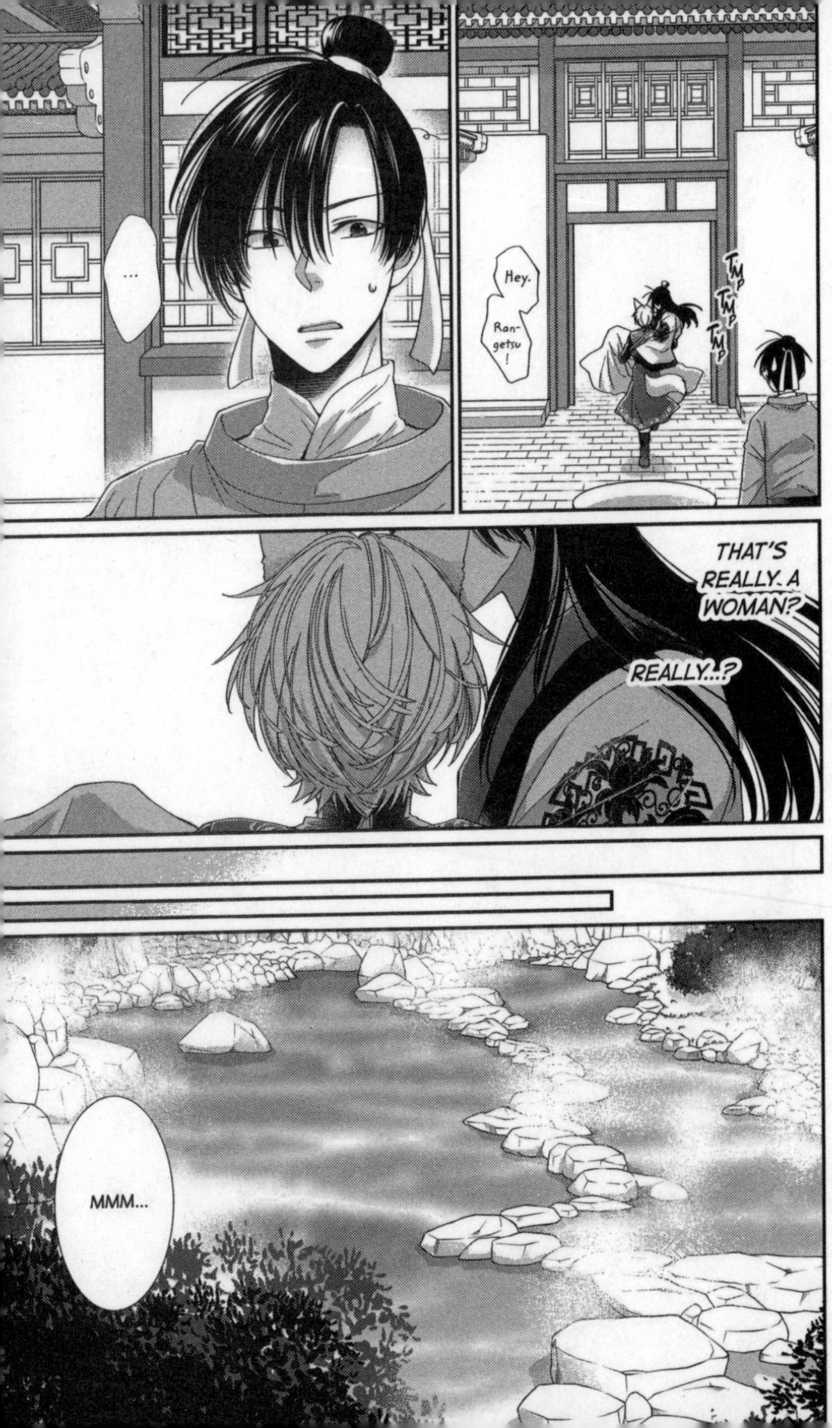
Hey.
Rangetsu!
TMP TMP TMP
...
THAT'S REALLY A WOMAN?
REALLY...?
MMM...

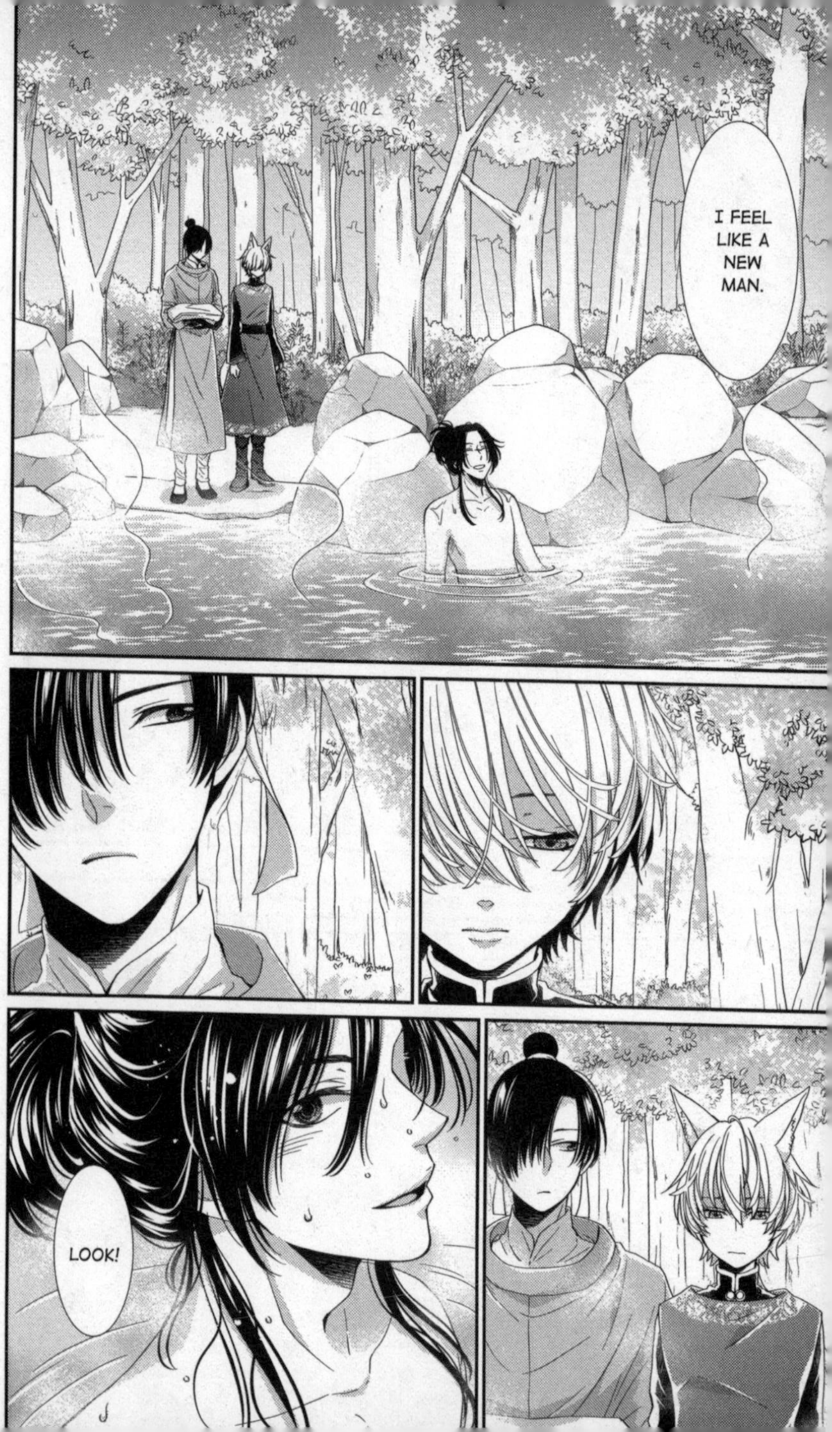
I FEEL LIKE A NEW MAN.
LOOK!

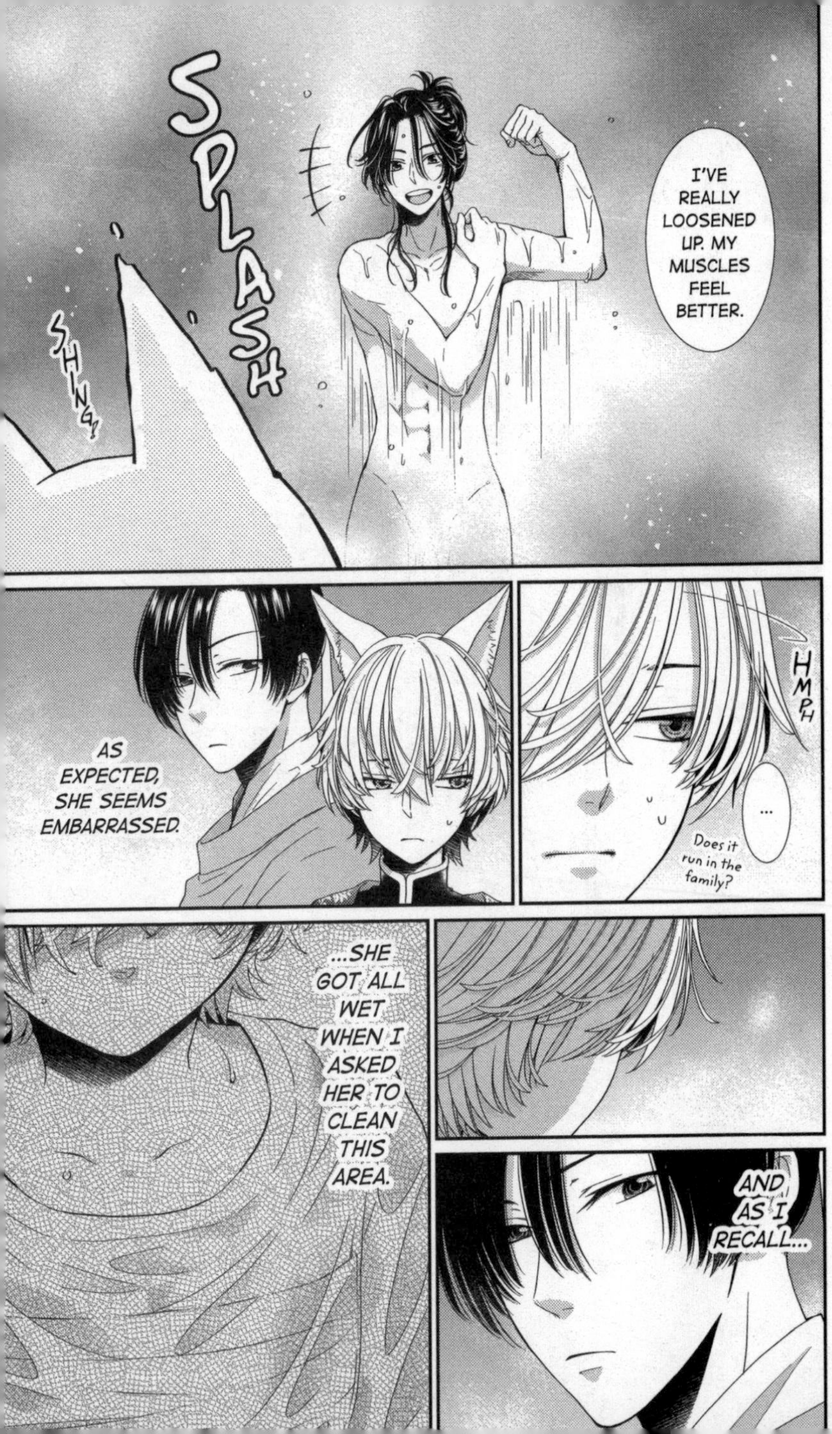
I'VE REALLY LOOSENED UP. MY MUSCLES FEEL BETTER.
SPLASH
SHING!
HMPH
...
Does it run in the family?
AS EXPECTED, SHE SEEMS EMBARRASSED.
...SHE GOT ALL WET WHEN I ASKED HER TO CLEAN THIS AREA.
AND AS I RECALL...

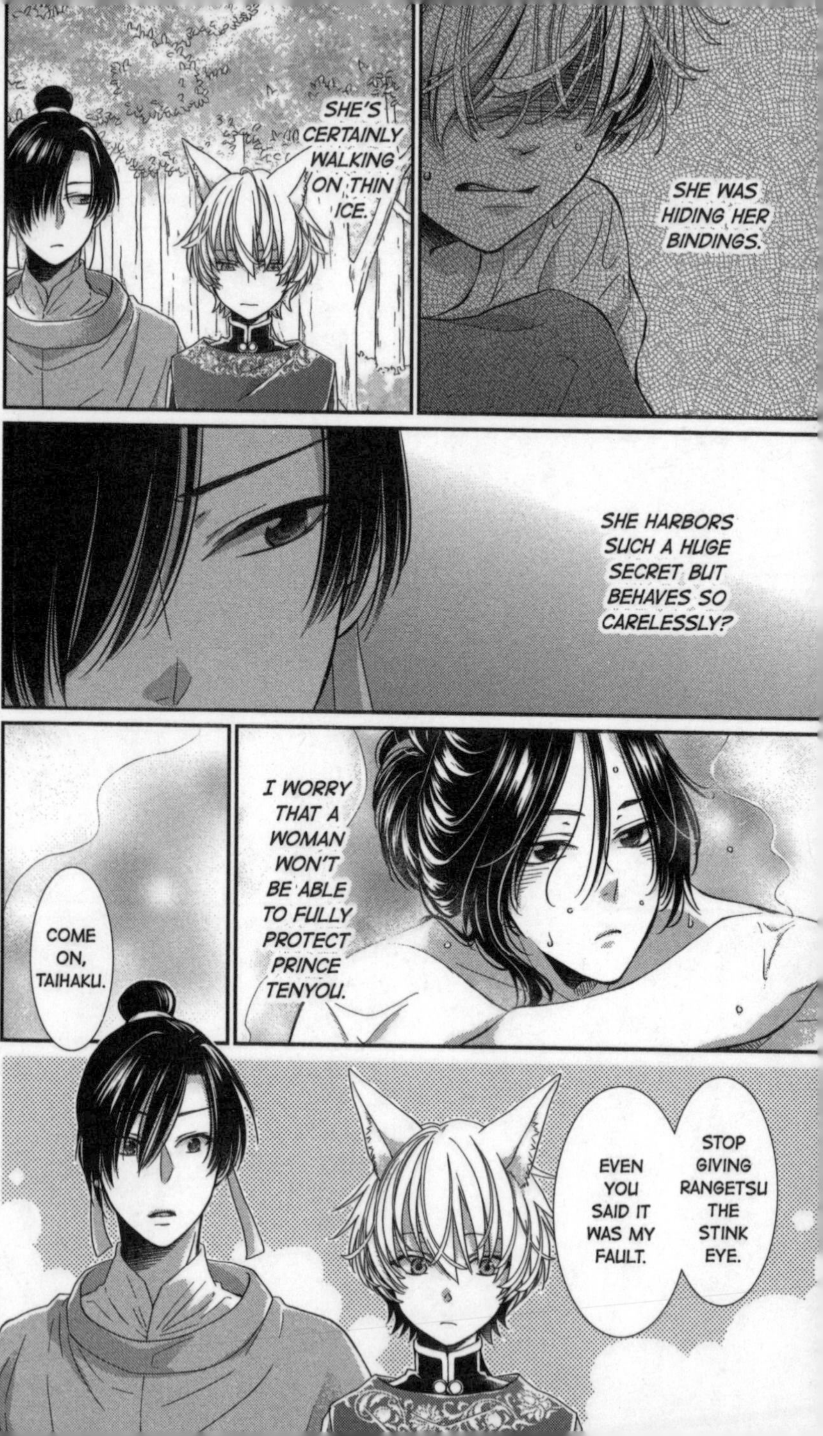
SHE WAS HIDING HER BINDINGS.
SHE'S CERTAINLY WALKING ON THIN ICE.
SHE HARBORS SUCH A HUGE SECRET BUT BEHAVES SO CARELESSLY?
I WORRY THAT A WOMAN WON'T BE ABLE TO FULLY PROTECT PRINCE TENYOU.
COME ON, TAIHAKU.
STOP GIVING RANGETSU THE STINK EYE.
EVEN YOU SAID IT WAS MY FAULT.

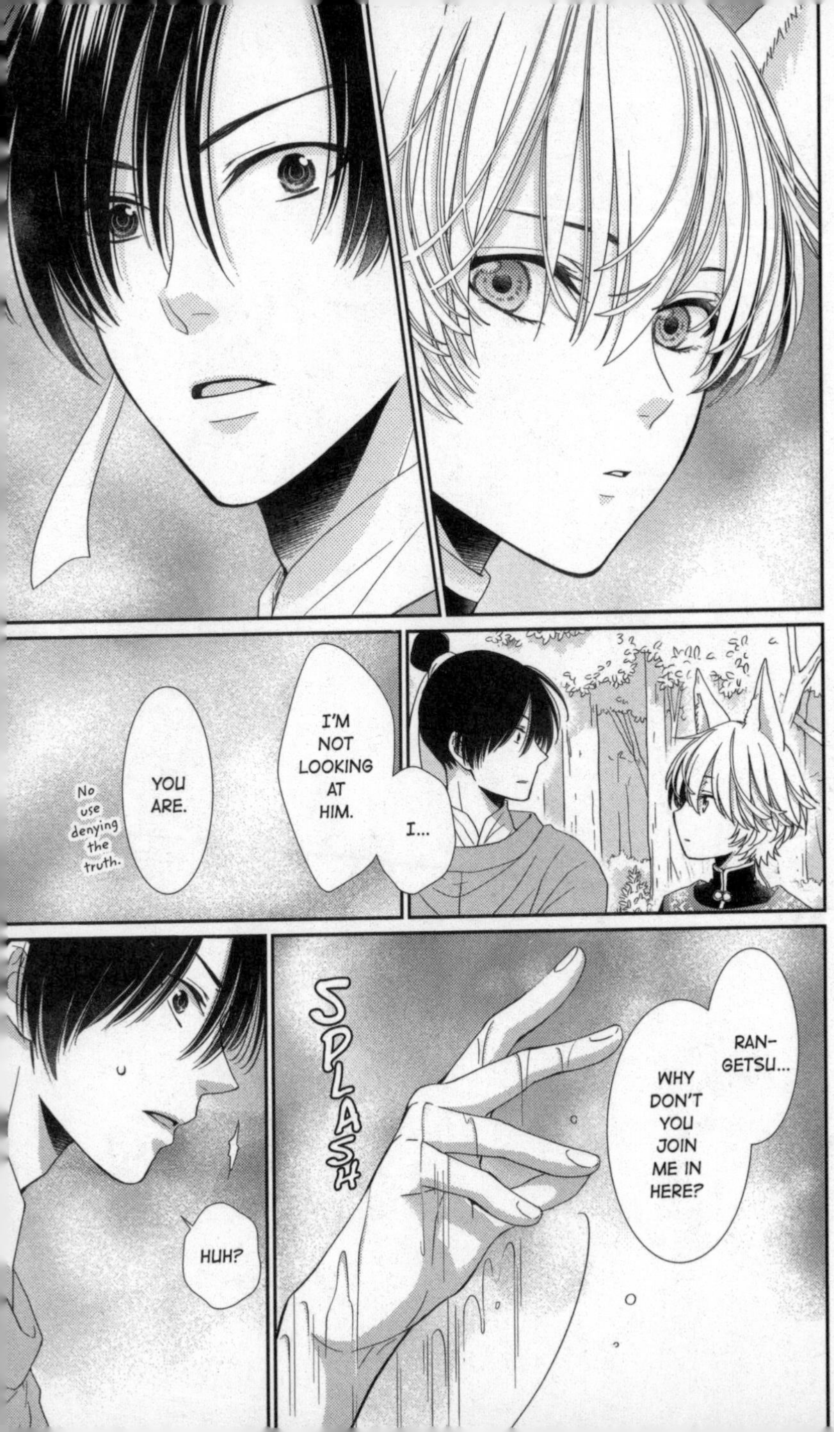
I...
I'M NOT LOOKING AT HIM.
YOU ARE.
No use denying the truth.
RAN-GETSU...
WHY DON'T YOU JOIN ME IN HERE?
SPLASH
HUH?

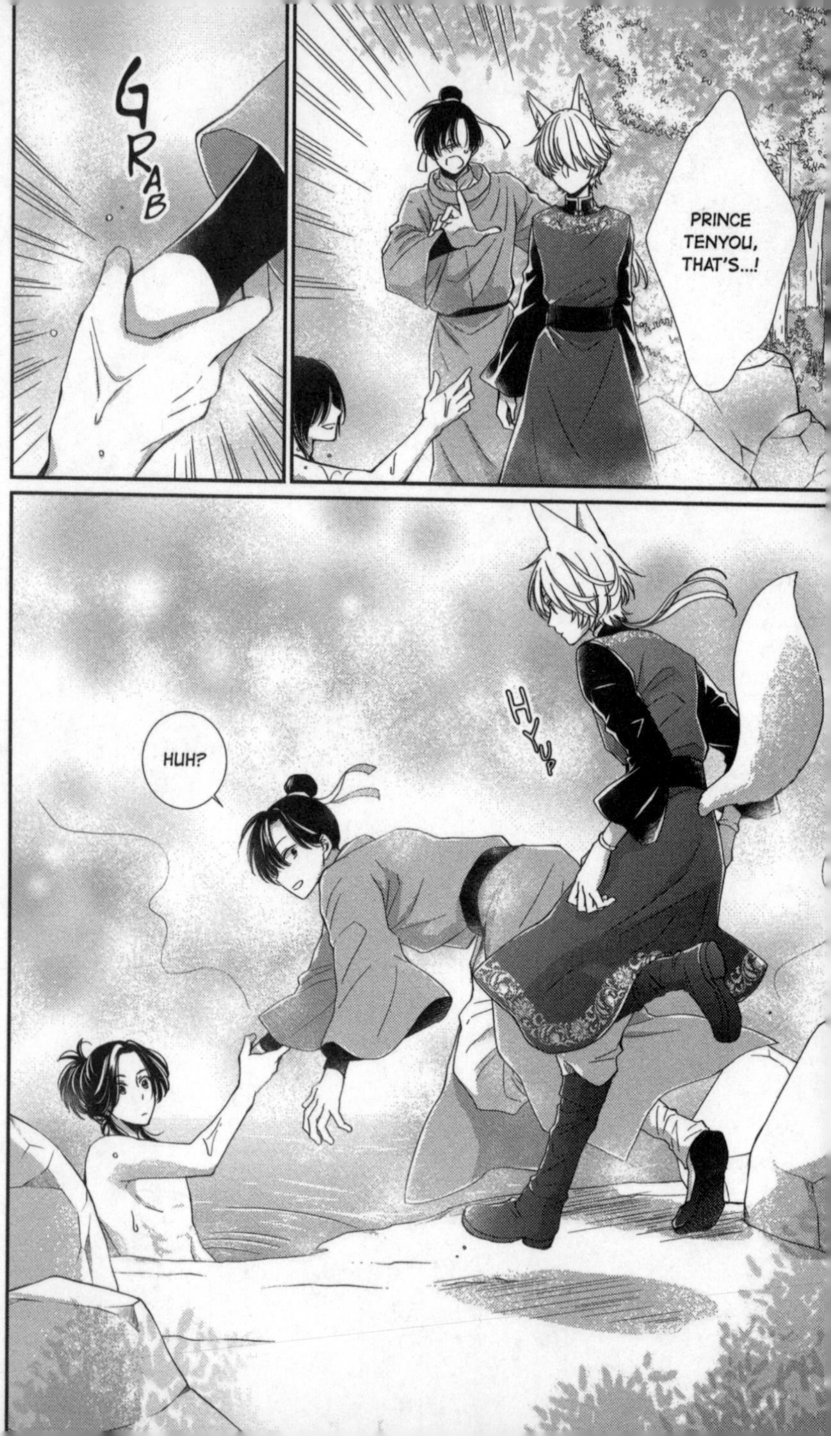
PRINCE TENYOU, THAT'S...!
GRAB
HYUP
HUH?

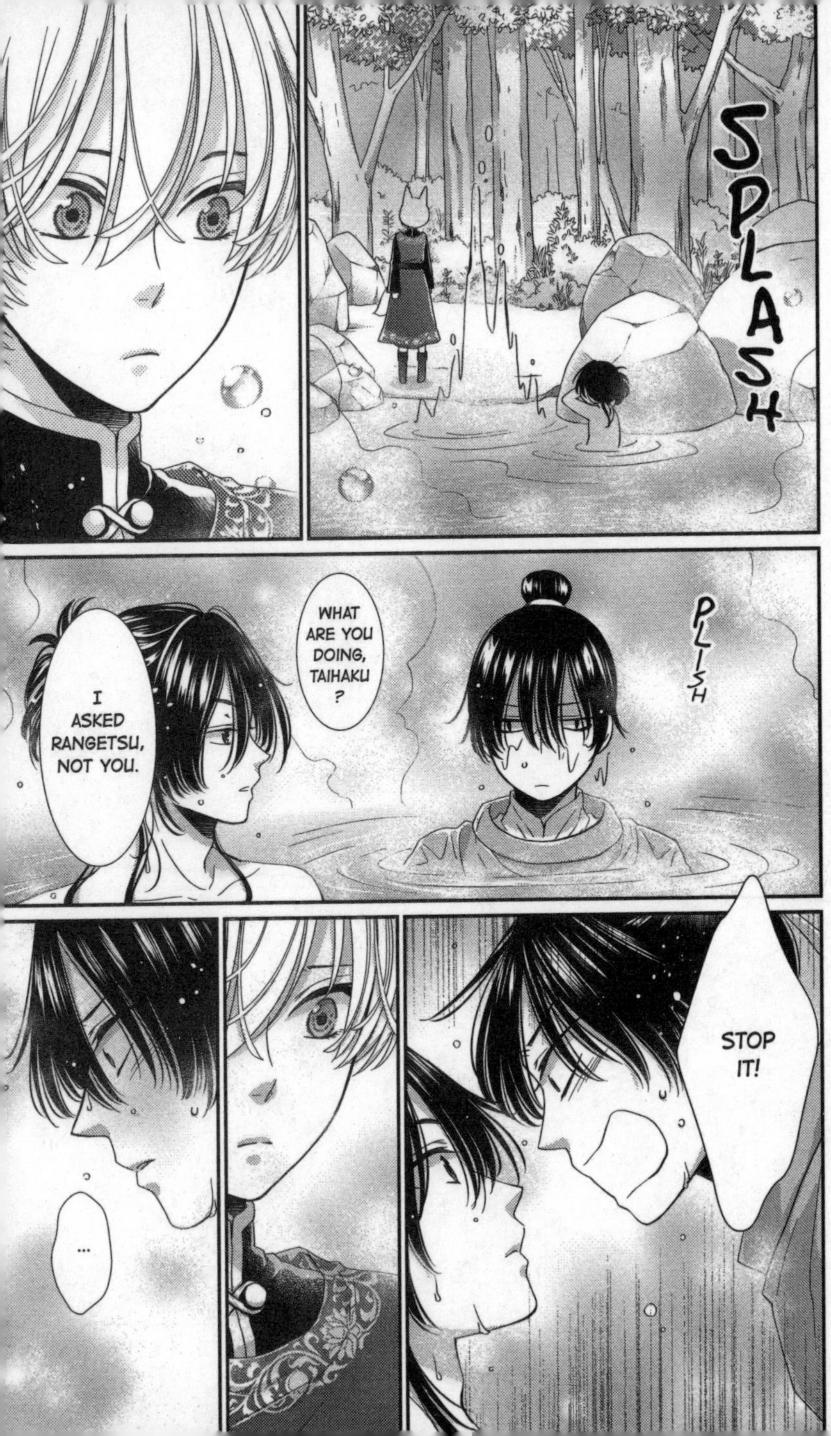
SPLASH
PLISH
WHAT ARE YOU DOING, TAIHAKU?
I ASKED RANGETSU, NOT YOU.
STOP IT!
...

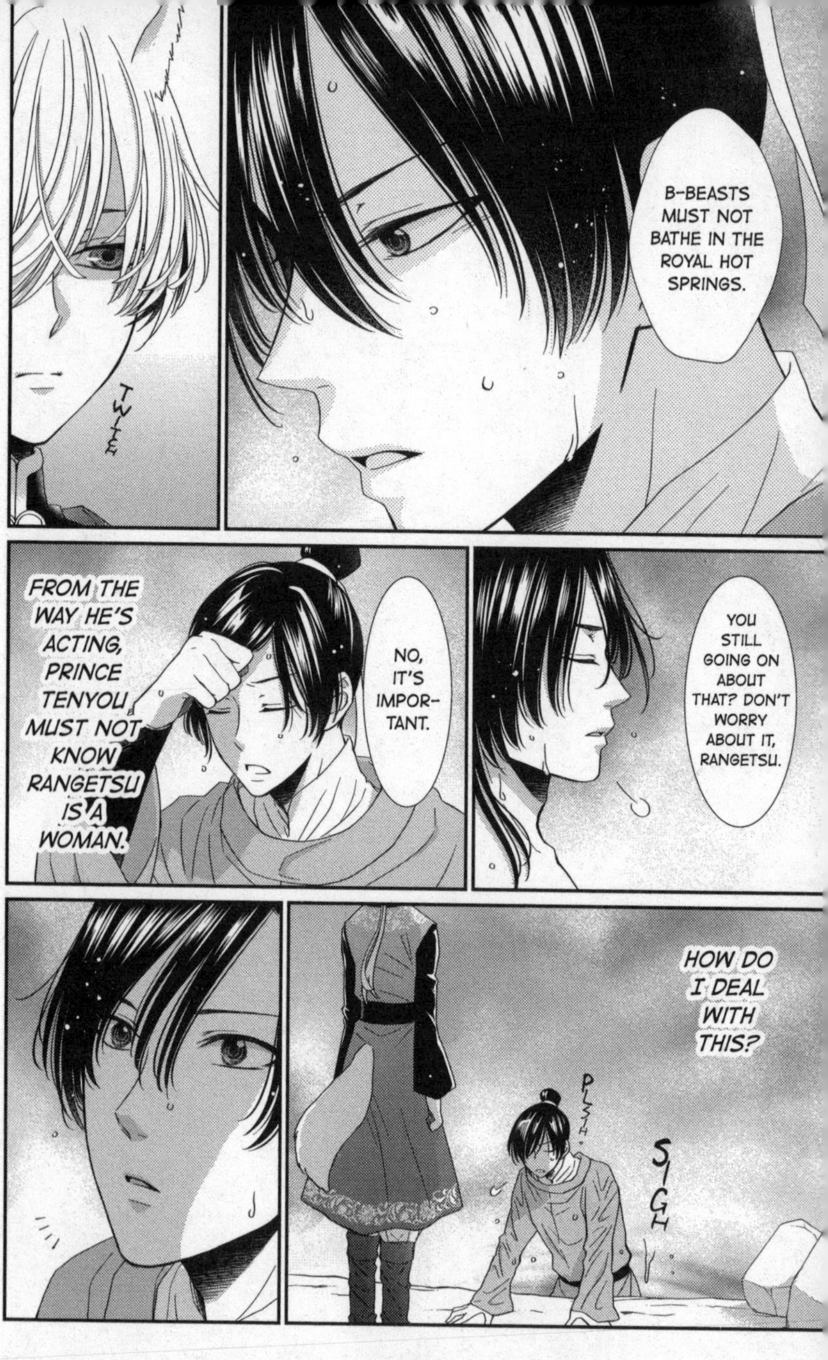
B-BEASTS MUST NOT BATHE IN THE ROYAL HOT SPRINGS.
TWITCH
YOU STILL GOING ON ABOUT THAT? DON'T WORRY ABOUT IT, RANGETSU.
NO, IT'S IMPORTANT.
FROM THE WAY HE'S ACTING, PRINCE TENYOU MUST NOT KNOW RANGETSU IS A WOMAN.
HOW DO I DEAL WITH THIS?
PLSH
SIGH

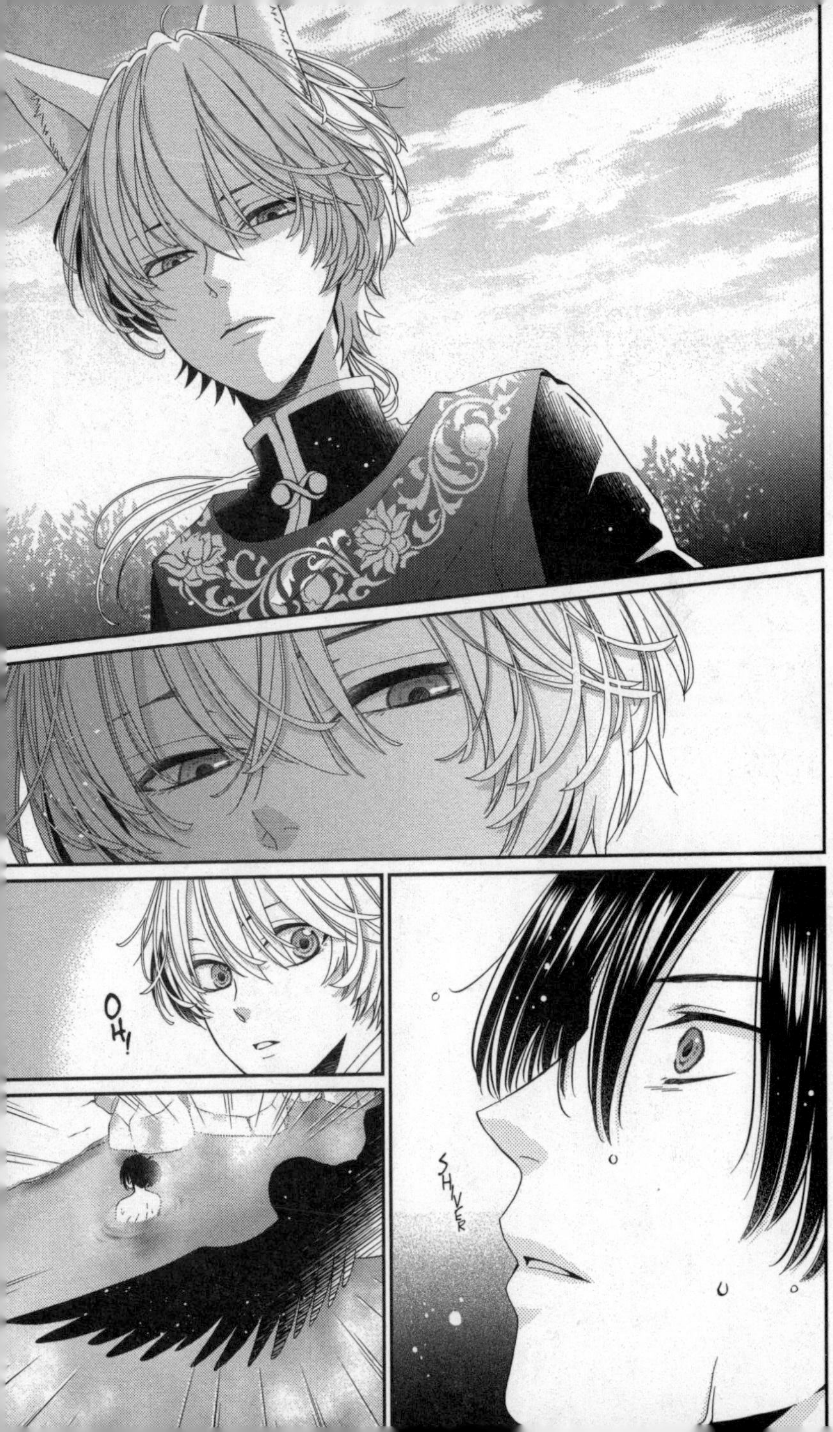
OH!
SHIVER

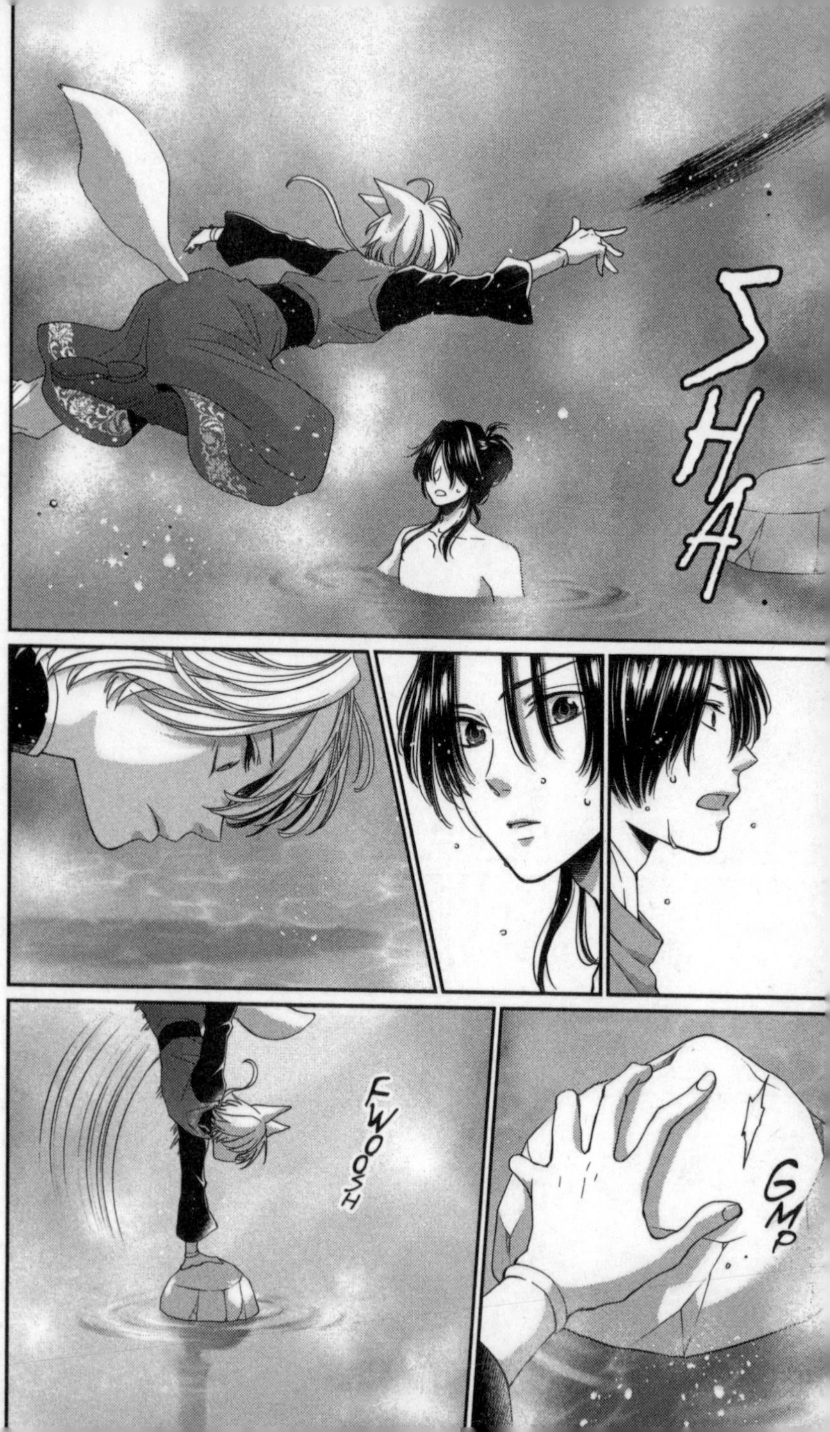
SHA
GMP
FWOOSH

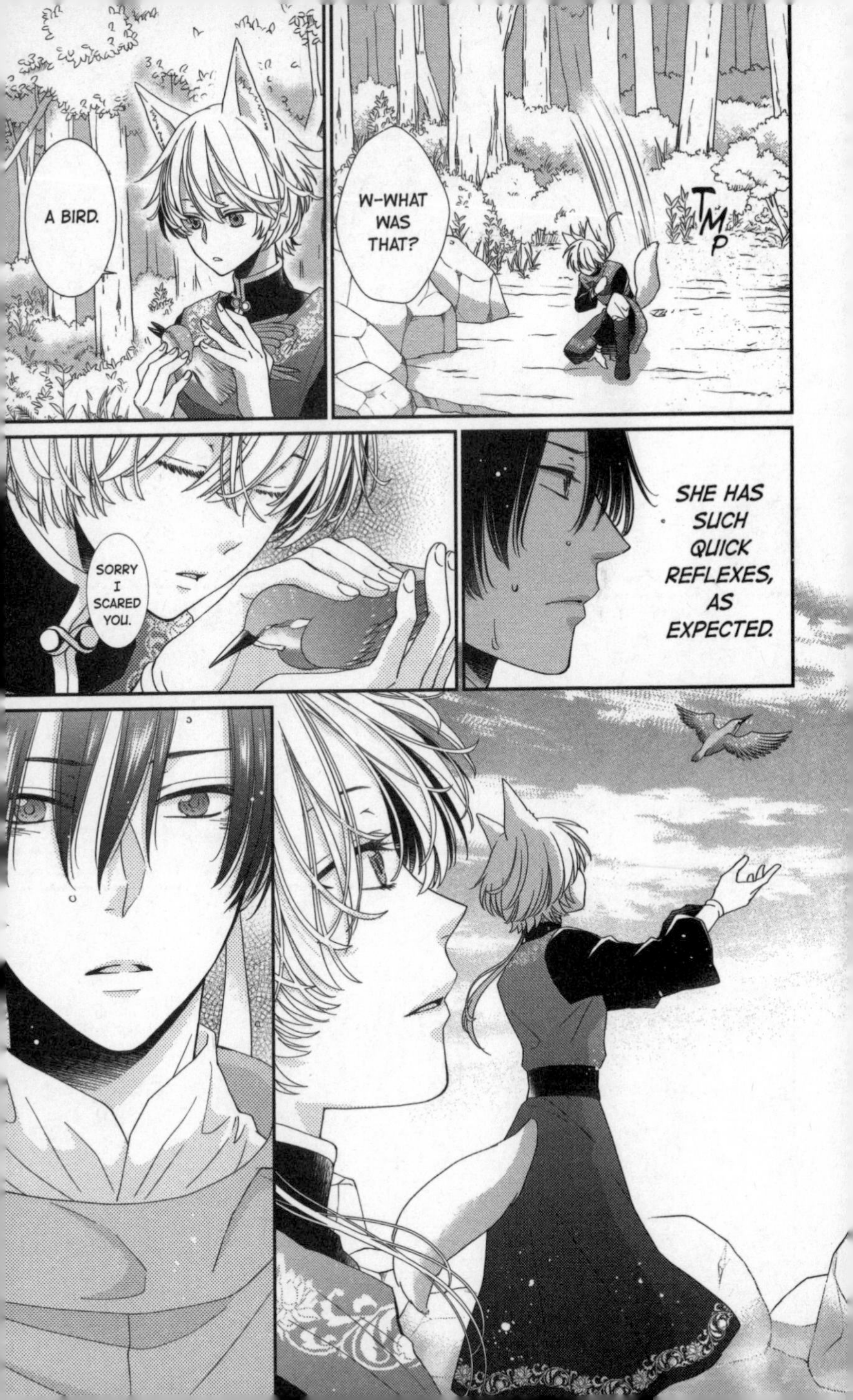
TMP
W-WHAT WAS THAT?
A BIRD.
SHE HAS SUCH QUICK REFLEXES, AS EXPECTED.
SORRY I SCARED YOU.

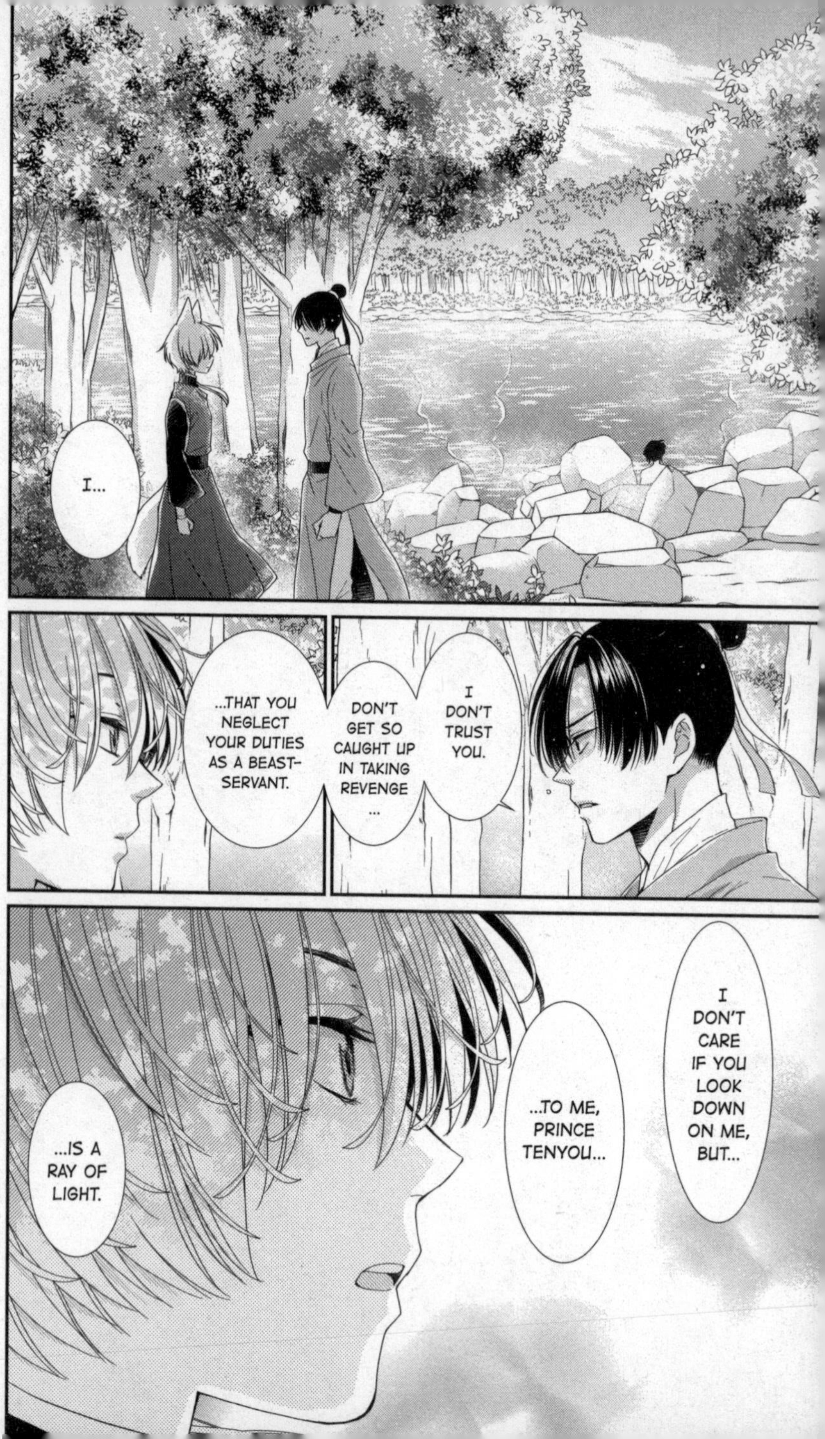
I...
I DON'T TRUST YOU.
DON'T GET SO CAUGHT UP IN TAKING REVENGE...
...THAT YOU NEGLECT YOUR DUTIES AS A BEAST-SERVANT.
I DON'T CARE IF YOU LOOK DOWN ON ME, BUT...
...TO ME, PRINCE TENYOU...
...IS A RAY OF LIGHT.

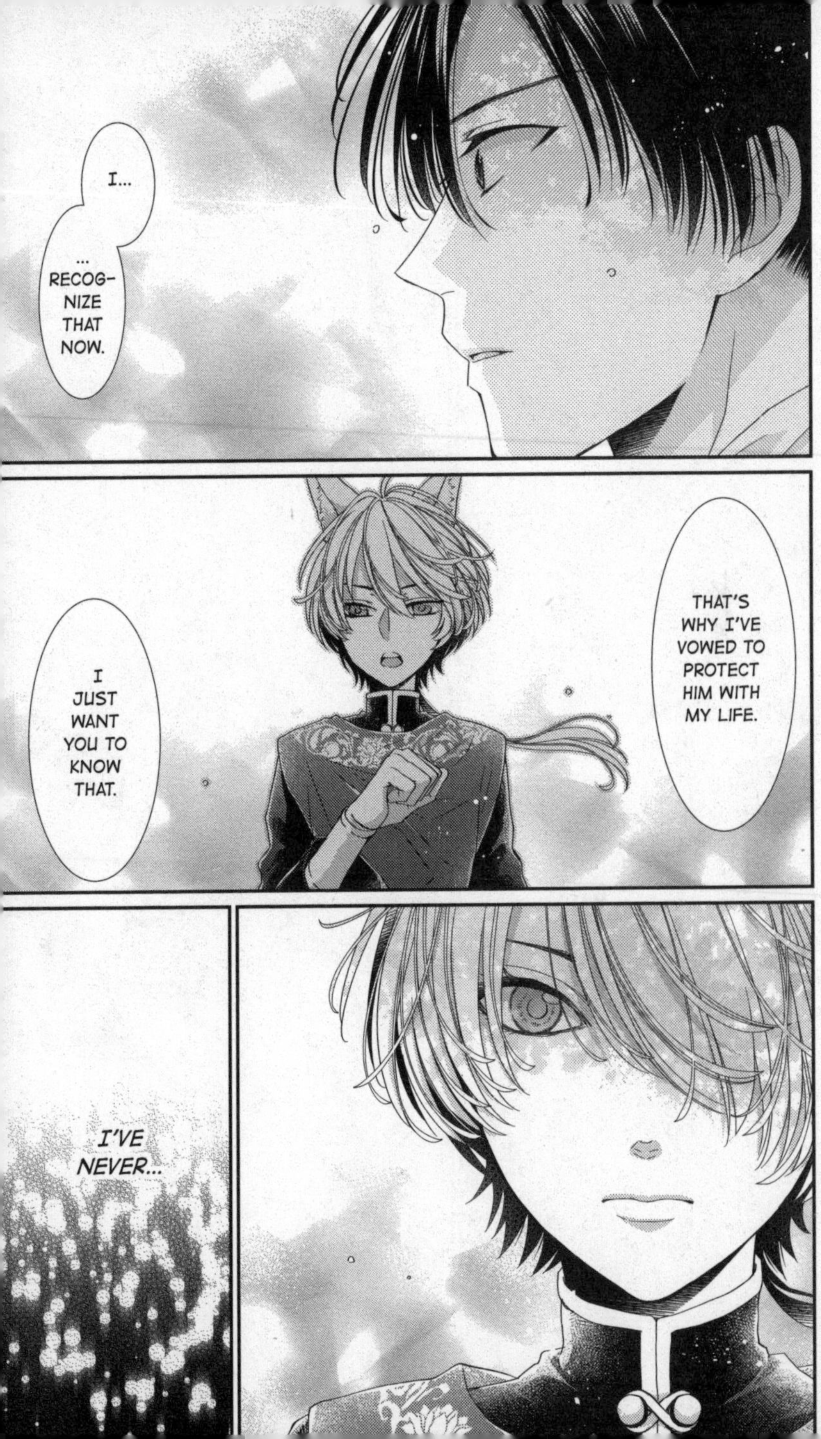
I...
...RECOG-NIZE THAT NOW.
THAT'S WHY I'VE VOWED TO PROTECT HIM WITH MY LIFE.
I JUST WANT YOU TO KNOW THAT.
I'VE NEVER...

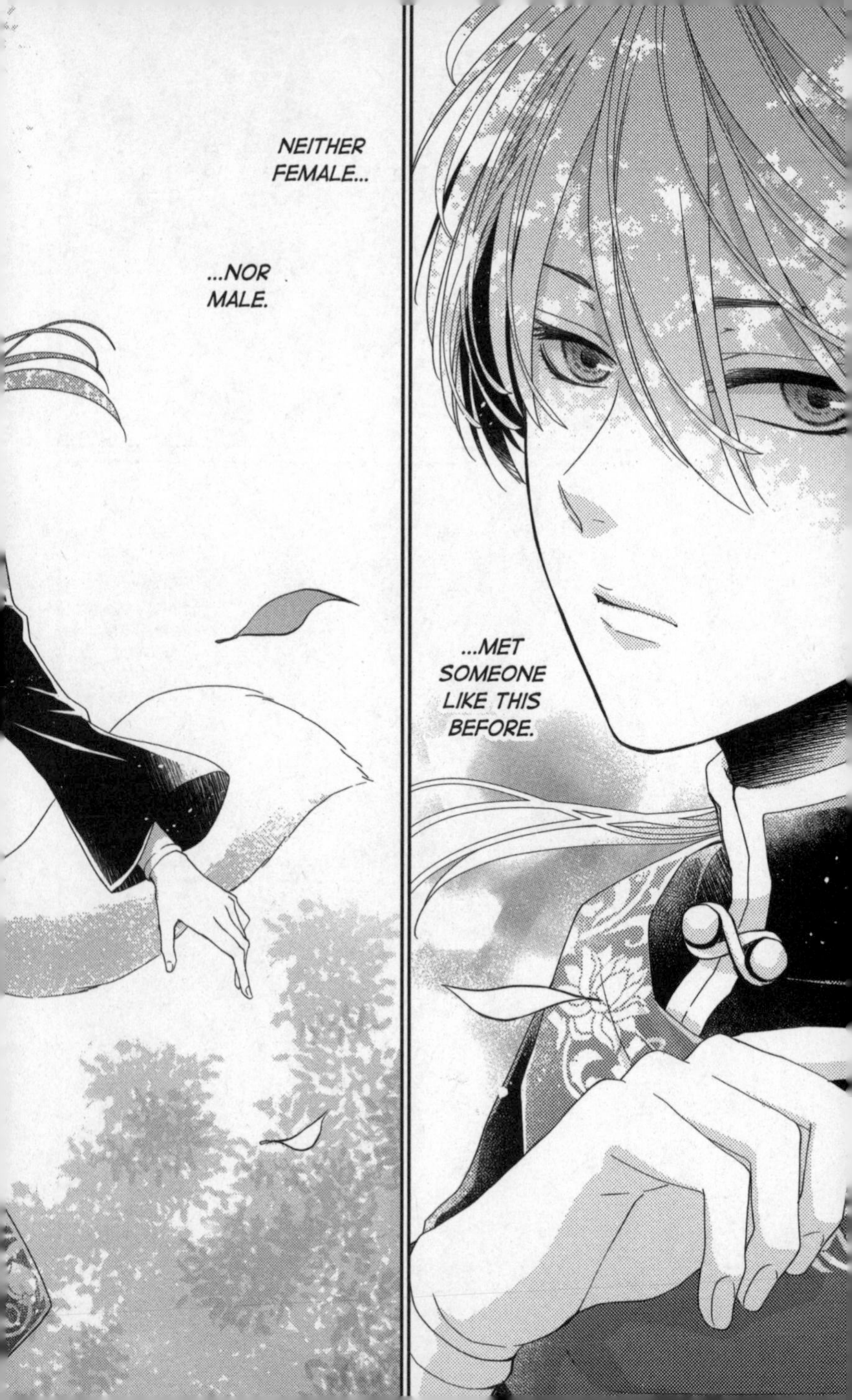
...MET SOMEONE LIKE THIS BEFORE.
NEITHER FEMALE...
...NOR MALE.

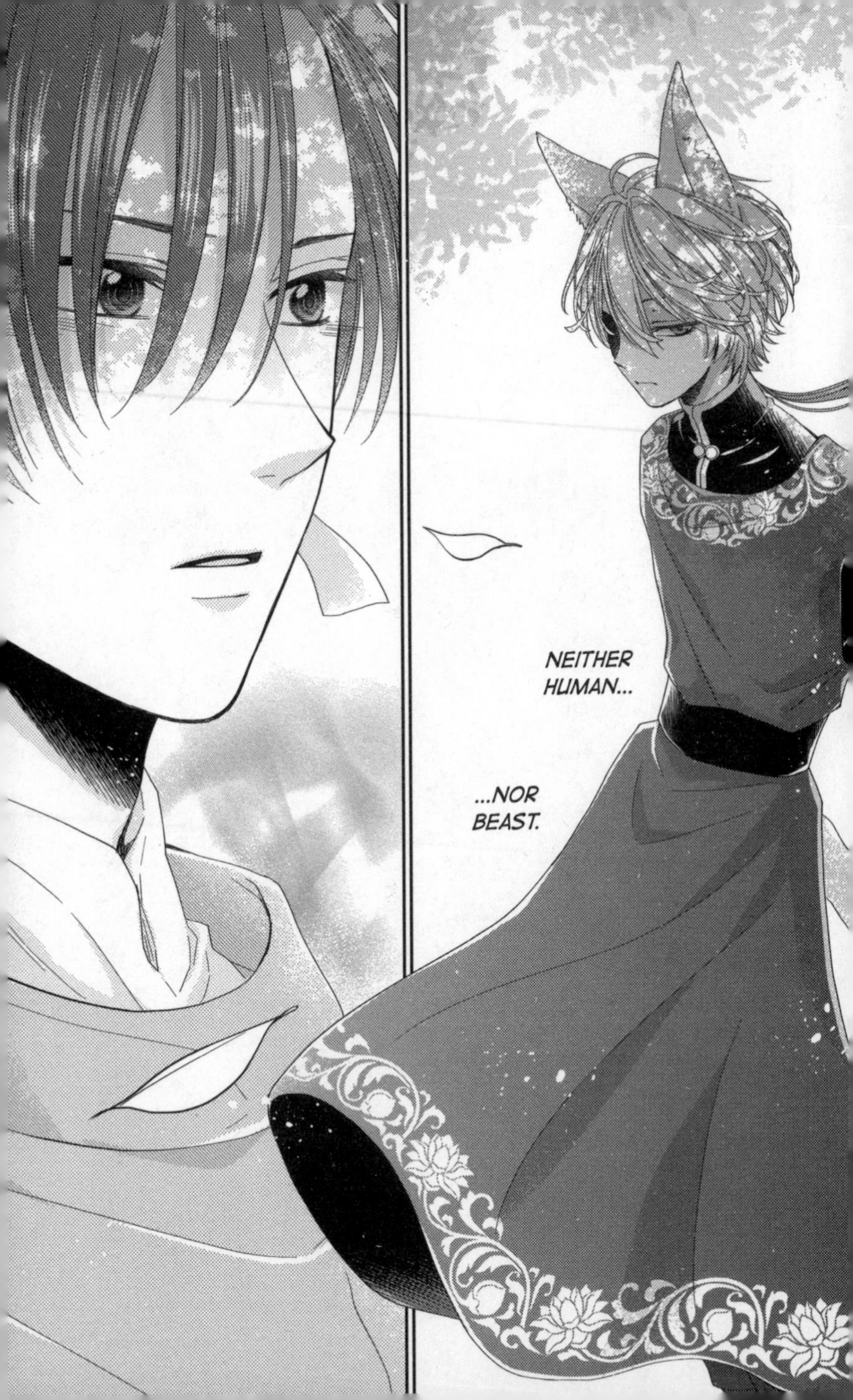
NEITHER HUMAN...
...NOR BEAST.

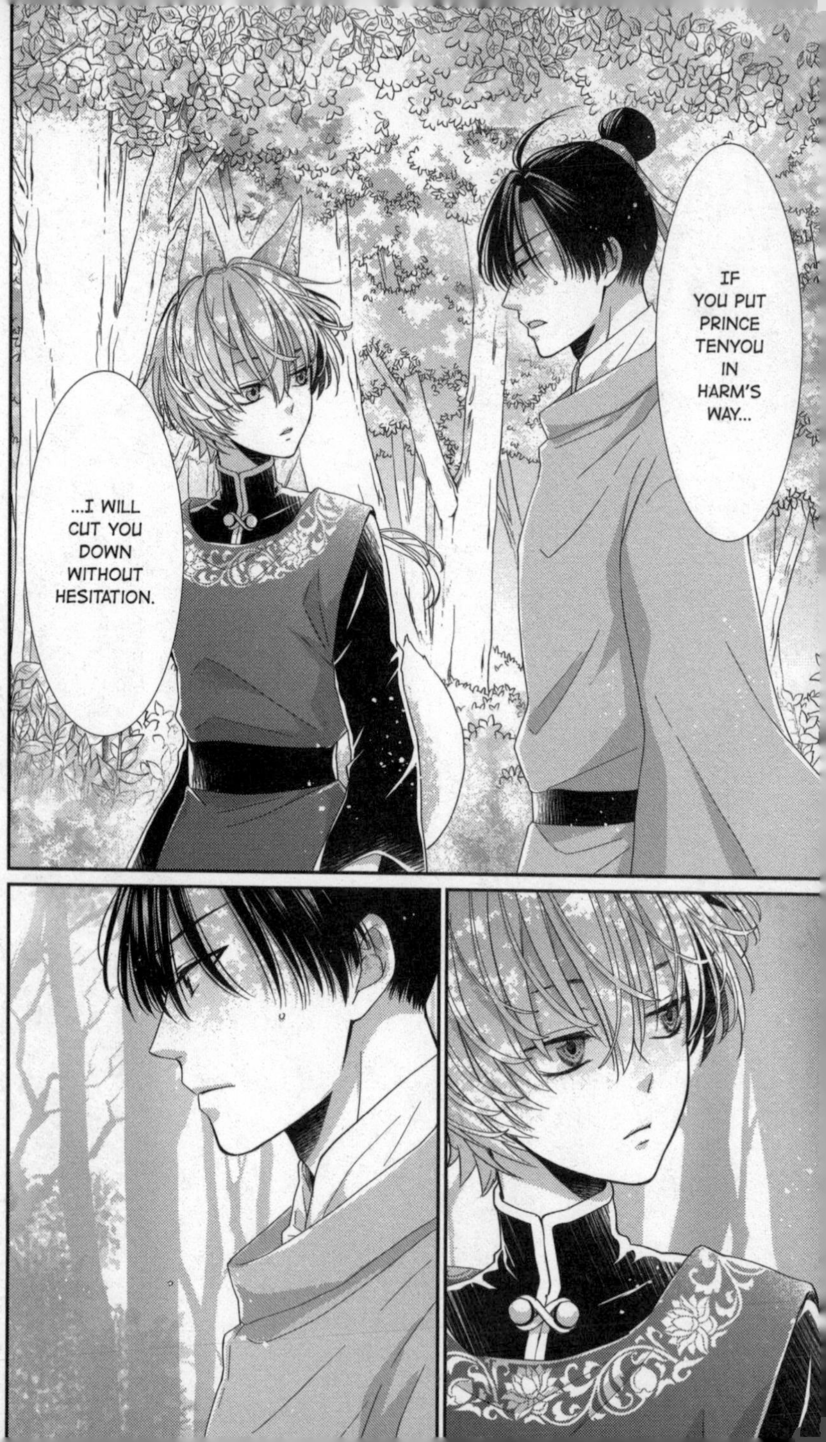
IF YOU PUT PRINCE TENYOU IN HARM'S WAY...
...I WILL CUT YOU DOWN WITHOUT HESITATION.

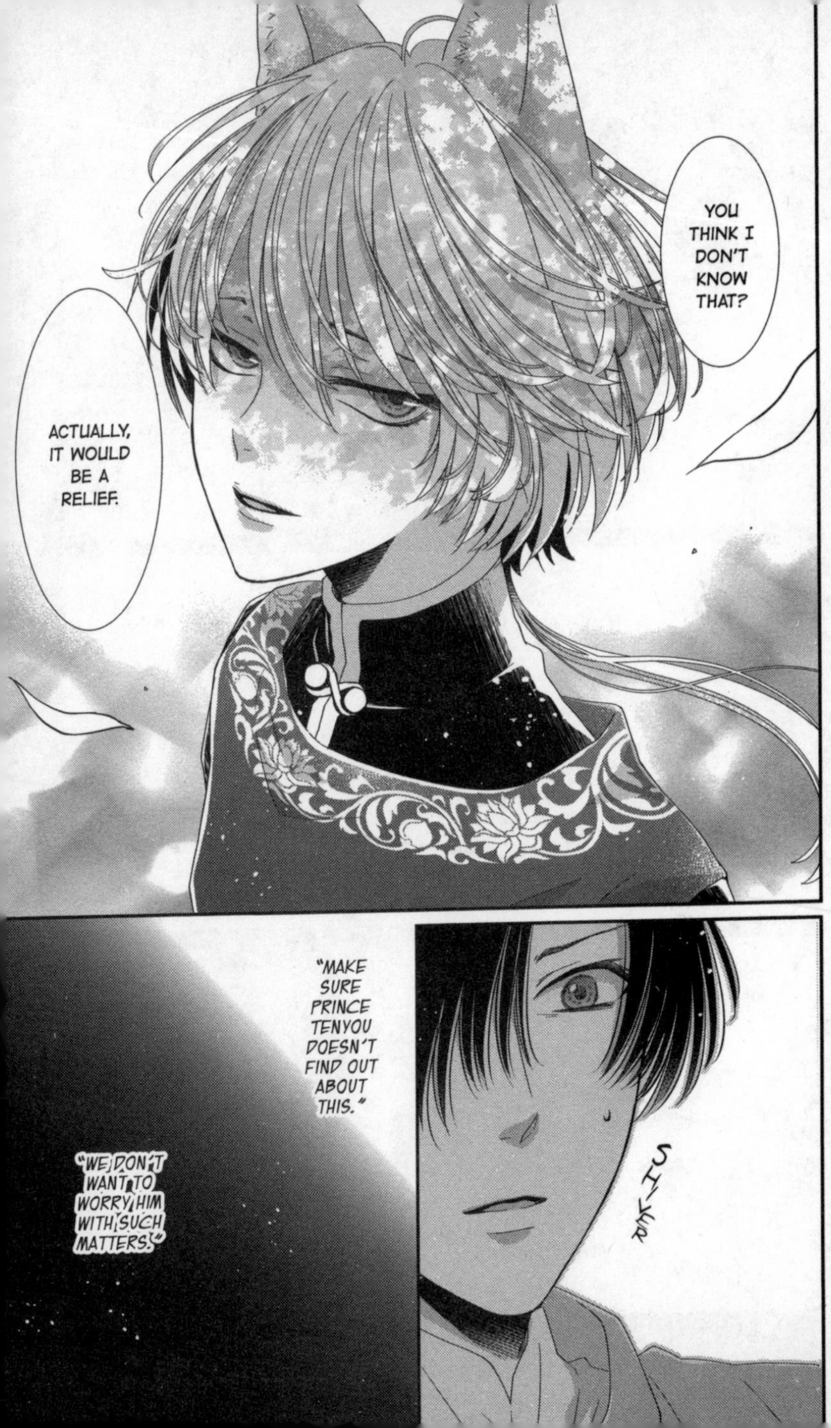
YOU THINK I DON'T KNOW THAT?
ACTUALLY, IT WOULD BE A RELIEF.
"MAKE SURE PRINCE TENYOU DOESN'T FIND OUT ABOUT THIS."
SHIVER
"WE DON'T WANT TO WORRY HIM WITH SUCH MATTERS."

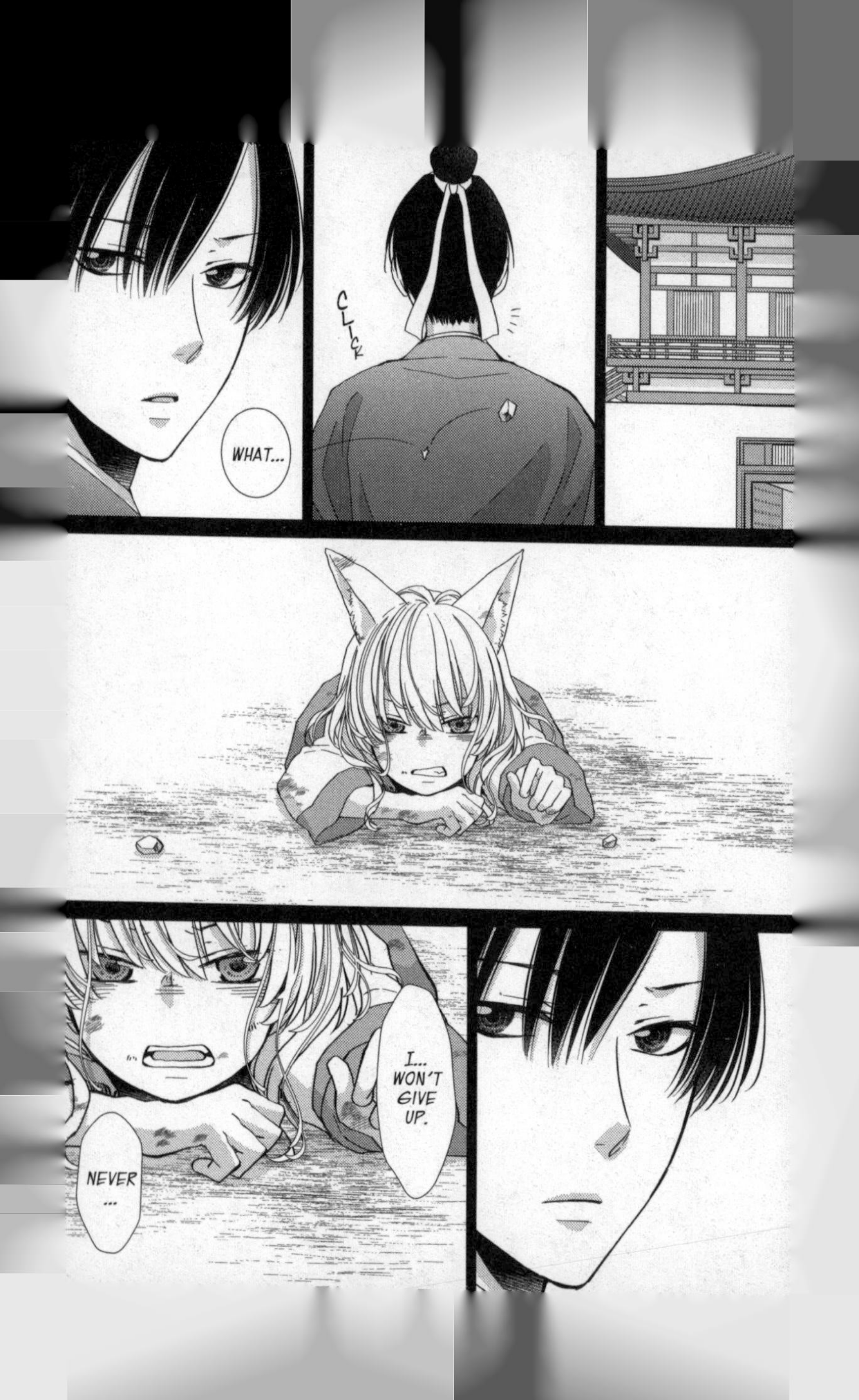
CLICK
WHAT...
I... WON'T GIVE UP.
NEVER...

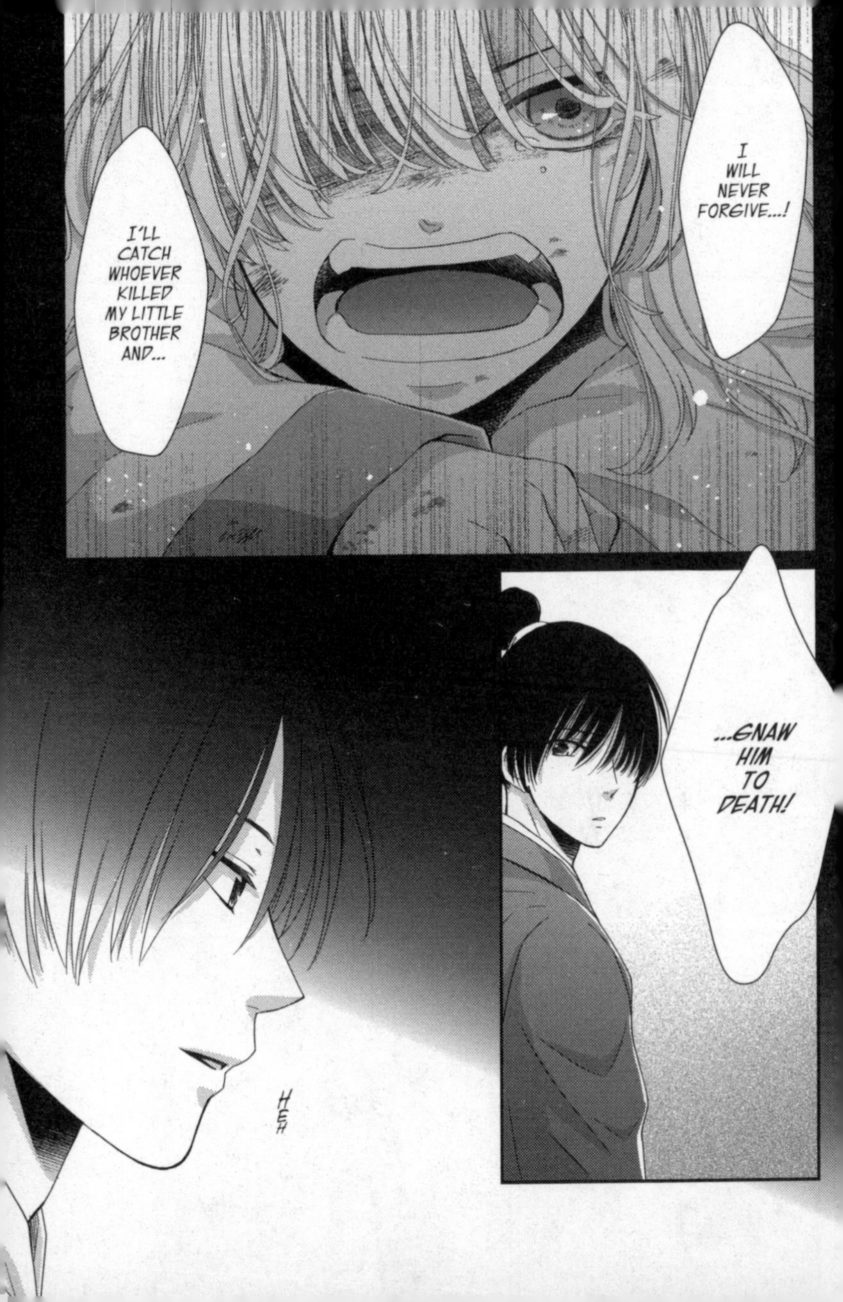
I WILL NEVER FORGIVE...!
I'LL CATCH WHOEVER KILLED MY LITTLE BROTHER AND...
...GNAW HIM TO DEATH!
HEH

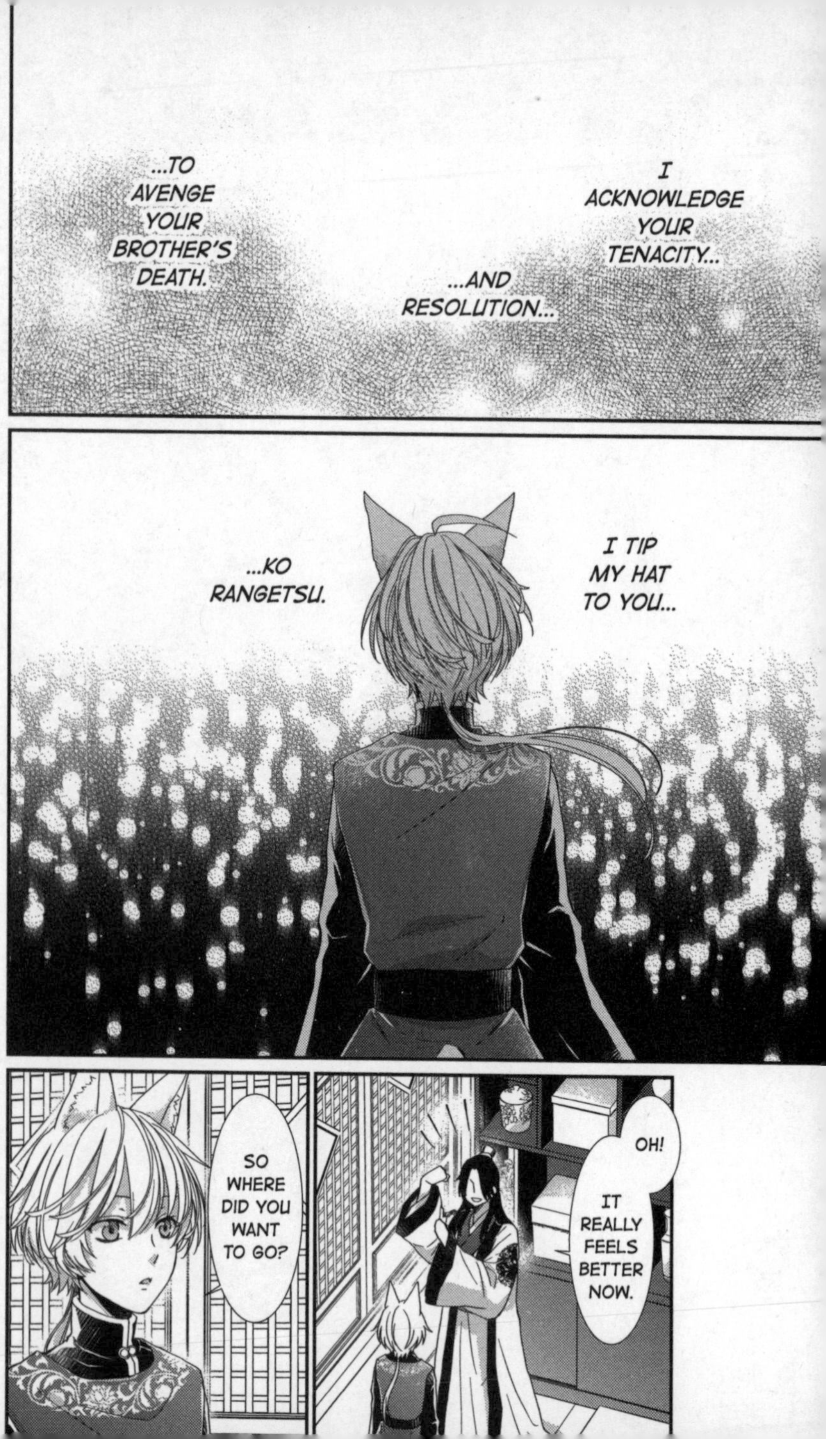
I ACKNOWLEDGE YOUR TENACITY...
...AND RESOLUTION...
...TO AVENGE YOUR BROTHER'S DEATH.
I TIP MY HAT TO YOU...
...KO RANGETSU.
OH!
IT REALLY FEELS BETTER NOW.
SO WHERE DID YOU WANT TO GO?

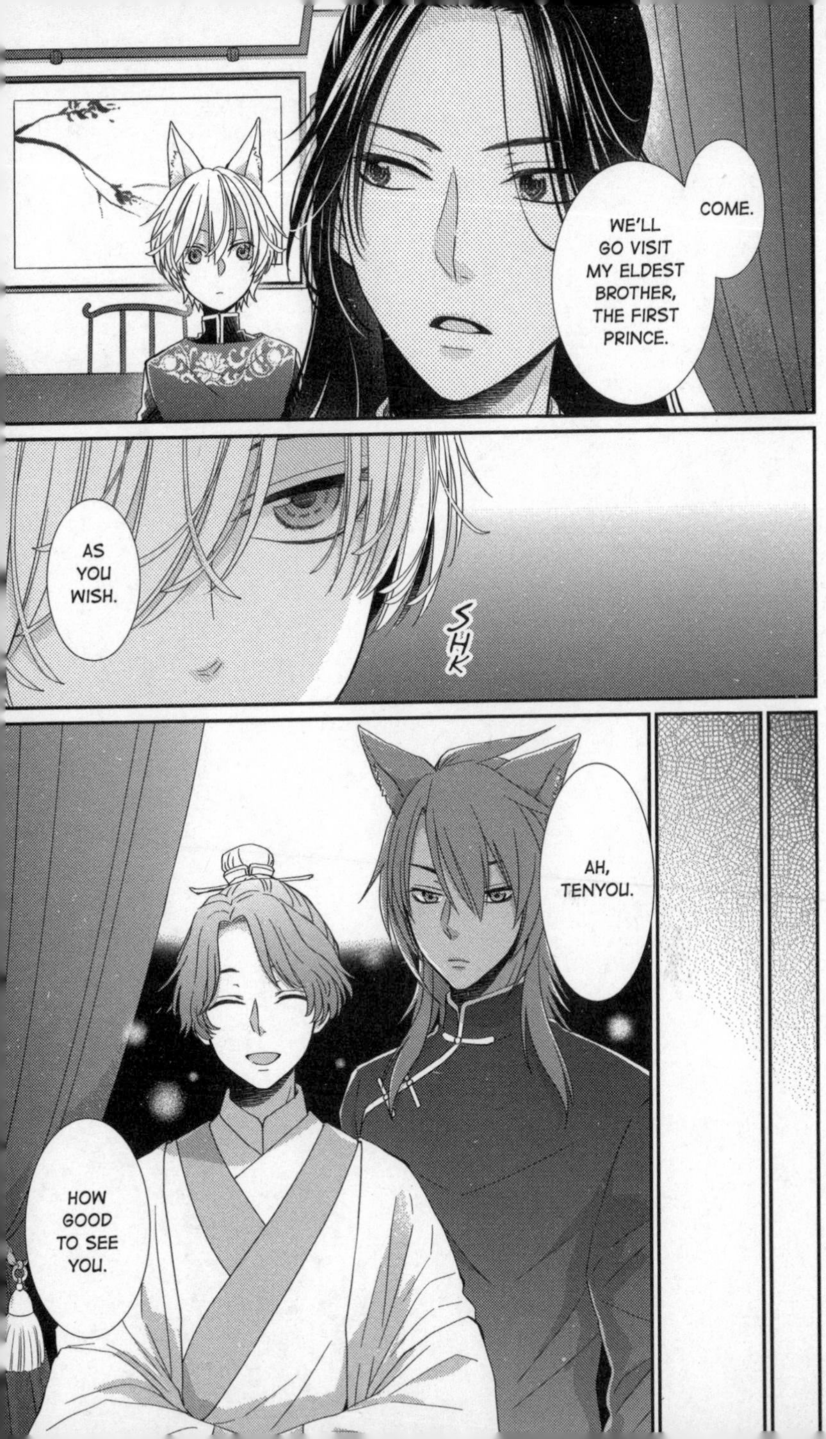
COME.
WE'LL GO VISIT MY ELDEST BROTHER, THE FIRST PRINCE.
SHK
AS YOU WISH.
AH, TENYOU.
HOW GOOD TO SEE YOU.

THE
KING'S
Beast

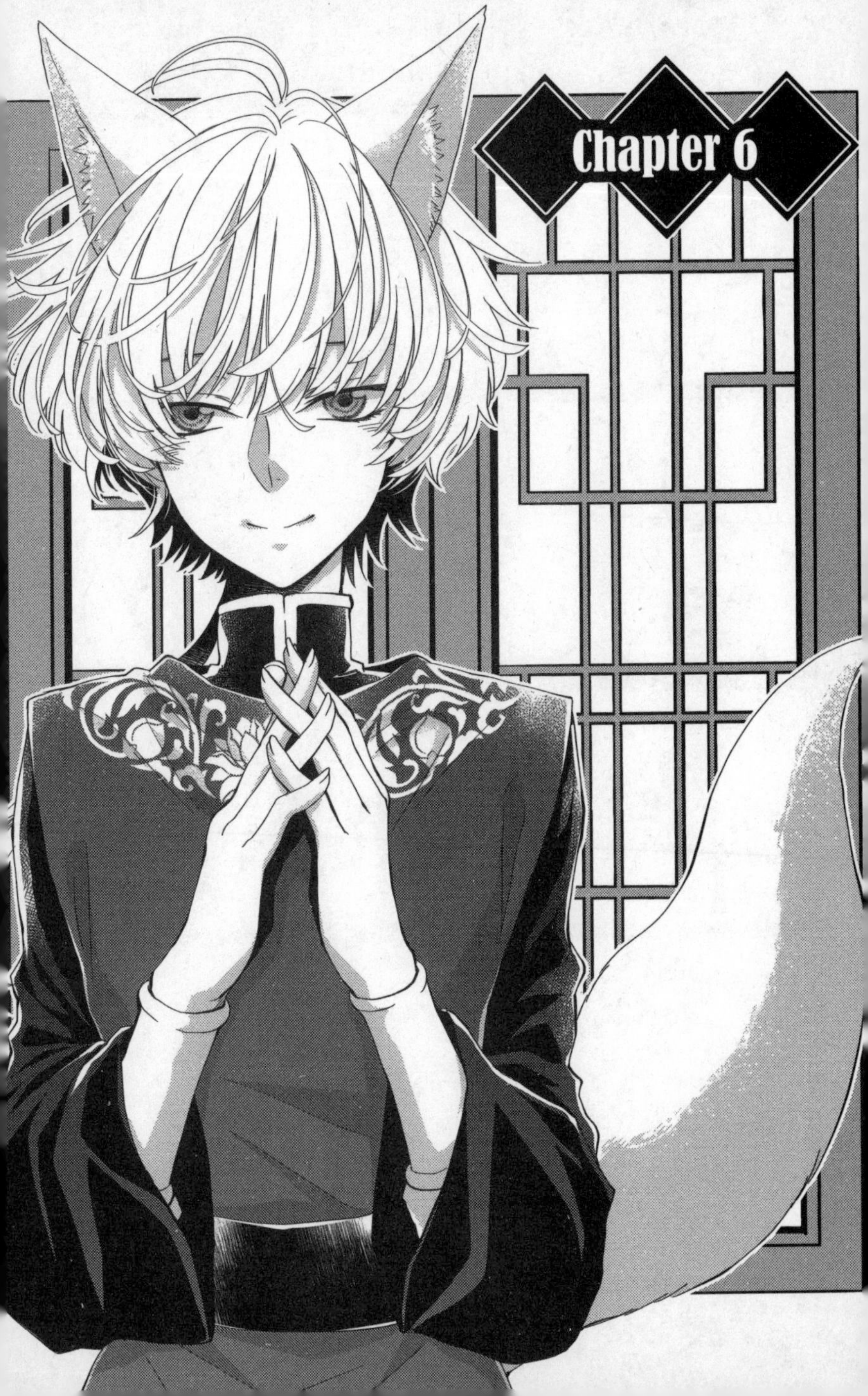
Chapter 6

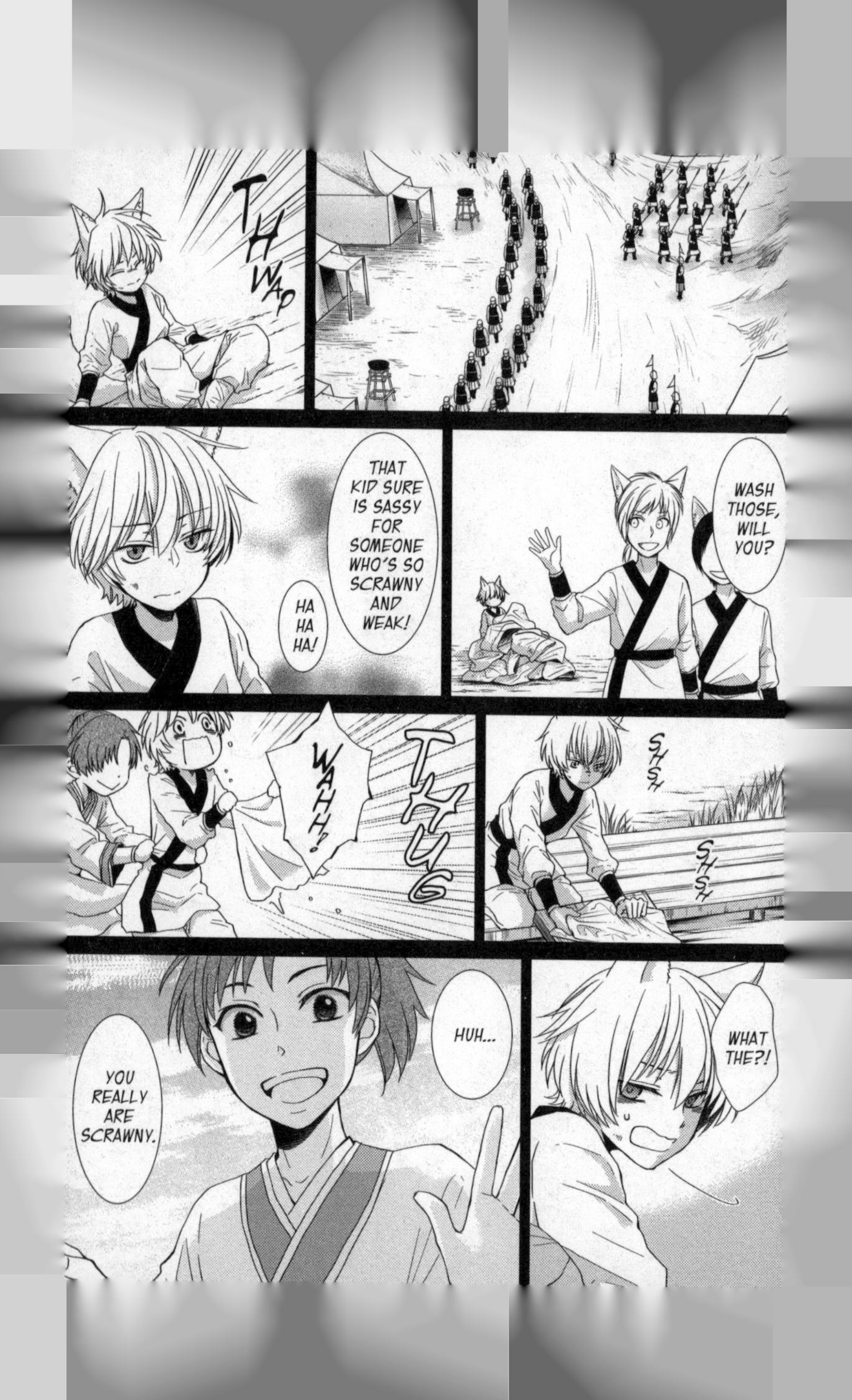
THWAP
WASH THOSE, WILL YOU?
THAT KID SURE IS SASSY FOR SOMEONE WHO'S SO SCRAWNY AND WEAK!
HA HA HA!
SHSH
SHSH
THUG
WAHH?!
WHAT THE?!
HUH...
YOU REALLY ARE SCRAWNY.

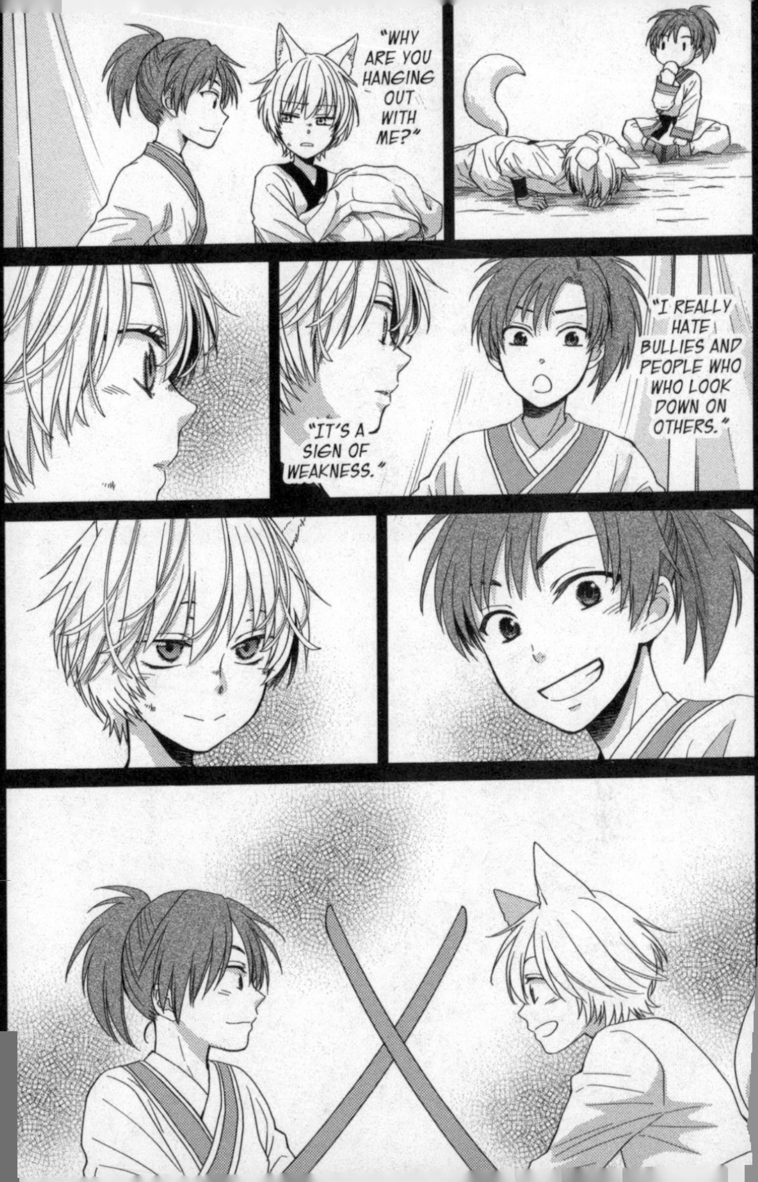
"WHY ARE YOU HANGING OUT WITH ME?"
"I REALLY HATE BULLIES AND PEOPLE WHO WHO LOOK DOWN ON OTHERS."
"IT'S A SIGN OF WEAKNESS."

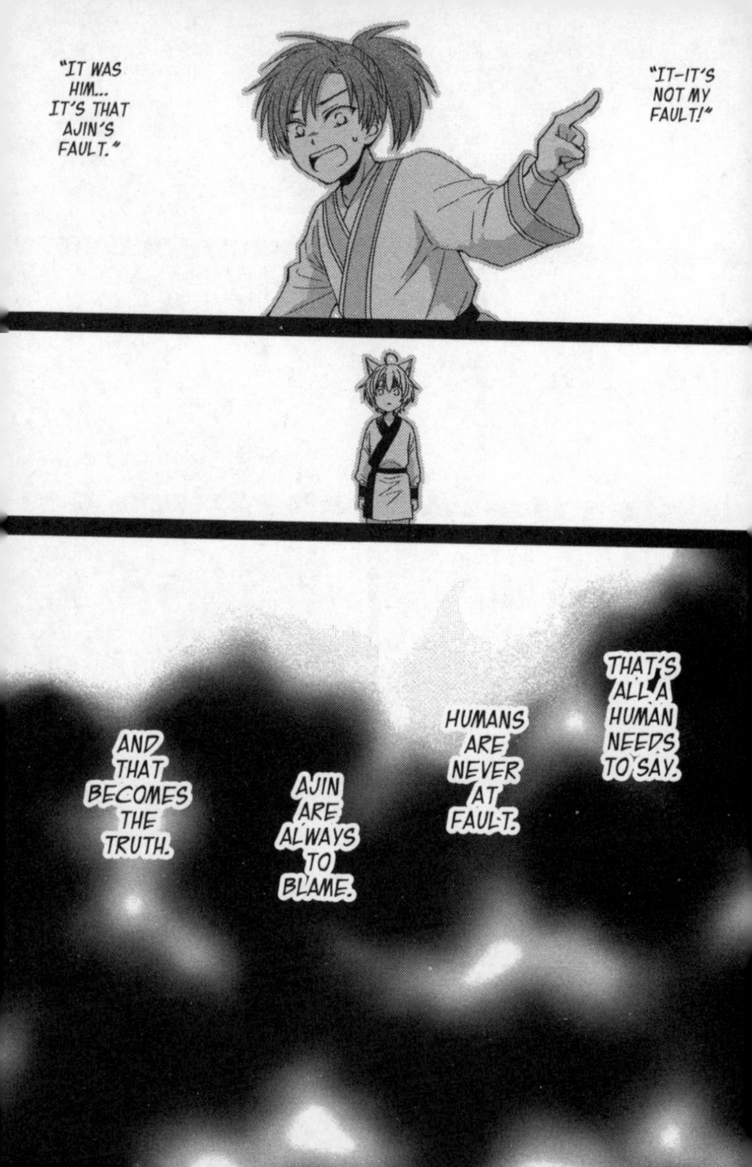
"IT-IT'S NOT MY FAULT!"
"IT WAS HIM... IT'S THAT AJIN'S FAULT."
THAT'S ALL A HUMAN NEEDS TO SAY.
HUMANS ARE NEVER AT FAULT.
AJIN ARE ALWAYS TO BLAME.
AND THAT BECOMES THE TRUTH.

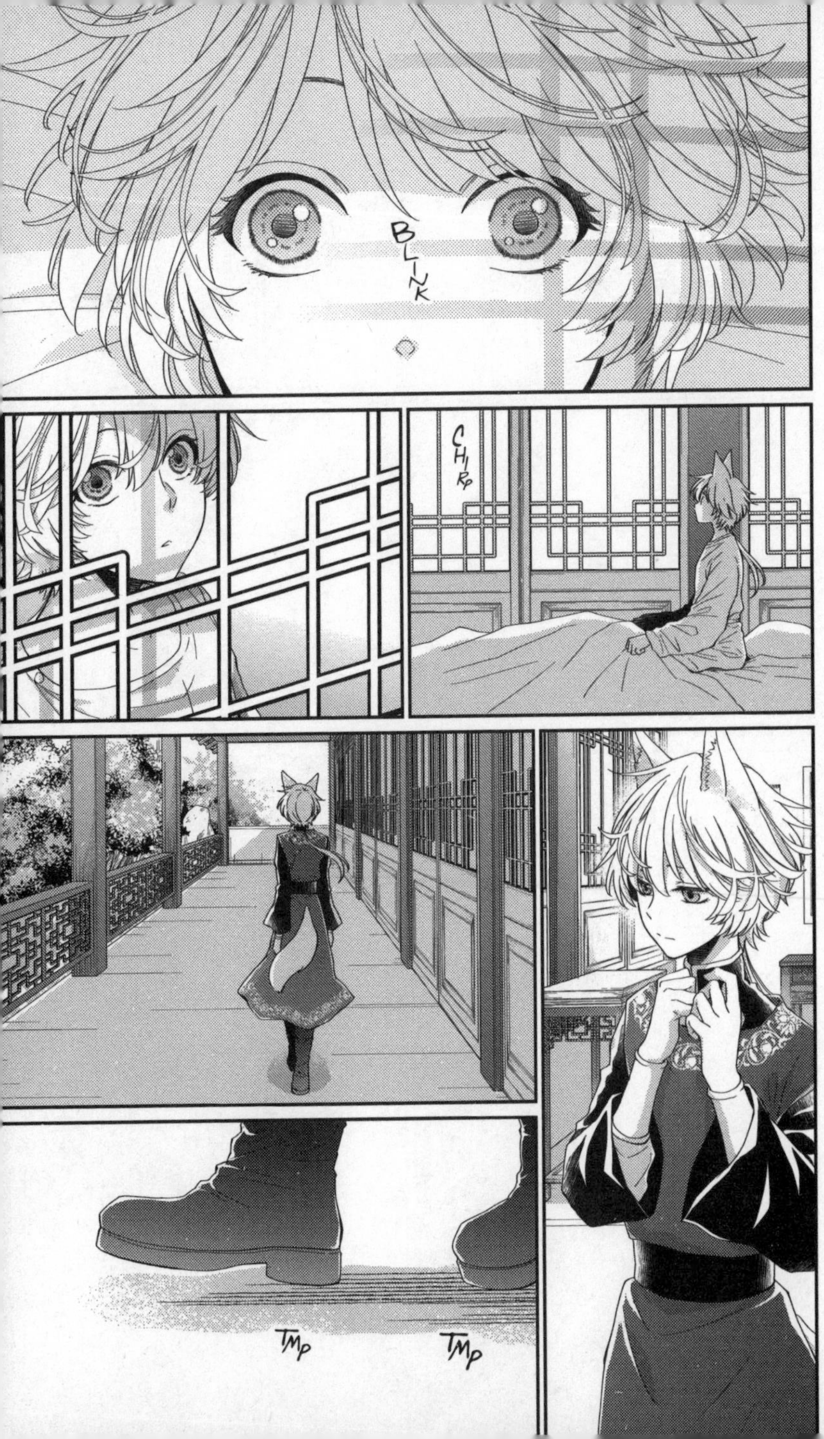
BLINK
CHIRP
TMP
TMP

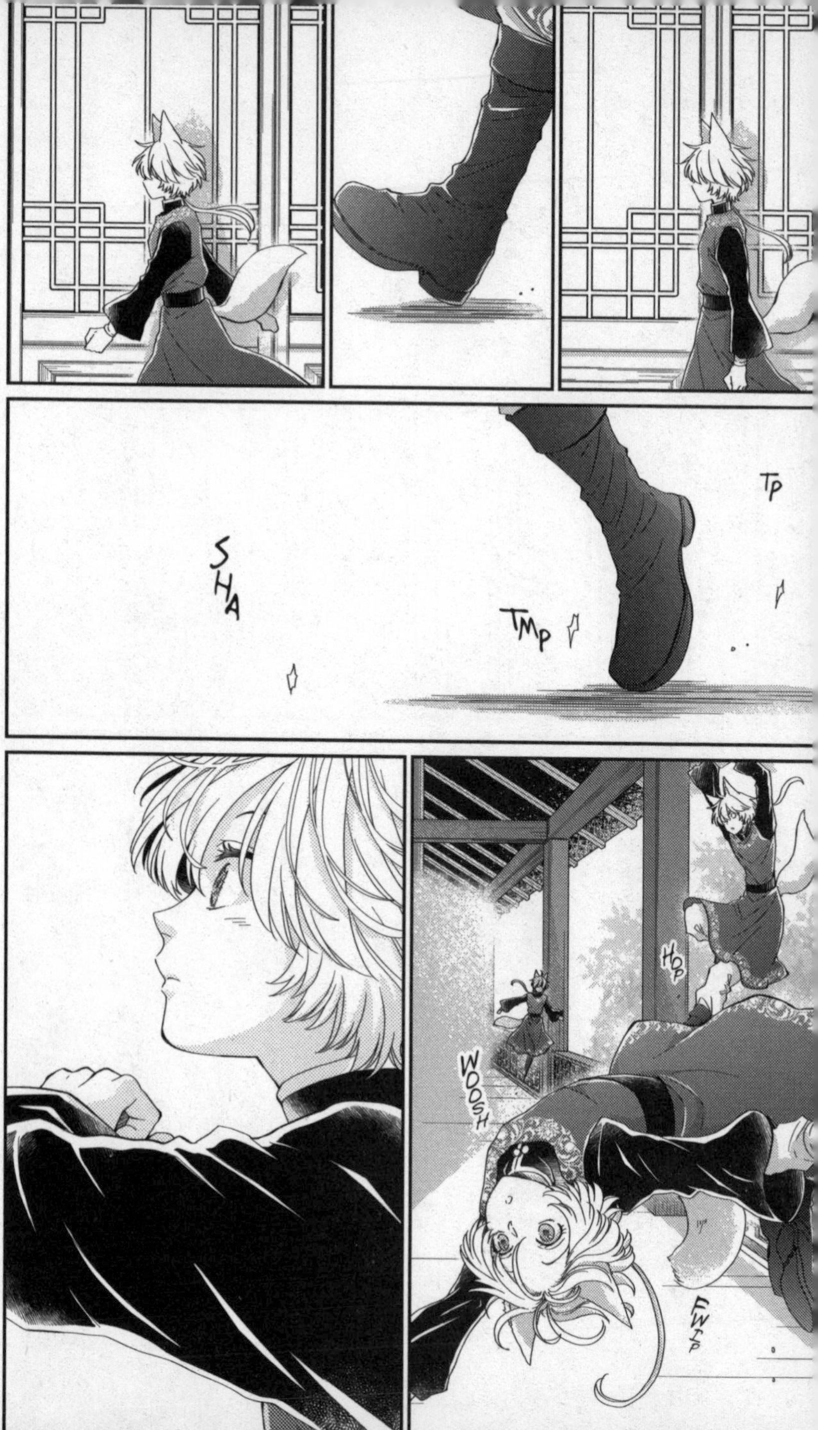
TP
TMP
SHA
HOP
WOOSH
FWIP

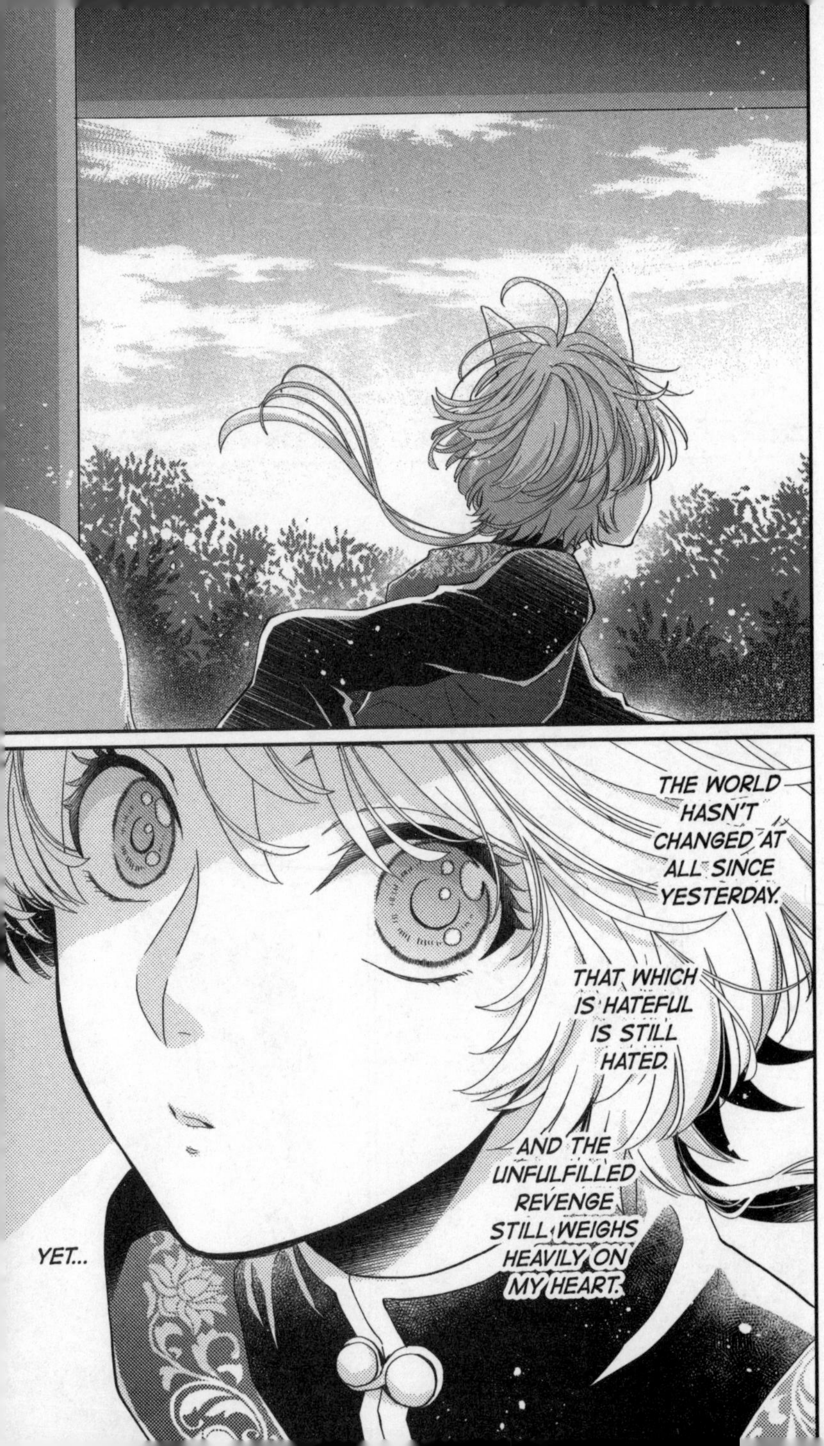
THE WORLD HASN'T CHANGED AT ALL SINCE YESTERDAY.
THAT WHICH IS HATEFUL IS STILL HATED.
AND THE UNFULFILLED REVENGE STILL WEIGHS HEAVILY ON MY HEART.
YET...

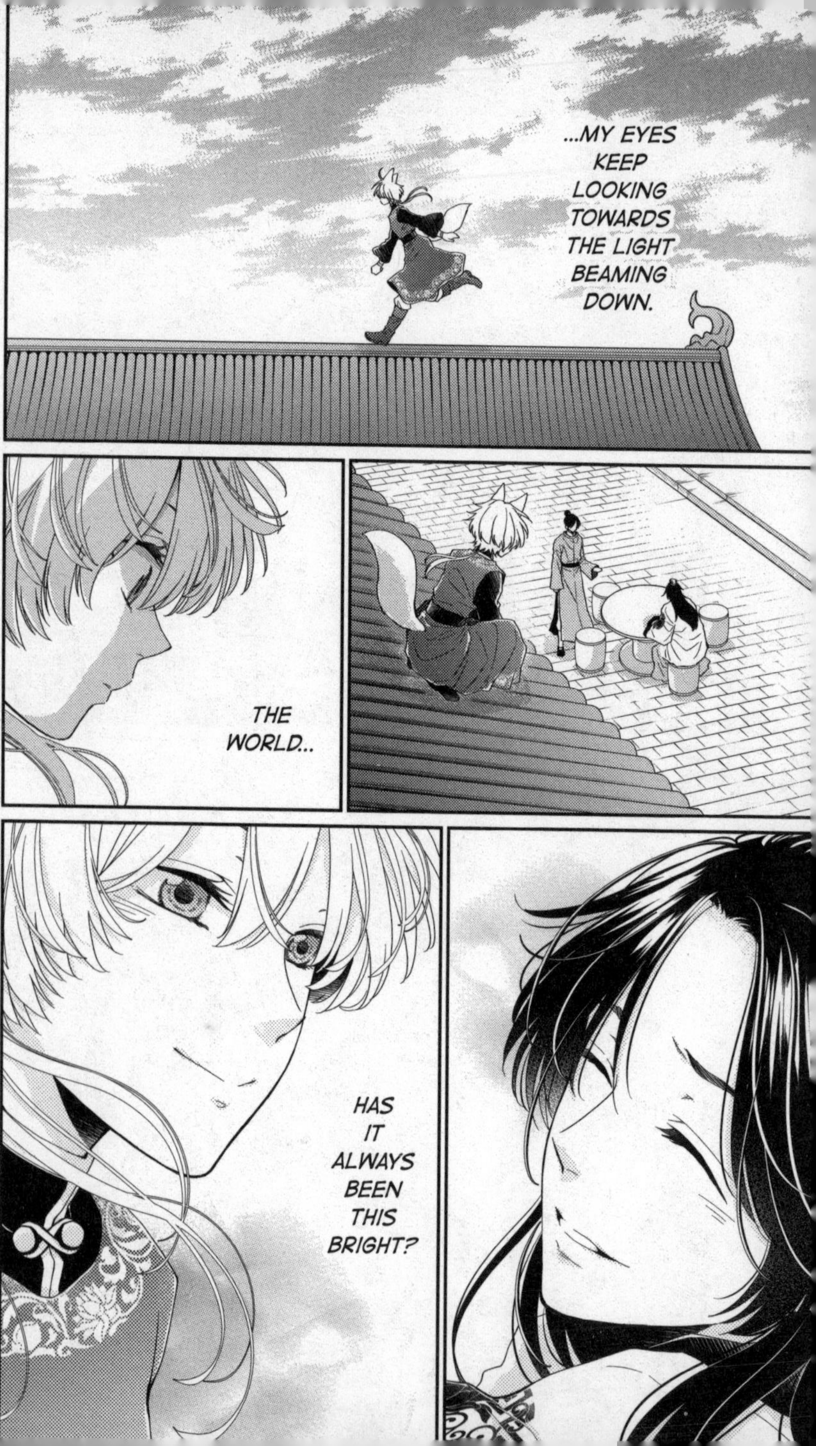
...MY EYES KEEP LOOKING TOWARDS THE LIGHT BEAMING DOWN.
THE WORLD...
HAS IT ALWAYS BEEN THIS BRIGHT?

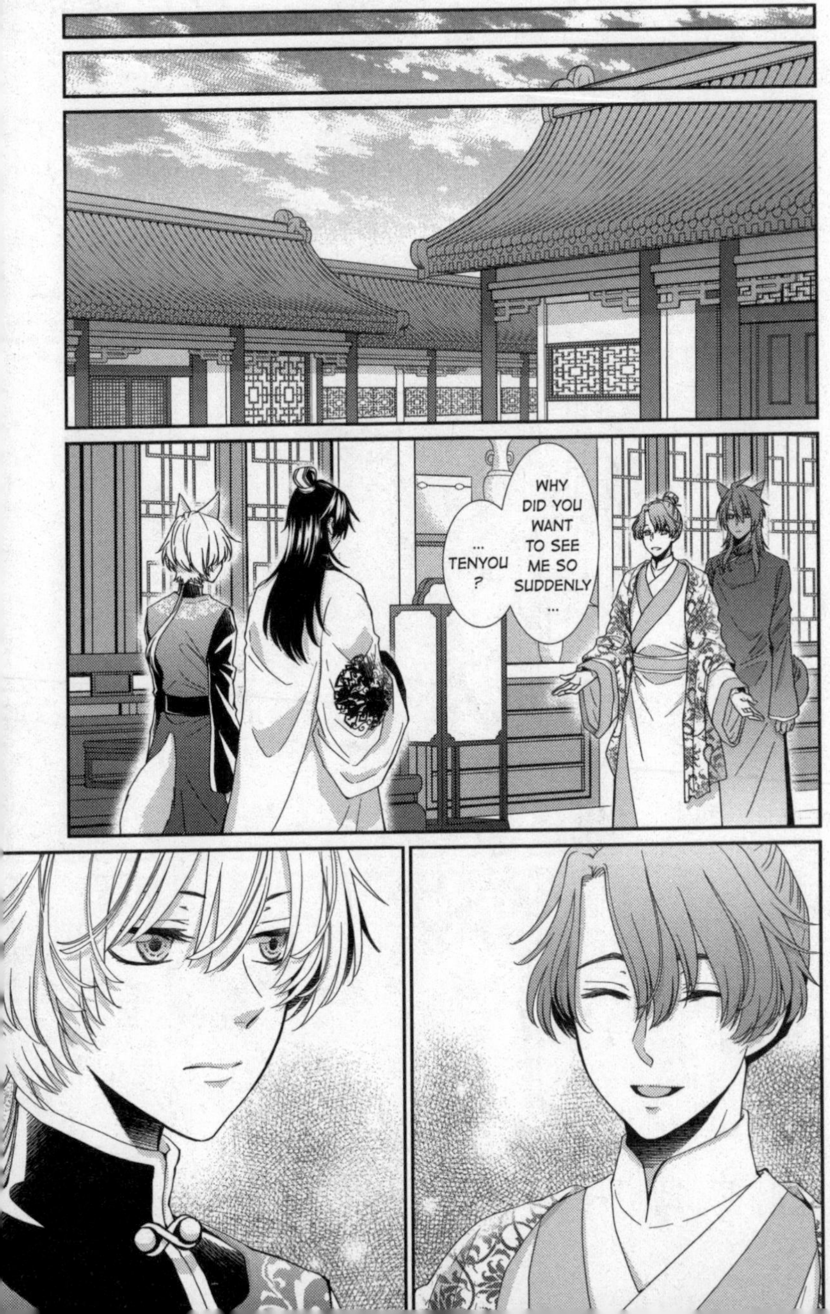
WHY DID YOU WANT TO SEE ME SO SUDDENLY ...
... TENYOU ?

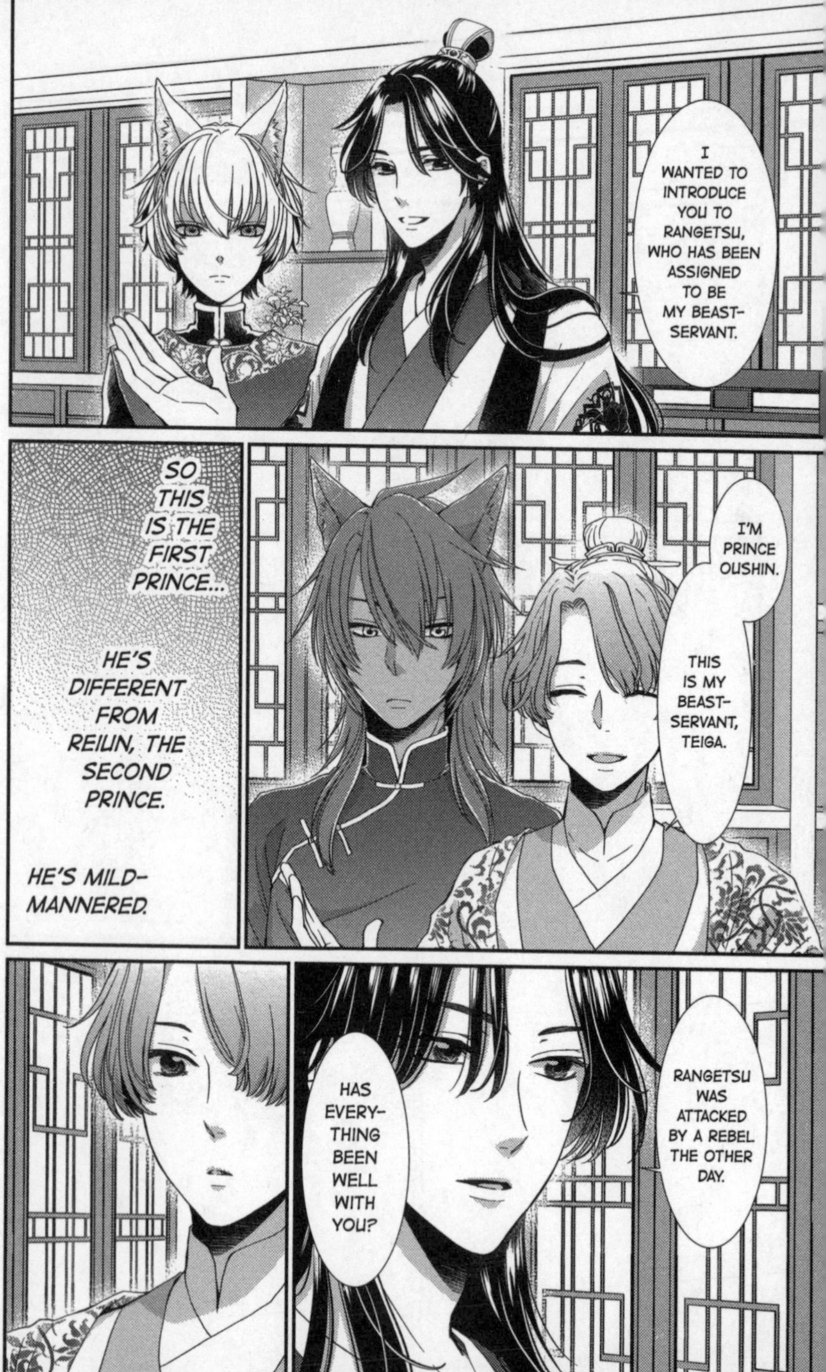
I WANTED TO INTRODUCE YOU TO RANGETSU, WHO HAS BEEN ASSIGNED TO BE MY BEAST-SERVANT.
I'M PRINCE OUSHIN.
THIS IS MY BEAST-SERVANT, TEIGA.
SO THIS IS THE FIRST PRINCE...
HE'S DIFFERENT FROM REIUN, THE SECOND PRINCE.
HE'S MILD-MANNERED.
RANGETSU WAS ATTACKED BY A REBEL THE OTHER DAY.
HAS EVERYTHING BEEN WELL WITH YOU?

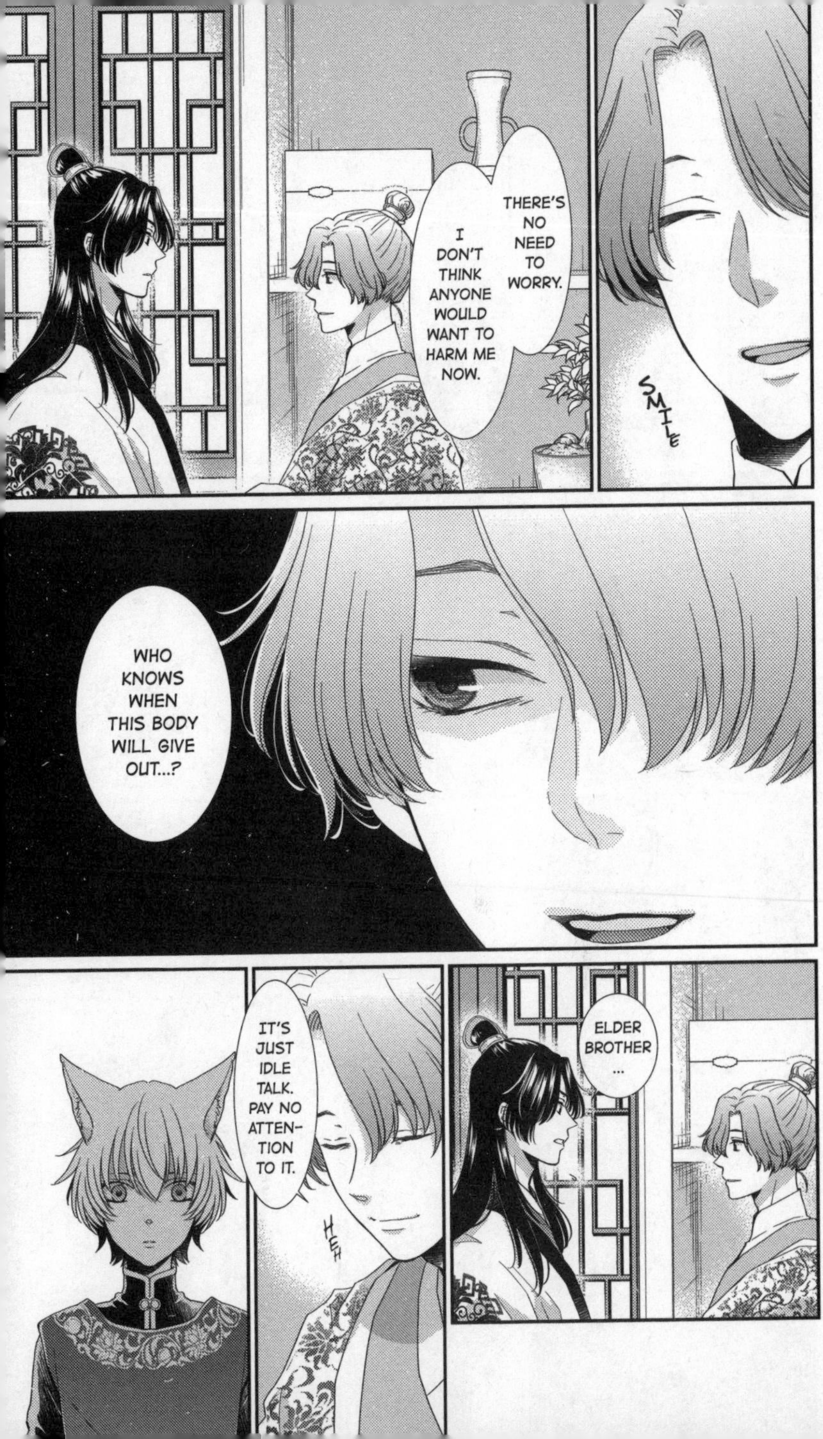
SMILE
THERE'S NO NEED TO WORRY.
I DON'T THINK ANYONE WOULD WANT TO HARM ME NOW.
WHO KNOWS WHEN THIS BODY WILL GIVE OUT...?
ELDER BROTHER ...
HEH
IT'S JUST IDLE TALK. PAY NO ATTEN-TION TO IT.

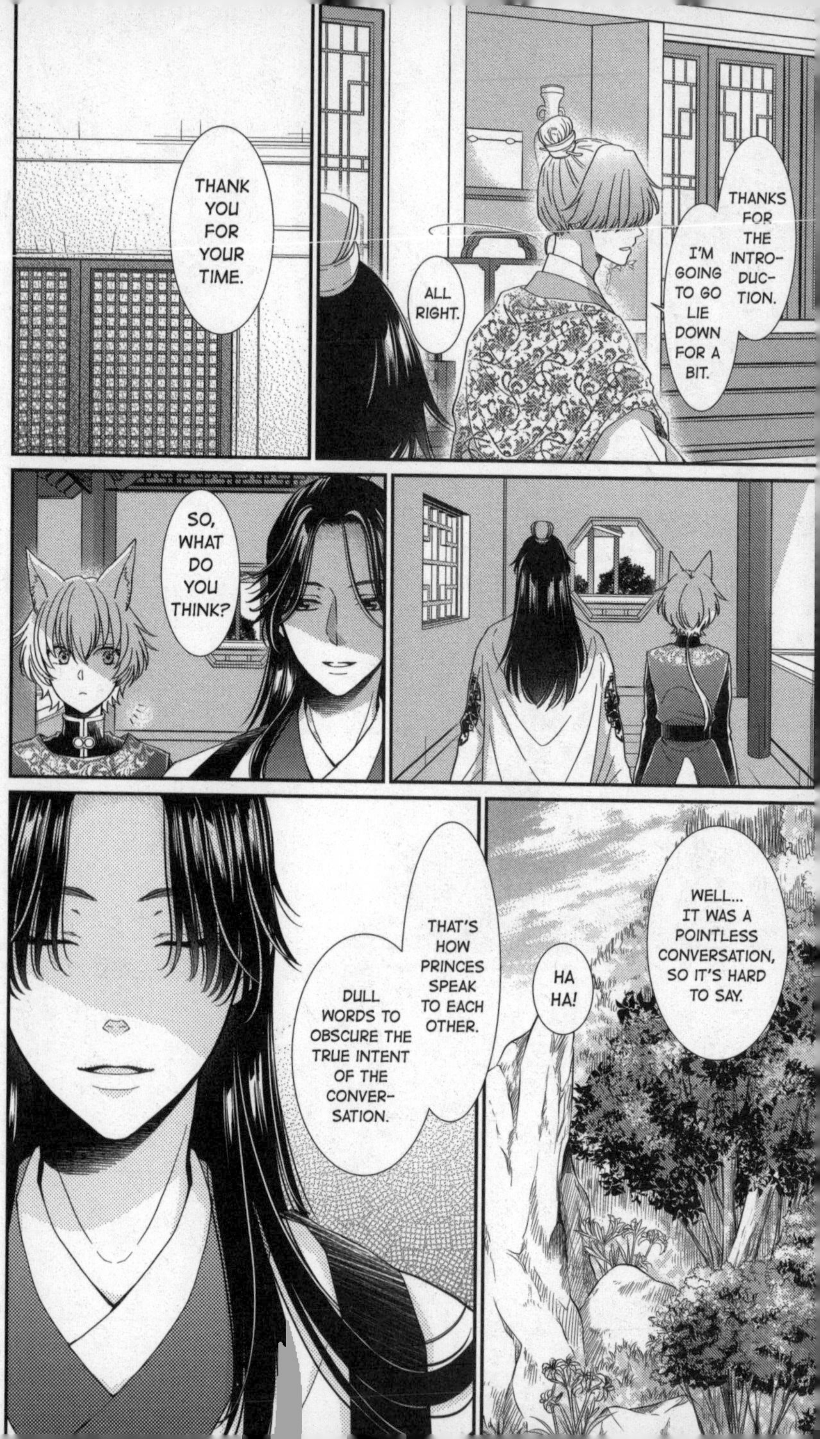
THANKS FOR THE INTRODUCTION.
I'M GOING TO GO LIE DOWN FOR A BIT.
ALL RIGHT.
THANK YOU FOR YOUR TIME.
SO, WHAT DO YOU THINK?
WELL... IT WAS A POINTLESS CONVERSATION, SO IT'S HARD TO SAY.
HA HA!
THAT'S HOW PRINCES SPEAK TO EACH OTHER.
DULL WORDS TO OBSCURE THE TRUE INTENT OF THE CONVERSATION.

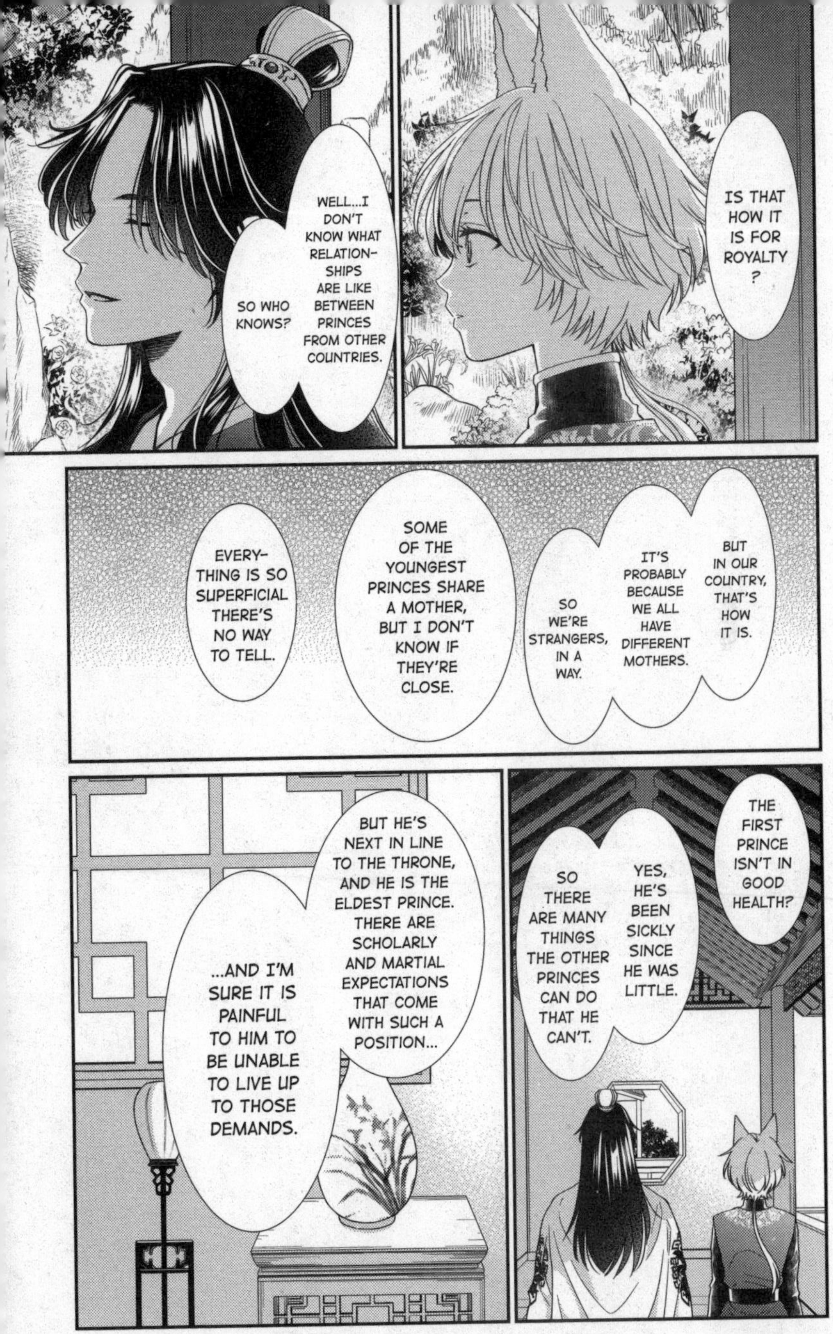
IS THAT HOW IT IS FOR ROYALTY?
WELL...I DON'T KNOW WHAT RELATION-SHIPS ARE LIKE BETWEEN PRINCES FROM OTHER COUNTRIES.
SO WHO KNOWS?
BUT IN OUR COUNTRY, THAT'S HOW IT IS.
IT'S PROBABLY BECAUSE WE ALL HAVE DIFFERENT MOTHERS.
SO WE'RE STRANGERS, IN A WAY.
SOME OF THE YOUNGEST PRINCES SHARE A MOTHER, BUT I DON'T KNOW IF THEY'RE CLOSE.
EVERY-THING IS SO SUPERFICIAL THERE'S NO WAY TO TELL.
THE FIRST PRINCE ISN'T IN GOOD HEALTH?
YES, HE'S BEEN SICKLY SINCE HE WAS LITTLE.
SO THERE ARE MANY THINGS THE OTHER PRINCES CAN DO THAT HE CAN'T.
BUT HE'S NEXT IN LINE TO THE THRONE, AND HE IS THE ELDEST PRINCE. THERE ARE SCHOLARLY AND MARTIAL EXPECTATIONS THAT COME WITH SUCH A POSITION...
...AND I'M SURE IT IS PAINFUL TO HIM TO BE UNABLE TO LIVE UP TO THOSE DEMANDS.

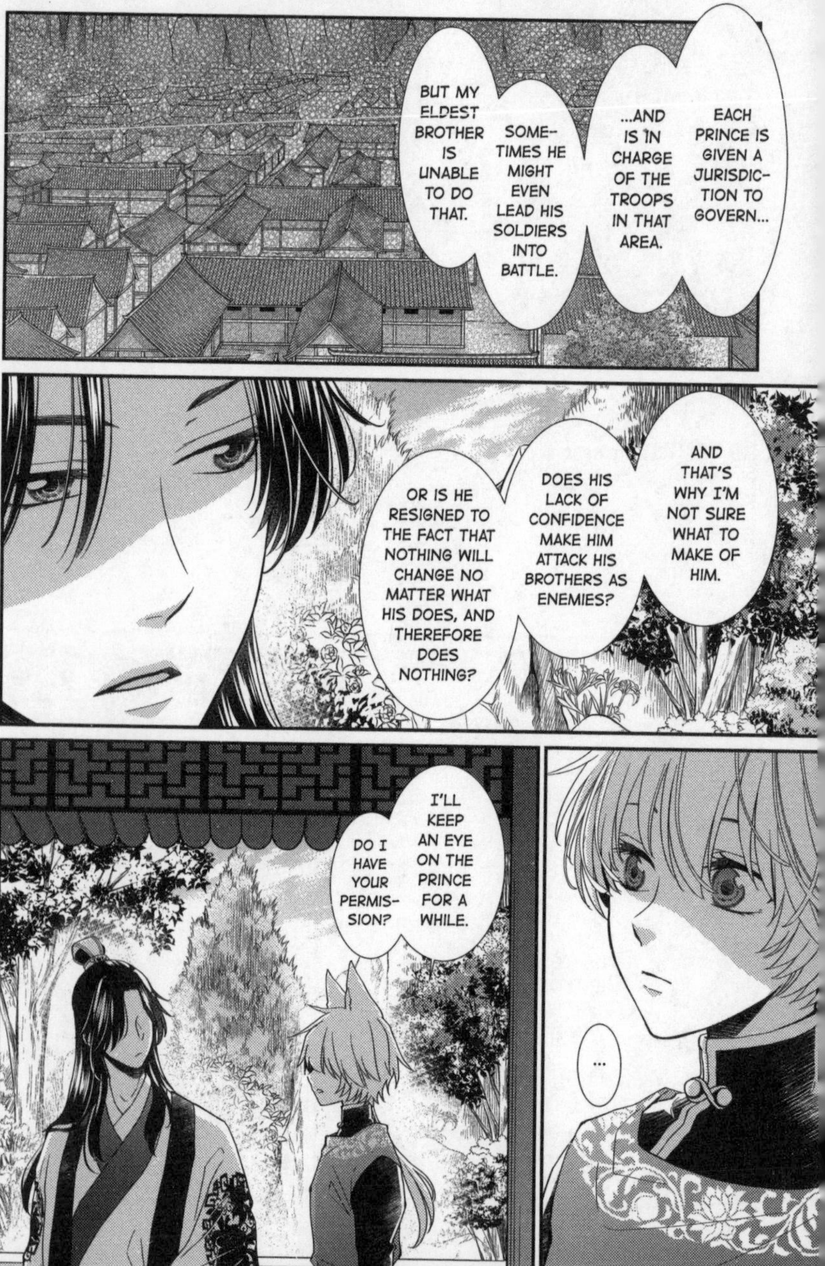
EACH PRINCE IS GIVEN A JURISDICTION TO GOVERN...
...AND IS IN CHARGE OF THE TROOPS IN THAT AREA.
SOMETIMES HE MIGHT EVEN LEAD HIS SOLDIERS INTO BATTLE.
BUT MY ELDEST BROTHER IS UNABLE TO DO THAT.
AND THAT'S WHY I'M NOT SURE WHAT TO MAKE OF HIM.
DOES HIS LACK OF CONFIDENCE MAKE HIM ATTACK HIS BROTHERS AS ENEMIES?
OR IS HE RESIGNED TO THE FACT THAT NOTHING WILL CHANGE NO MATTER WHAT HIS DOES, AND THEREFORE DOES NOTHING?
...
I'LL KEEP AN EYE ON THE PRINCE FOR A WHILE.
DO I HAVE YOUR PERMISSION?

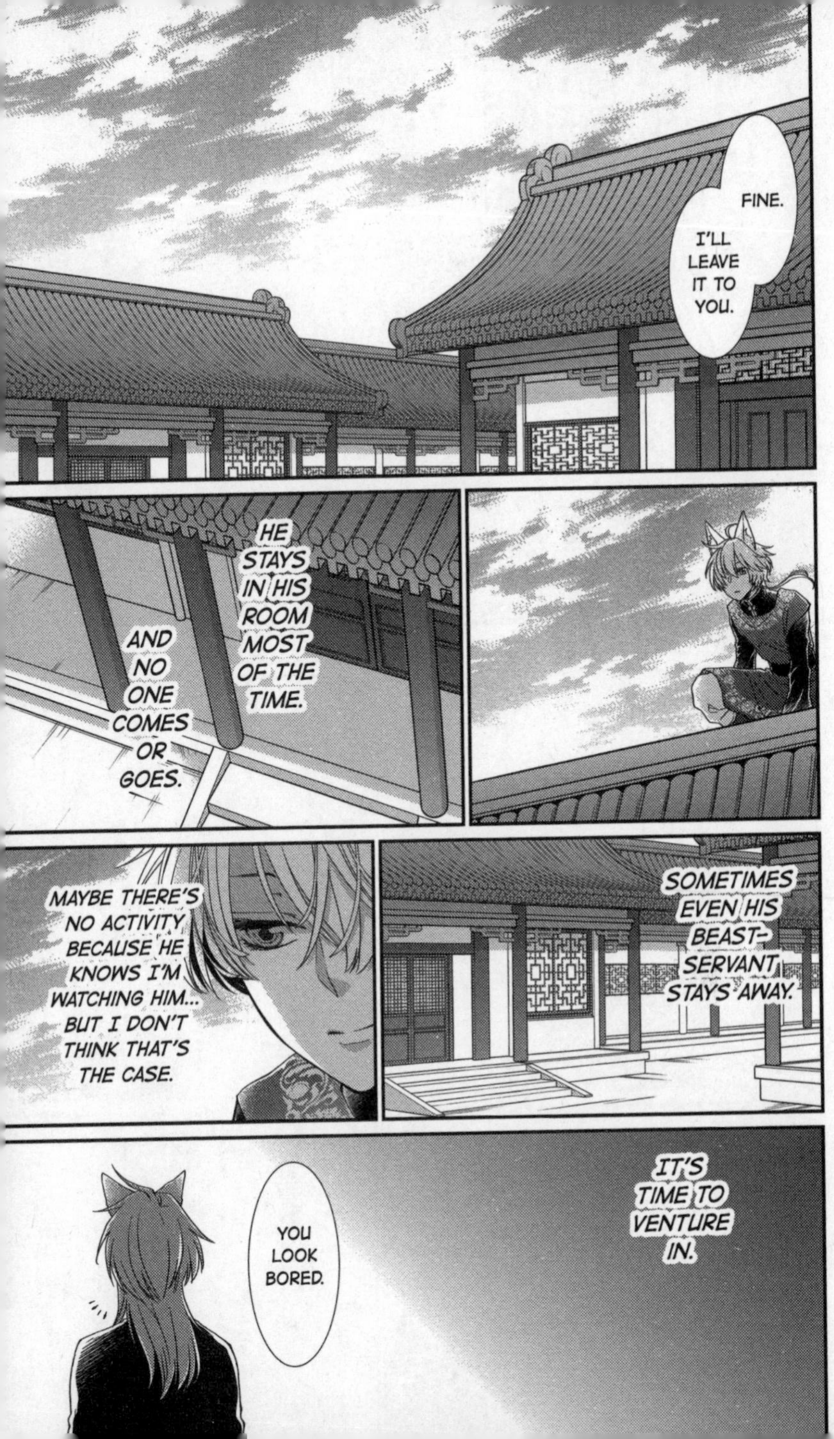
FINE.
I'LL LEAVE IT TO YOU.
HE STAYS IN HIS ROOM MOST OF THE TIME.
AND NO ONE COMES OR GOES.
SOMETIMES EVEN HIS BEAST-SERVANT STAYS AWAY.
MAYBE THERE'S NO ACTIVITY BECAUSE HE KNOWS I'M WATCHING HIM... BUT I DON'T THINK THAT'S THE CASE.
IT'S TIME TO VENTURE IN.
YOU LOOK BORED.

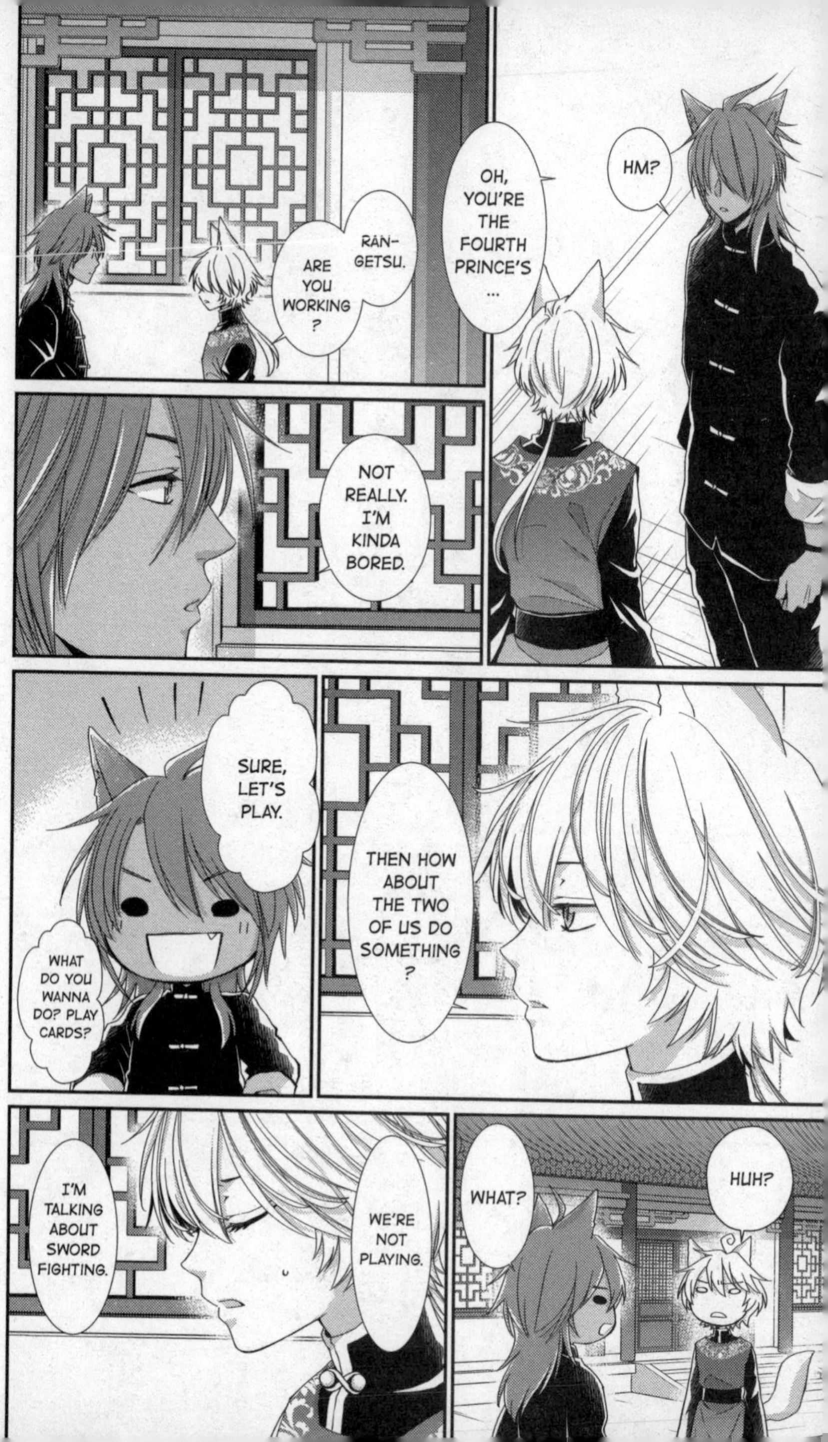
HM?
OH, YOU'RE THE FOURTH PRINCE'S ...
RAN-GETSU.
ARE YOU WORKING?
NOT REALLY. I'M KINDA BORED.
THEN HOW ABOUT THE TWO OF US DO SOMETHING?
SURE, LET'S PLAY.
WHAT DO YOU WANNA DO? PLAY CARDS?
HUH?
WHAT?
WE'RE NOT PLAYING.
I'M TALKING ABOUT SWORD FIGHTING.

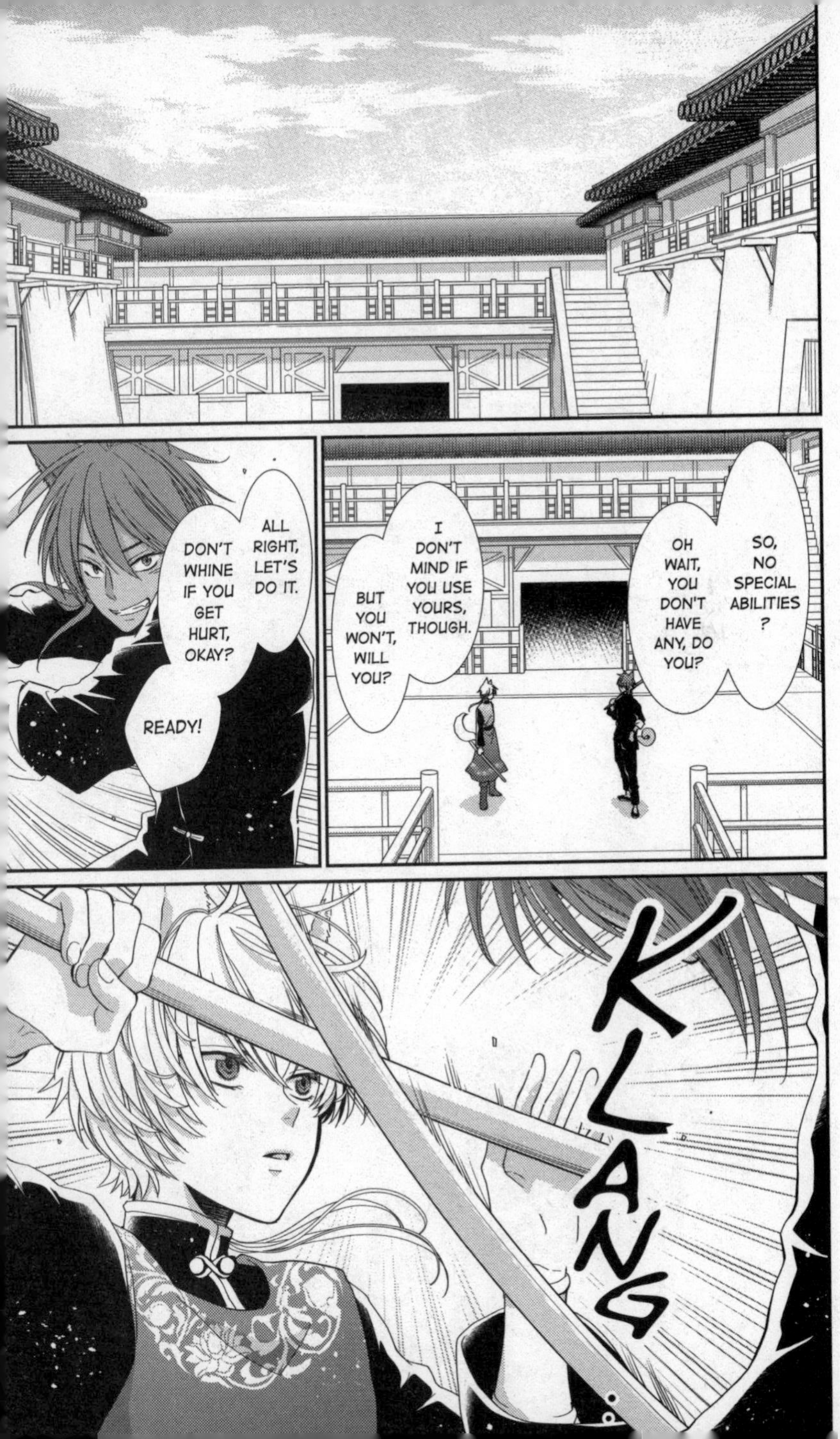
SO, NO SPECIAL ABILITIES?
OH WAIT, YOU DON'T HAVE ANY, DO YOU?
I DON'T MIND IF YOU USE YOURS, THOUGH.
BUT YOU WON'T, WILL YOU?
ALL RIGHT, LET'S DO IT.
DON'T WHINE IF YOU GET HURT, OKAY?
READY!
KLANG

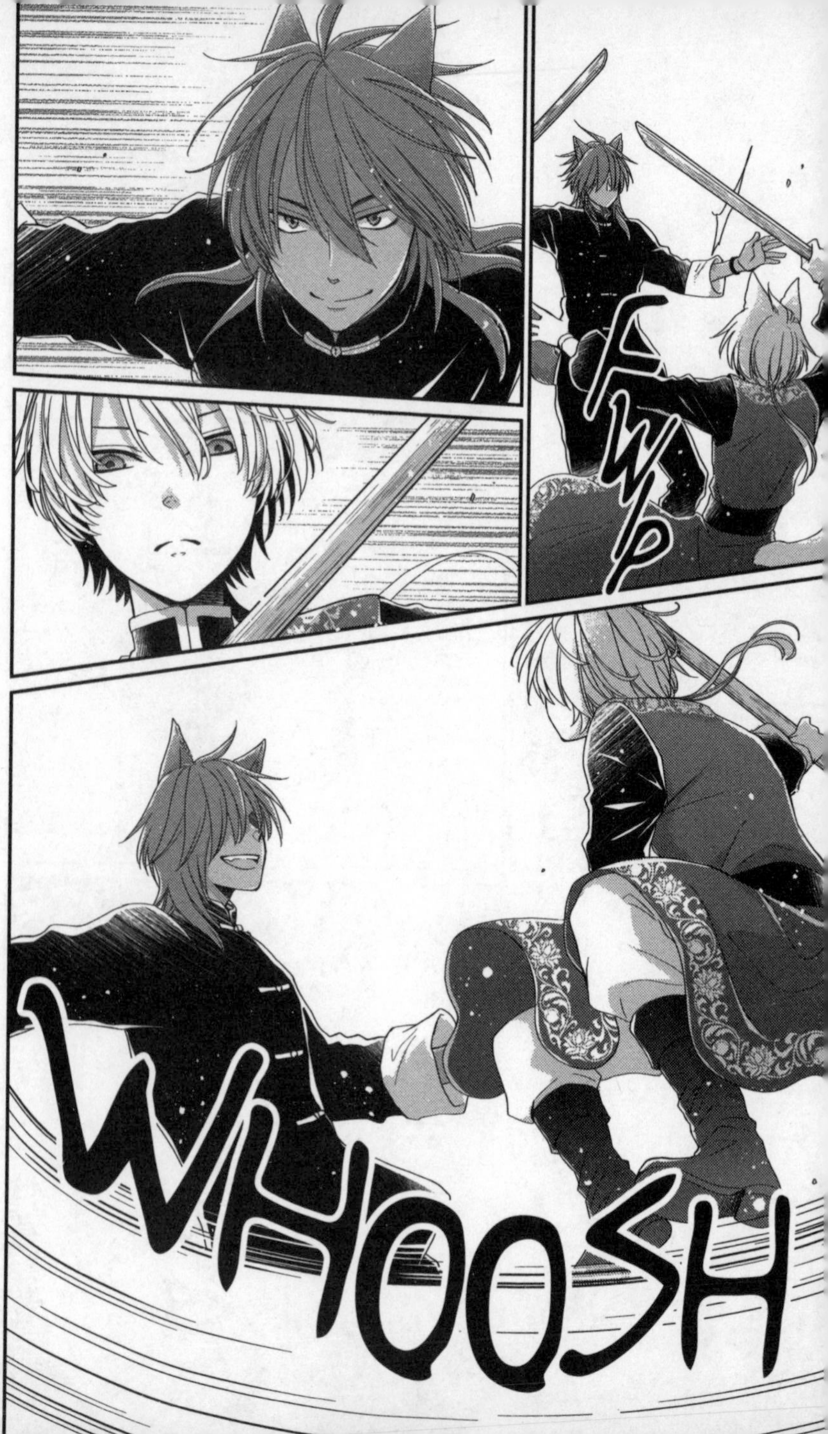
FWIP
WHOOSH

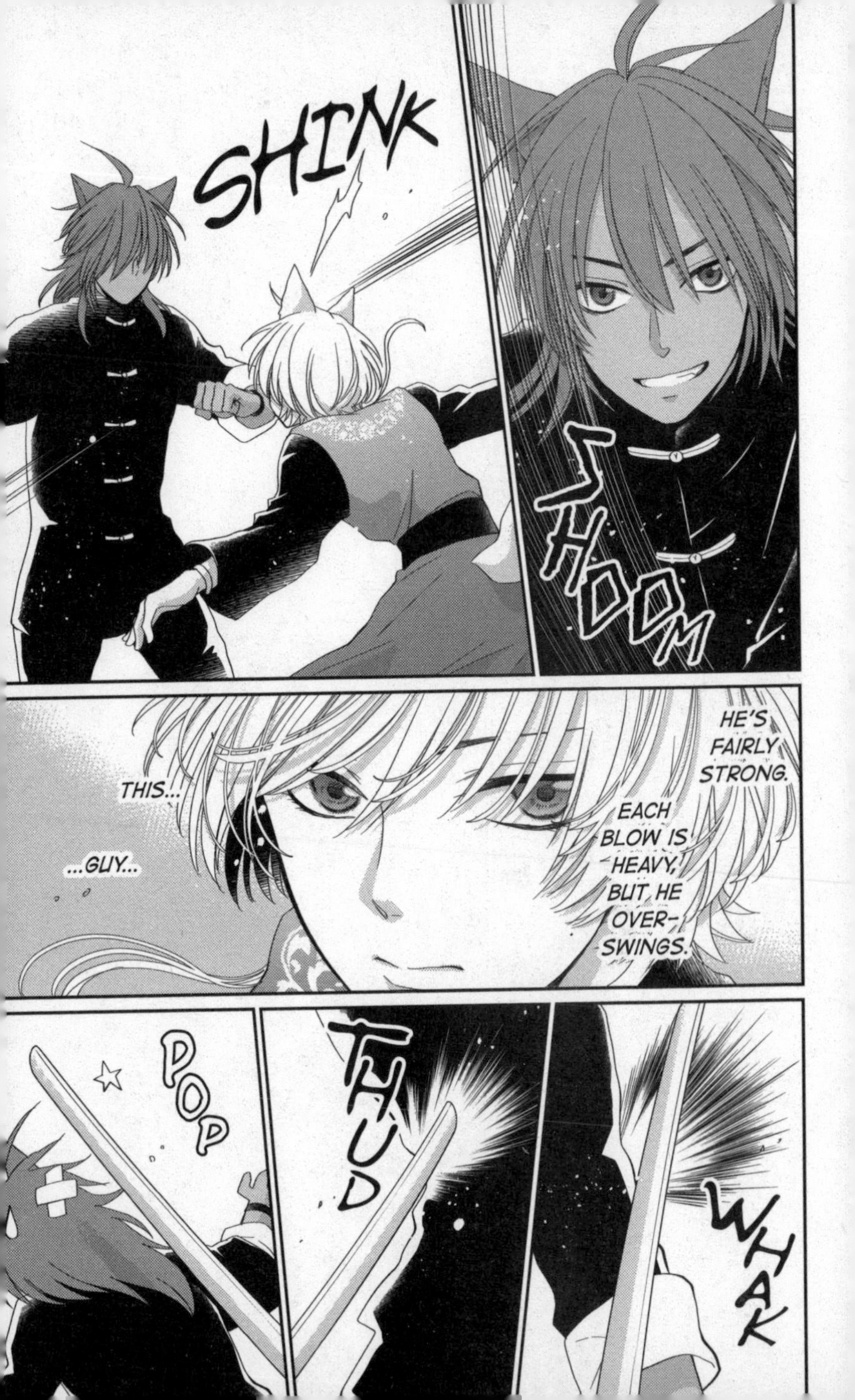
SHOOM
SHINK
HE'S FAIRLY STRONG.
EACH BLOW IS HEAVY, BUT HE OVER-SWINGS.
THIS...
...GUY...
WHAK
THUD
POP

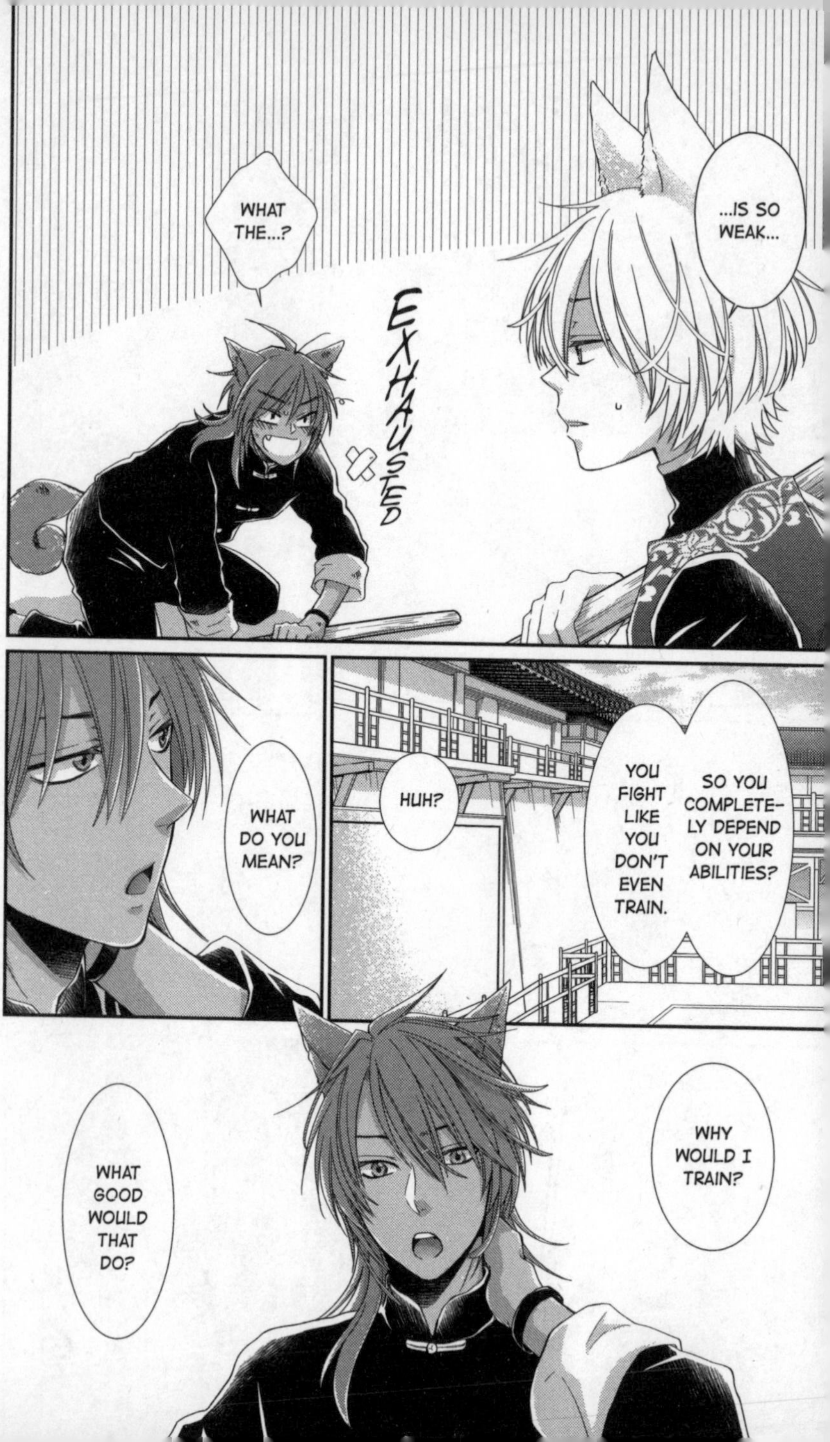
...IS SO WEAK...
WHAT THE...?
EXHAUSTED
SO YOU COMPLETE-LY DEPEND ON YOUR ABILITIES?
YOU FIGHT LIKE YOU DON'T EVEN TRAIN.
HUH?
WHAT DO YOU MEAN?
WHY WOULD I TRAIN?
WHAT GOOD WOULD THAT DO?

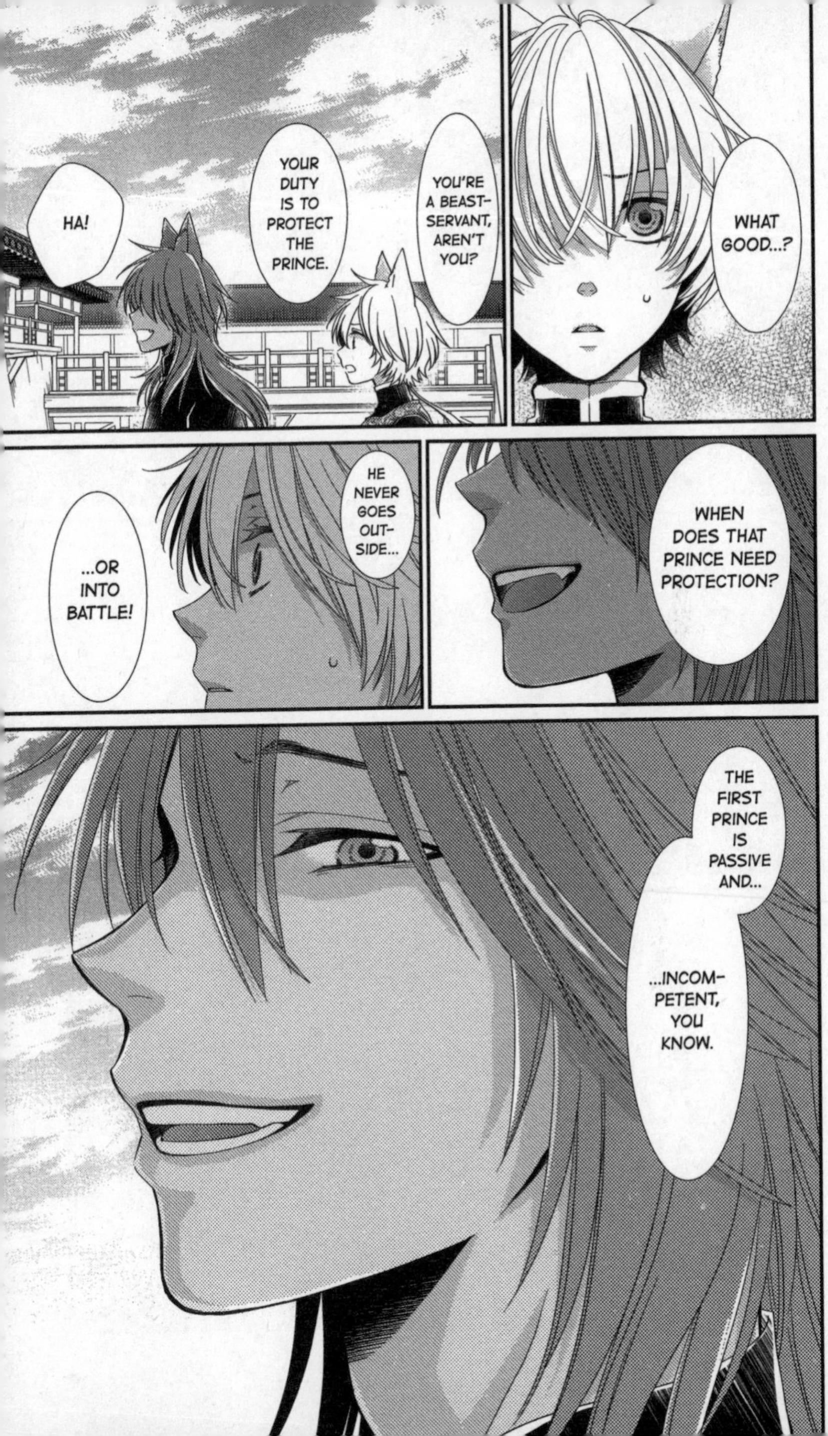
WHAT GOOD...?
YOU'RE A BEAST-SERVANT, AREN'T YOU?
YOUR DUTY IS TO PROTECT THE PRINCE.
HA!
WHEN DOES THAT PRINCE NEED PROTECTION?
HE NEVER GOES OUT-SIDE...
...OR INTO BATTLE!
THE FIRST PRINCE IS PASSIVE AND...
...INCOM-PETENT, YOU KNOW.

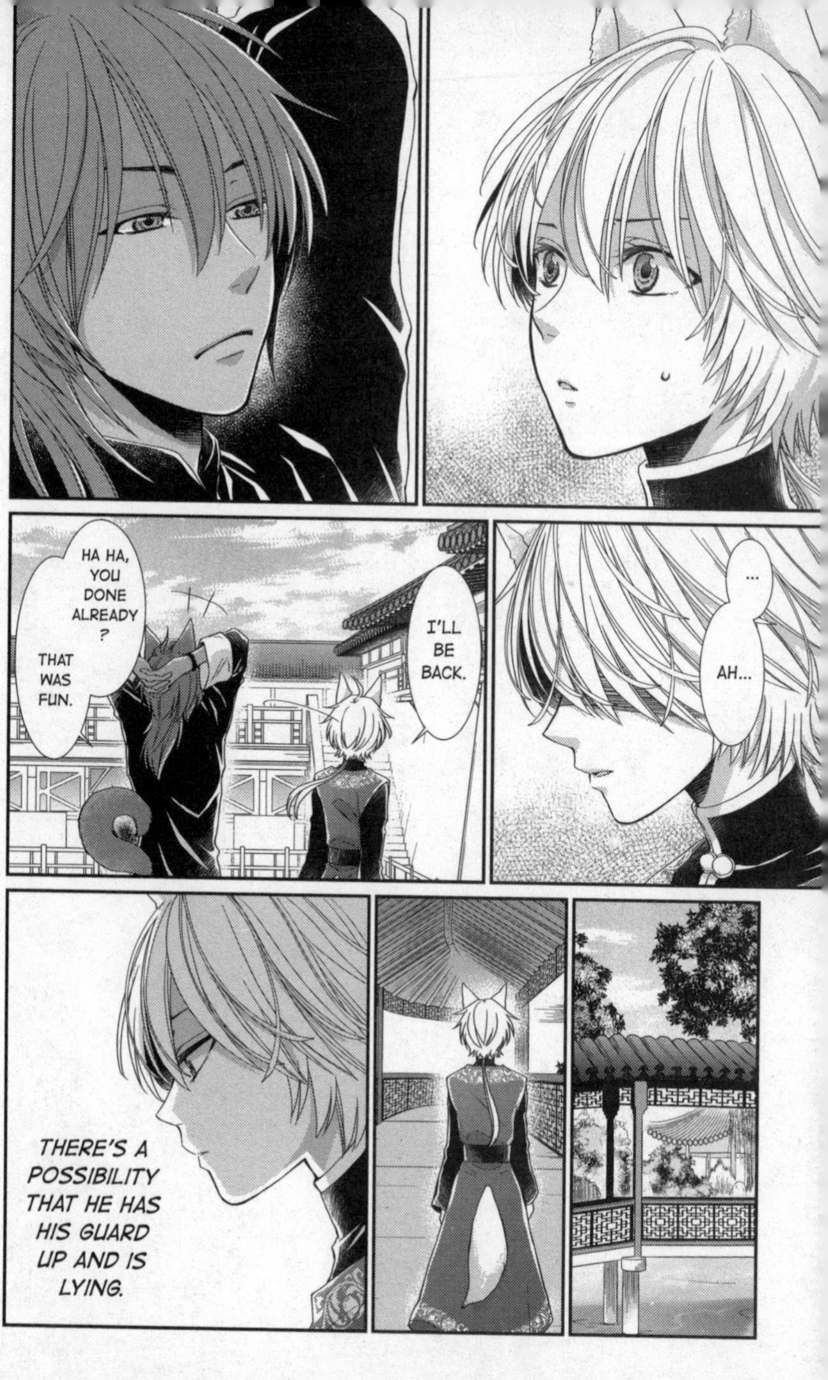
...
AH...
I'LL BE BACK.
HA HA, YOU DONE ALREADY?
THAT WAS FUN.
THERE'S A POSSIBILITY THAT HE HAS HIS GUARD UP AND IS LYING.

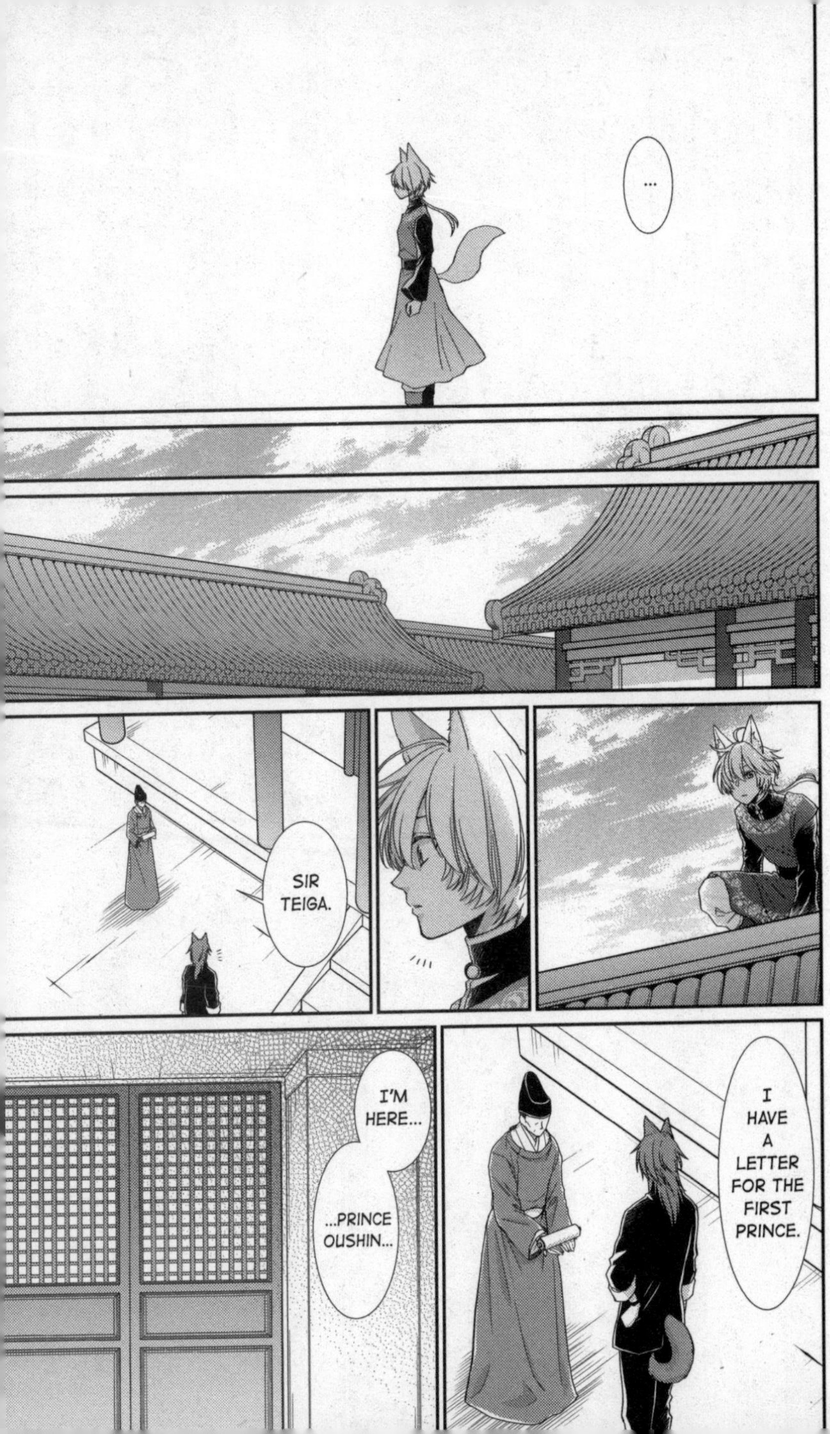
...
SIR TEIGA.
I HAVE A LETTER FOR THE FIRST PRINCE.
I'M HERE...
...PRINCE OUSHIN...

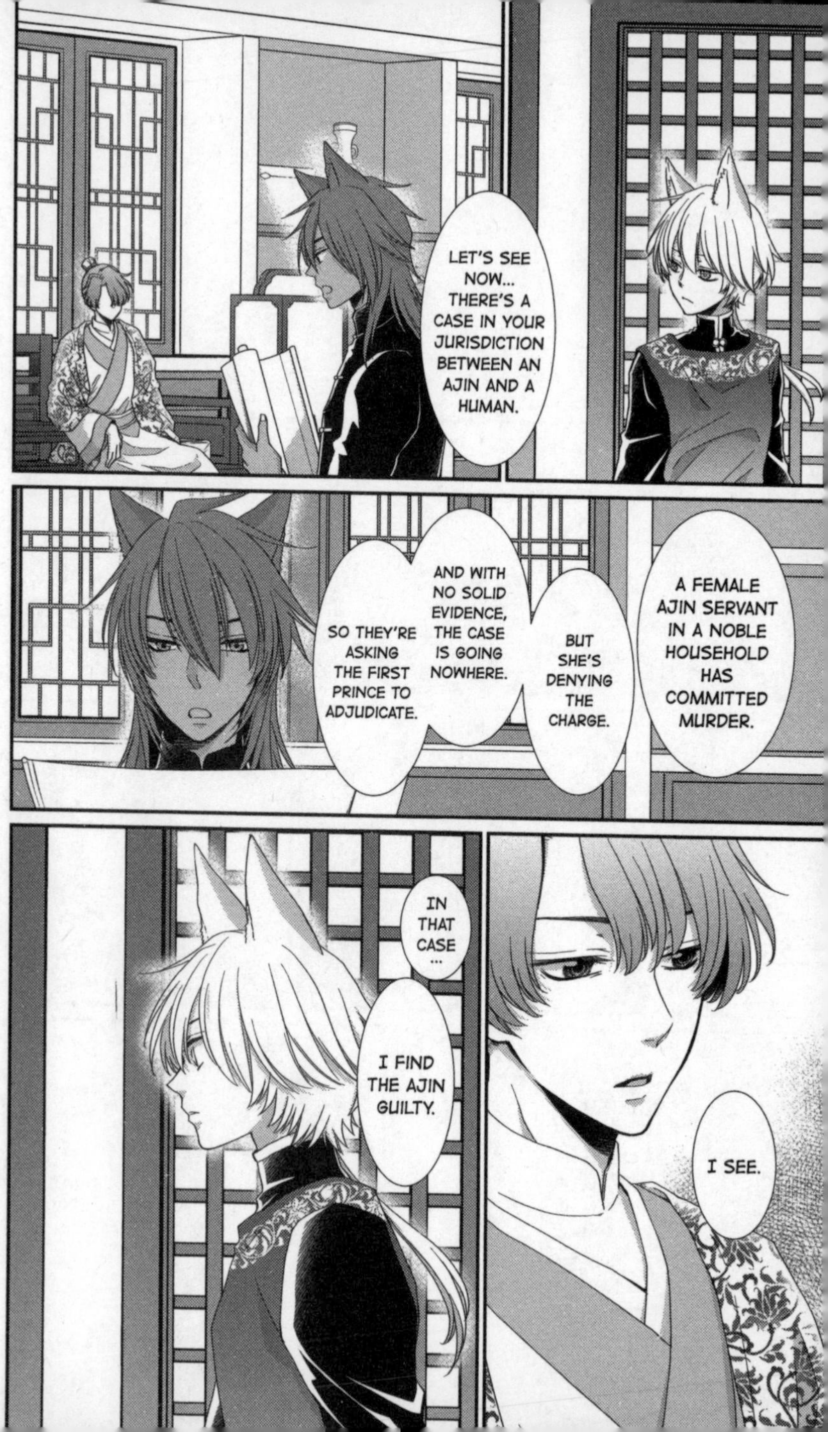
LET'S SEE NOW... THERE'S A CASE IN YOUR JURISDICTION BETWEEN AN AJIN AND A HUMAN.
A FEMALE AJIN SERVANT IN A NOBLE HOUSEHOLD HAS COMMITTED MURDER.
BUT SHE'S DENYING THE CHARGE.
AND WITH NO SOLID EVIDENCE, THE CASE IS GOING NOWHERE.
SO THEY'RE ASKING THE FIRST PRINCE TO ADJUDICATE.
I SEE.
IN THAT CASE...
I FIND THE AJIN GUILTY.

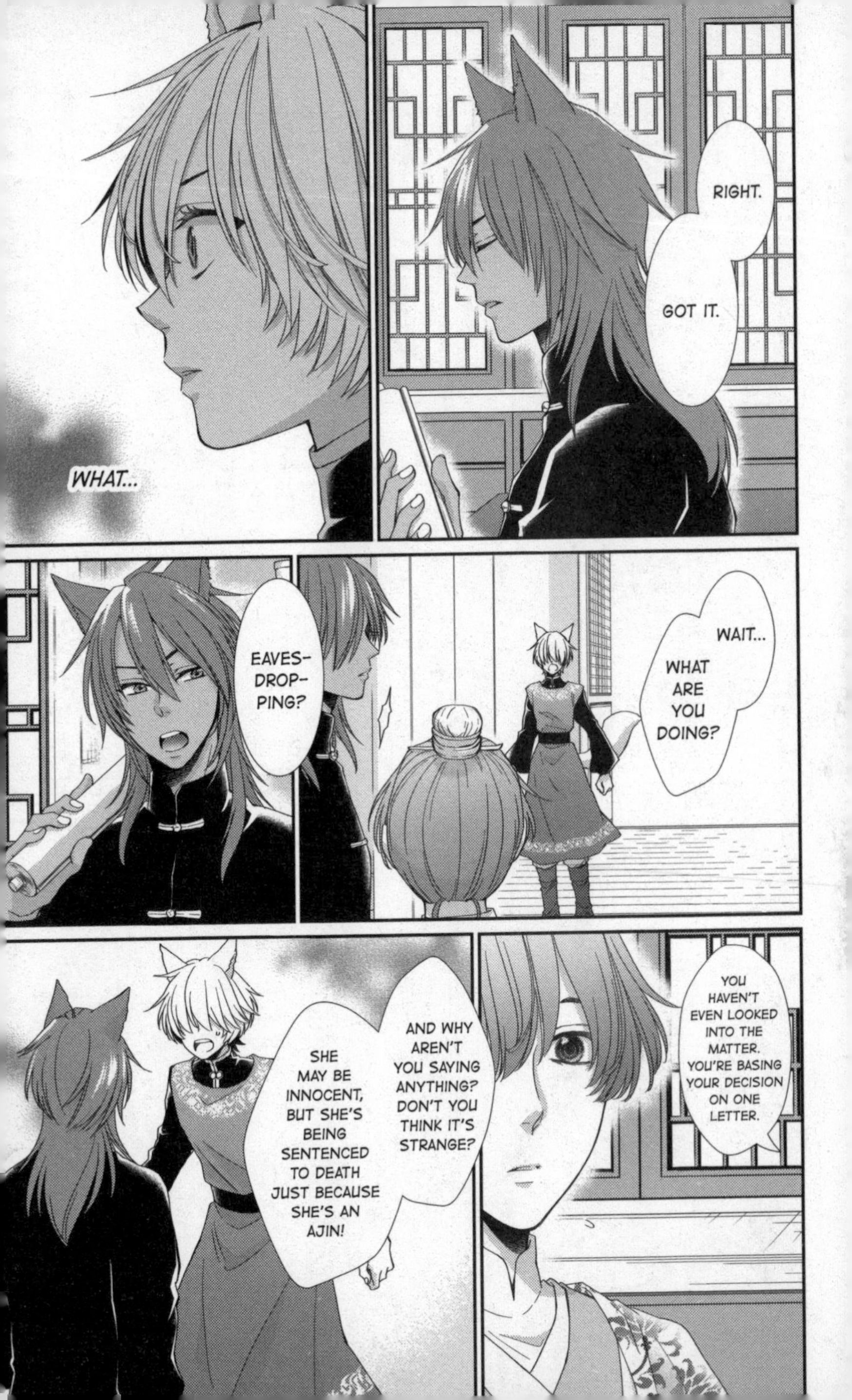
RIGHT.
GOT IT.
WHAT...
WAIT...
WHAT ARE YOU DOING?
EAVES-DROP-PING?
YOU HAVEN'T EVEN LOOKED INTO THE MATTER. YOU'RE BASING YOUR DECISION ON ONE LETTER.
AND WHY AREN'T YOU SAYING ANYTHING? DON'T YOU THINK IT'S STRANGE?
SHE MAY BE INNOCENT, BUT SHE'S BEING SENTENCED TO DEATH JUST BECAUSE SHE'S AN AJIN!

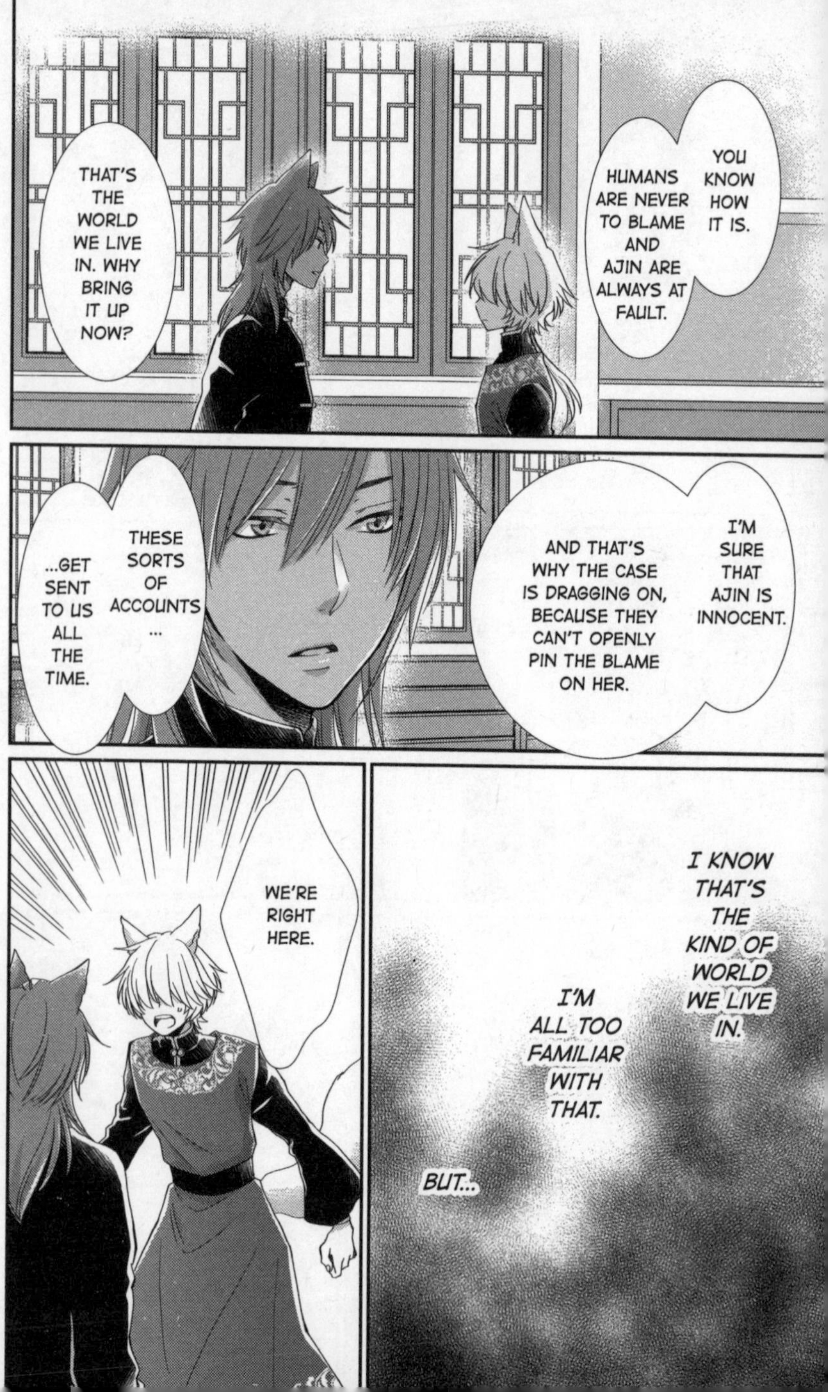
YOU KNOW HOW IT IS.
HUMANS ARE NEVER TO BLAME AND AJIN ARE ALWAYS AT FAULT.
THAT'S THE WORLD WE LIVE IN. WHY BRING IT UP NOW?
I'M SURE THAT AJIN IS INNOCENT.
AND THAT'S WHY THE CASE IS DRAGGING ON, BECAUSE THEY CAN'T OPENLY PIN THE BLAME ON HER.
THESE SORTS OF ACCOUNTS...
...GET SENT TO US ALL THE TIME.
I KNOW THAT'S THE KIND OF WORLD WE LIVE IN.
I'M ALL TOO FAMILIAR WITH THAT.
BUT...
WE'RE RIGHT HERE.

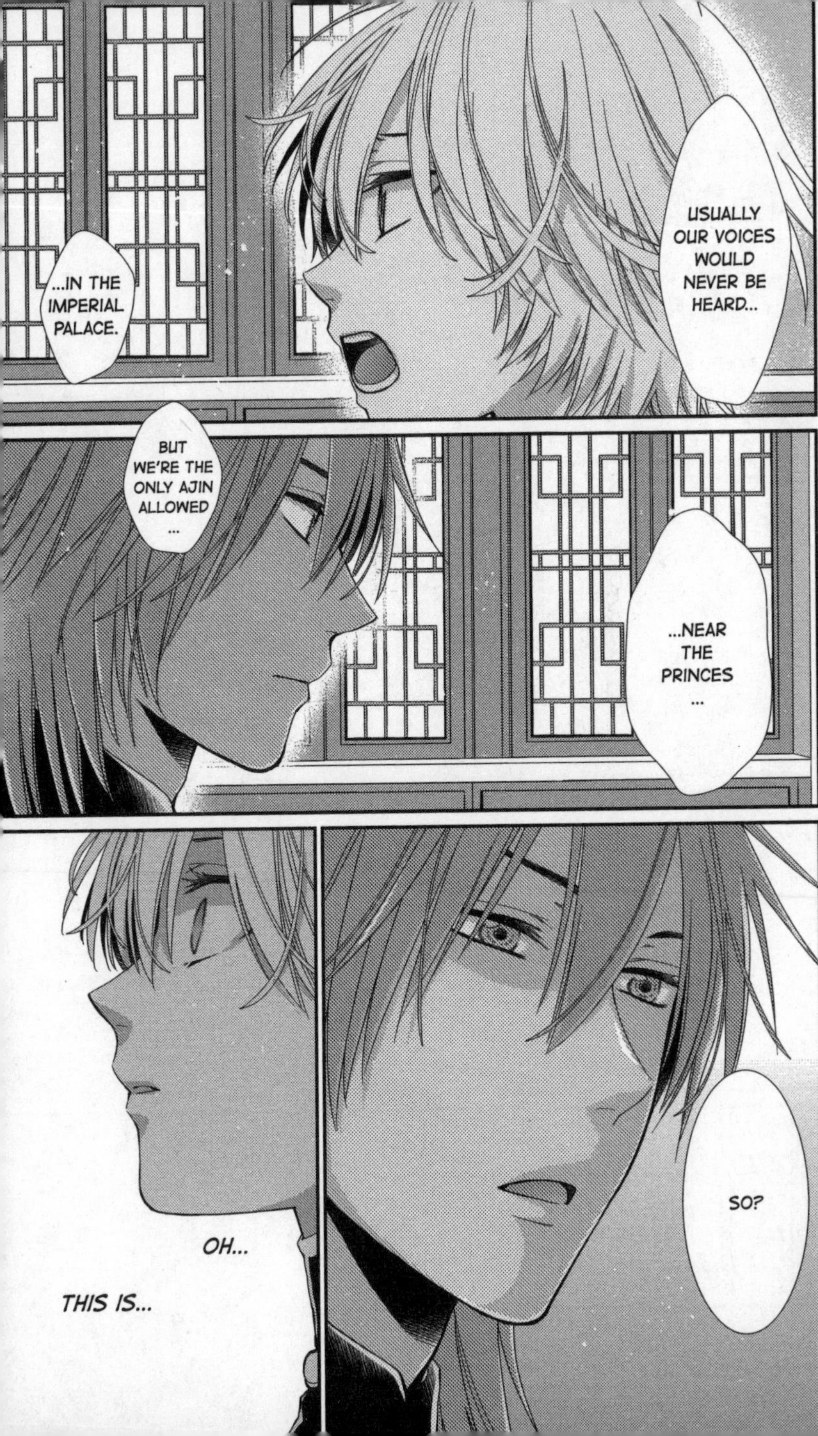
USUALLY OUR VOICES WOULD NEVER BE HEARD...
...IN THE IMPERIAL PALACE.
BUT WE'RE THE ONLY AJIN ALLOWED ...
...NEAR THE PRINCES ...
SO?
OH...
THIS IS...

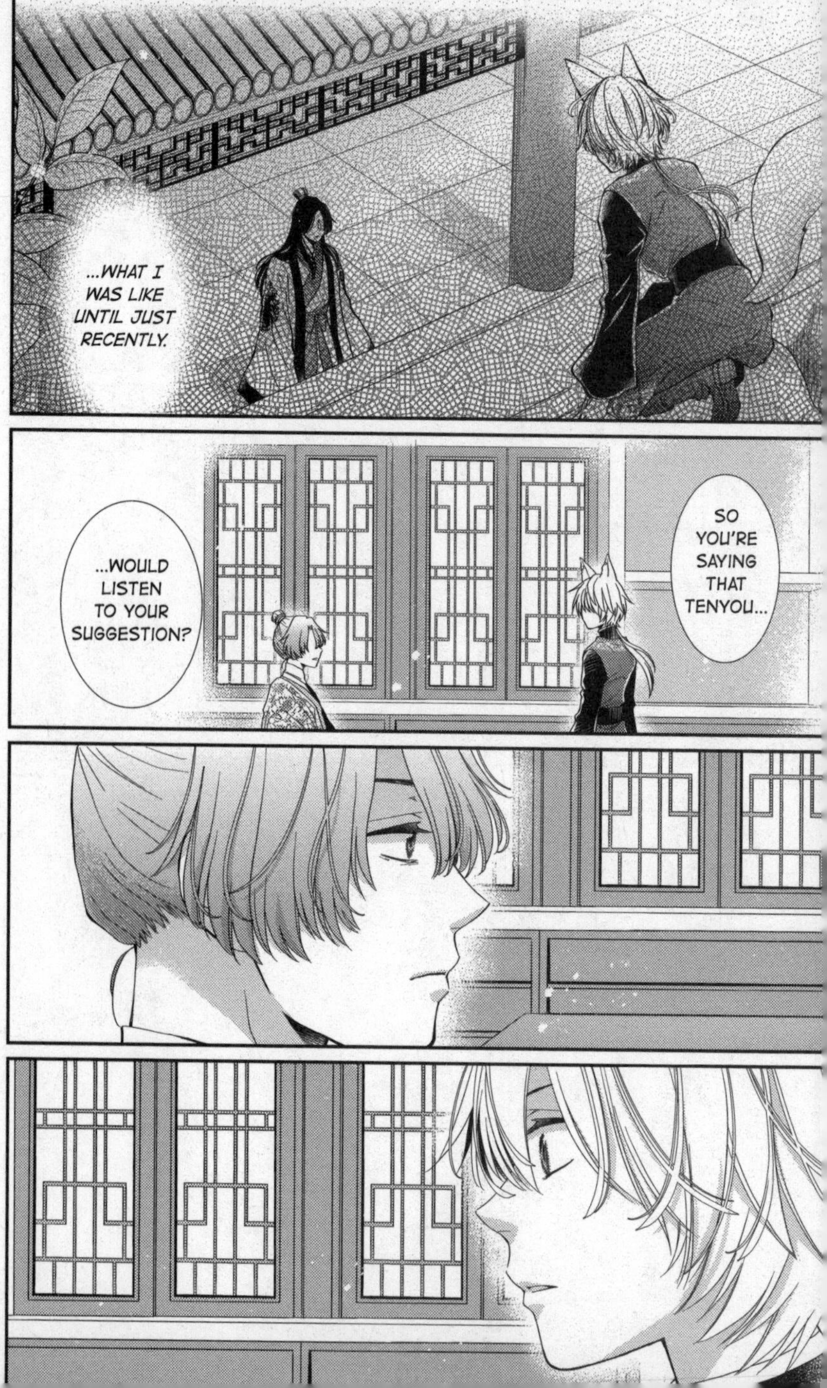
...WHAT I WAS LIKE UNTIL JUST RECENTLY.
SO YOU'RE SAYING THAT TENYOU...
...WOULD LISTEN TO YOUR SUGGESTION?

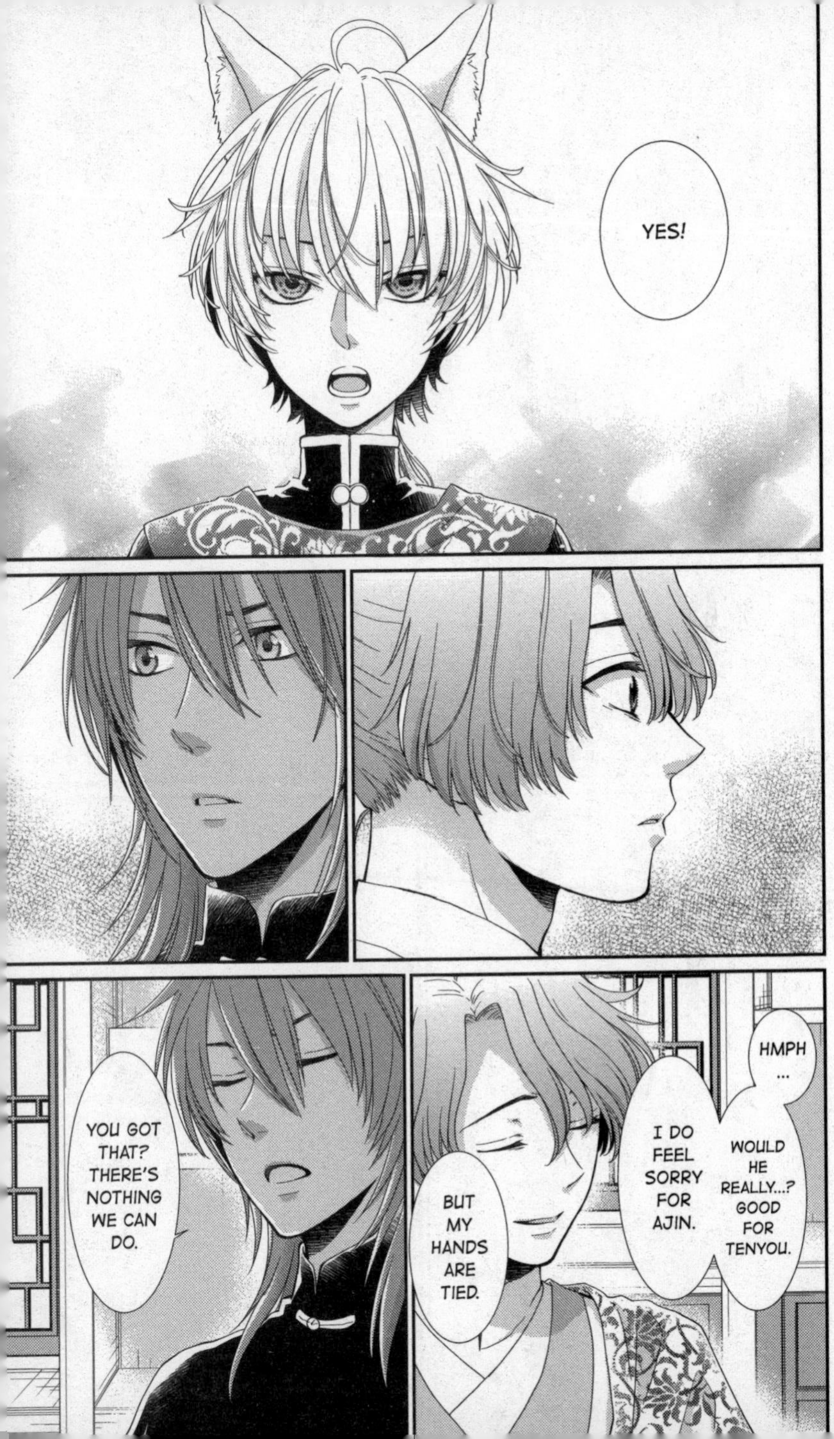
YES!
HMPH ...
WOULD HE REALLY...? GOOD FOR TENYOU.
I DO FEEL SORRY FOR AJIN.
BUT MY HANDS ARE TIED.
YOU GOT THAT? THERE'S NOTHING WE CAN DO.

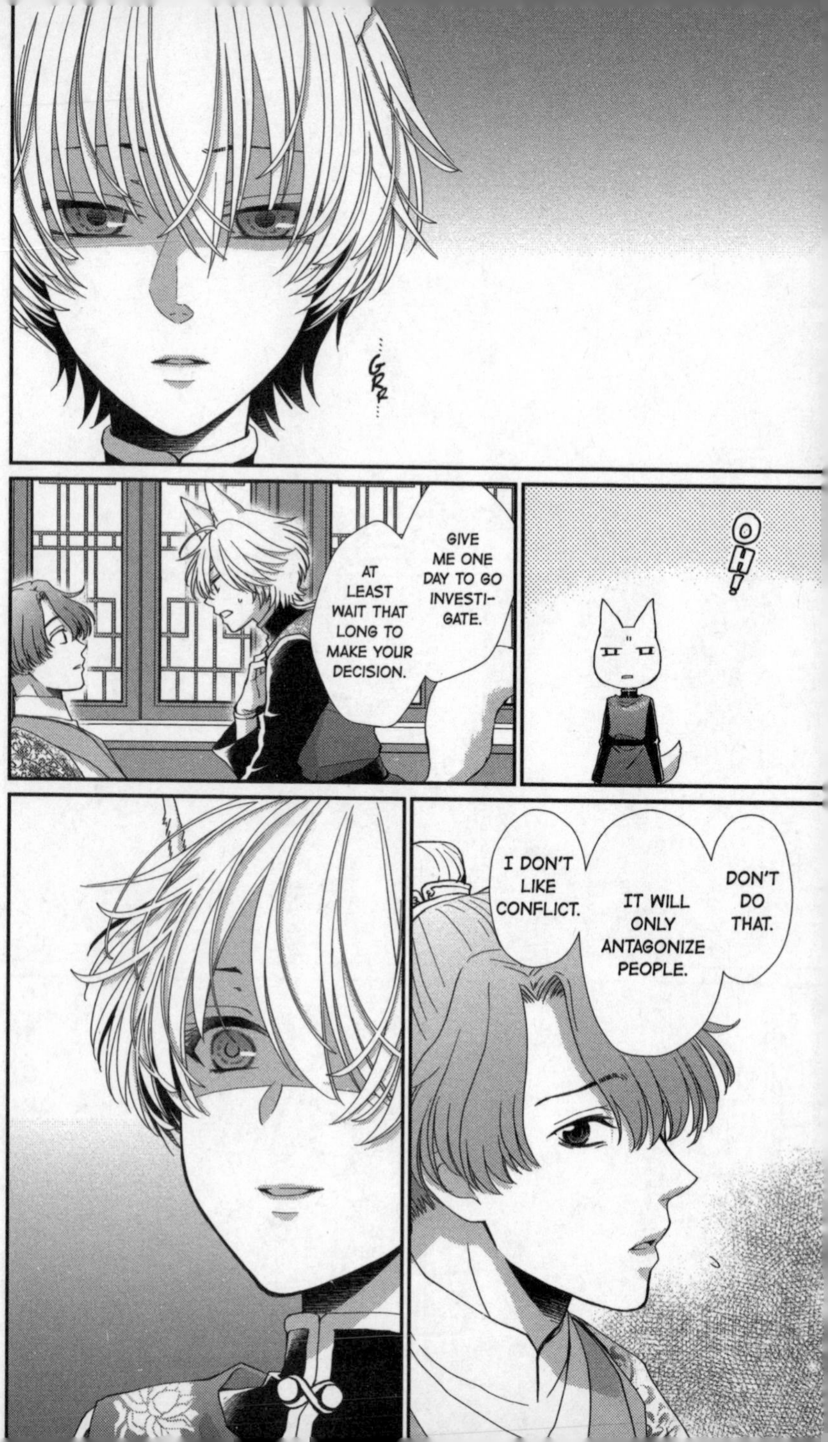
...GRR...
OH!
GIVE ME ONE DAY TO GO INVESTI-GATE.
AT LEAST WAIT THAT LONG TO MAKE YOUR DECISION.
DON'T DO THAT.
IT WILL ONLY ANTAGONIZE PEOPLE.
I DON'T LIKE CONFLICT.

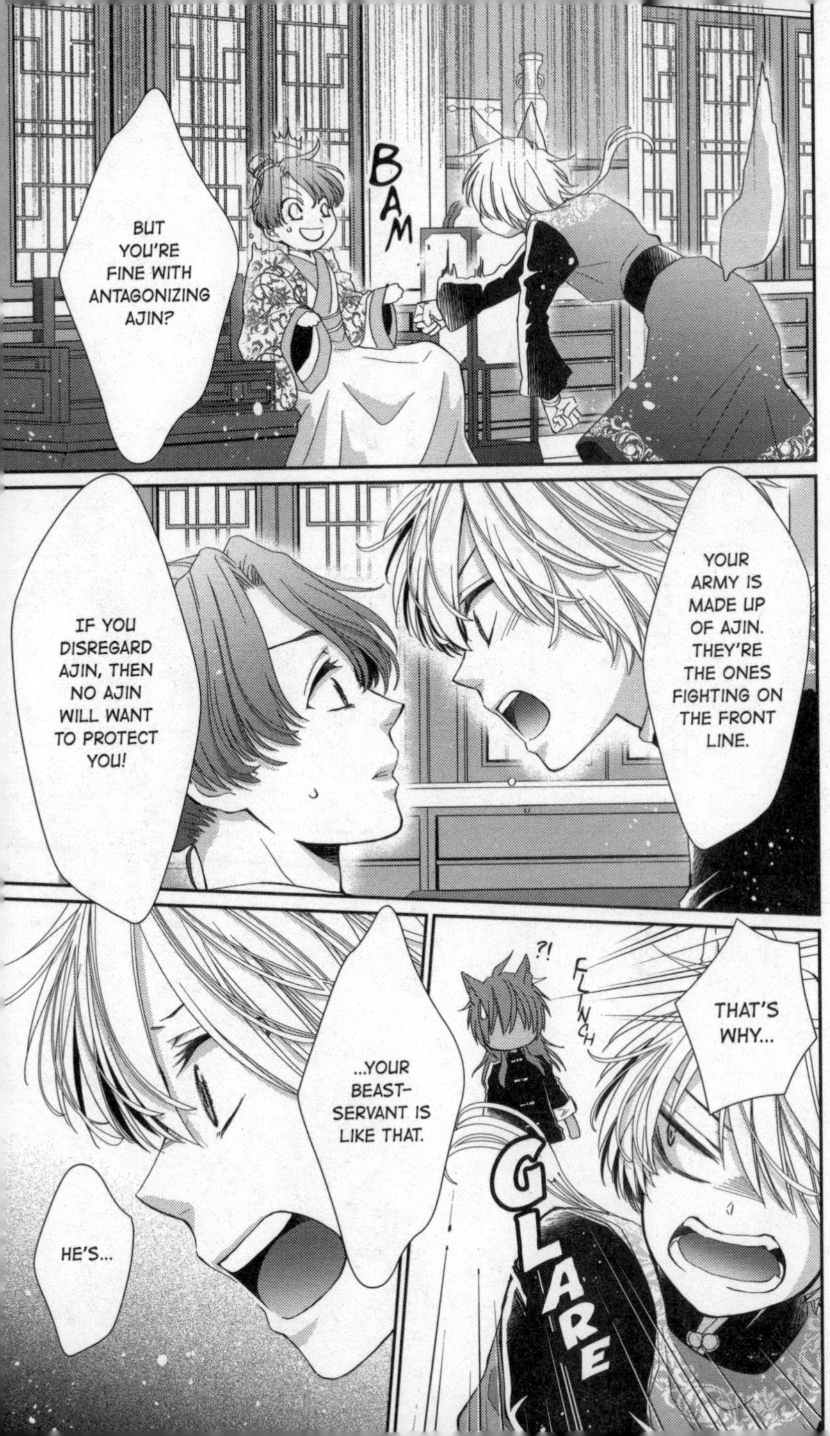
BAM
BUT YOU'RE FINE WITH ANTAGONIZING AJIN?
YOUR ARMY IS MADE UP OF AJIN. THEY'RE THE ONES FIGHTING ON THE FRONT LINE.
IF YOU DISREGARD AJIN, THEN NO AJIN WILL WANT TO PROTECT YOU!
THAT'S WHY...
?!
FLINCH
GLARE
...YOUR BEAST-SERVANT IS LIKE THAT.
HE'S...

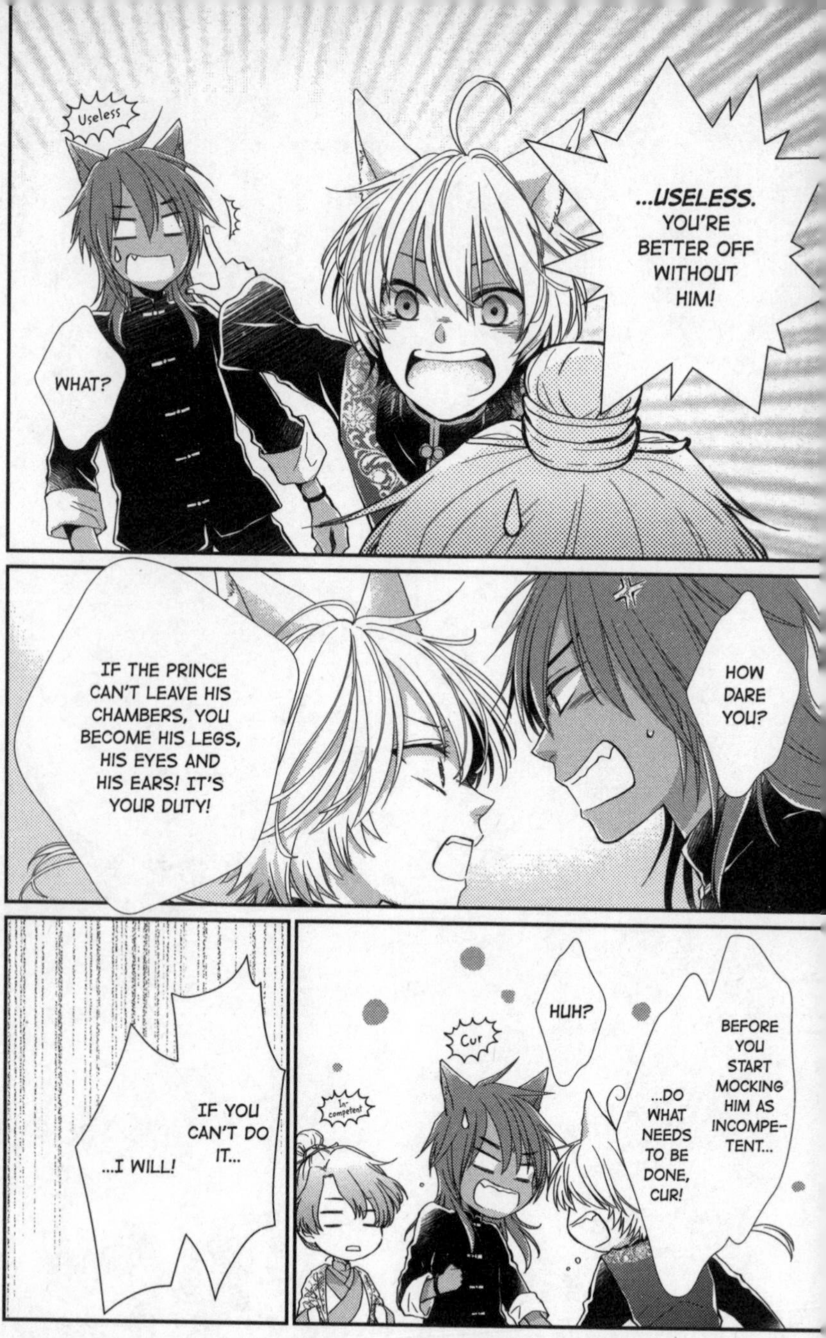
...USELESS. YOU'RE BETTER OFF WITHOUT HIM!
Useless
WHAT?
HOW DARE YOU?
IF THE PRINCE CAN'T LEAVE HIS CHAMBERS, YOU BECOME HIS LEGS, HIS EYES AND HIS EARS! IT'S YOUR DUTY!
BEFORE YOU START MOCKING HIM AS INCOMPE-TENT...
...DO WHAT NEEDS TO BE DONE, CUR!
HUH?
Cur
In-competent
IF YOU CAN'T DO IT...
...I WILL!

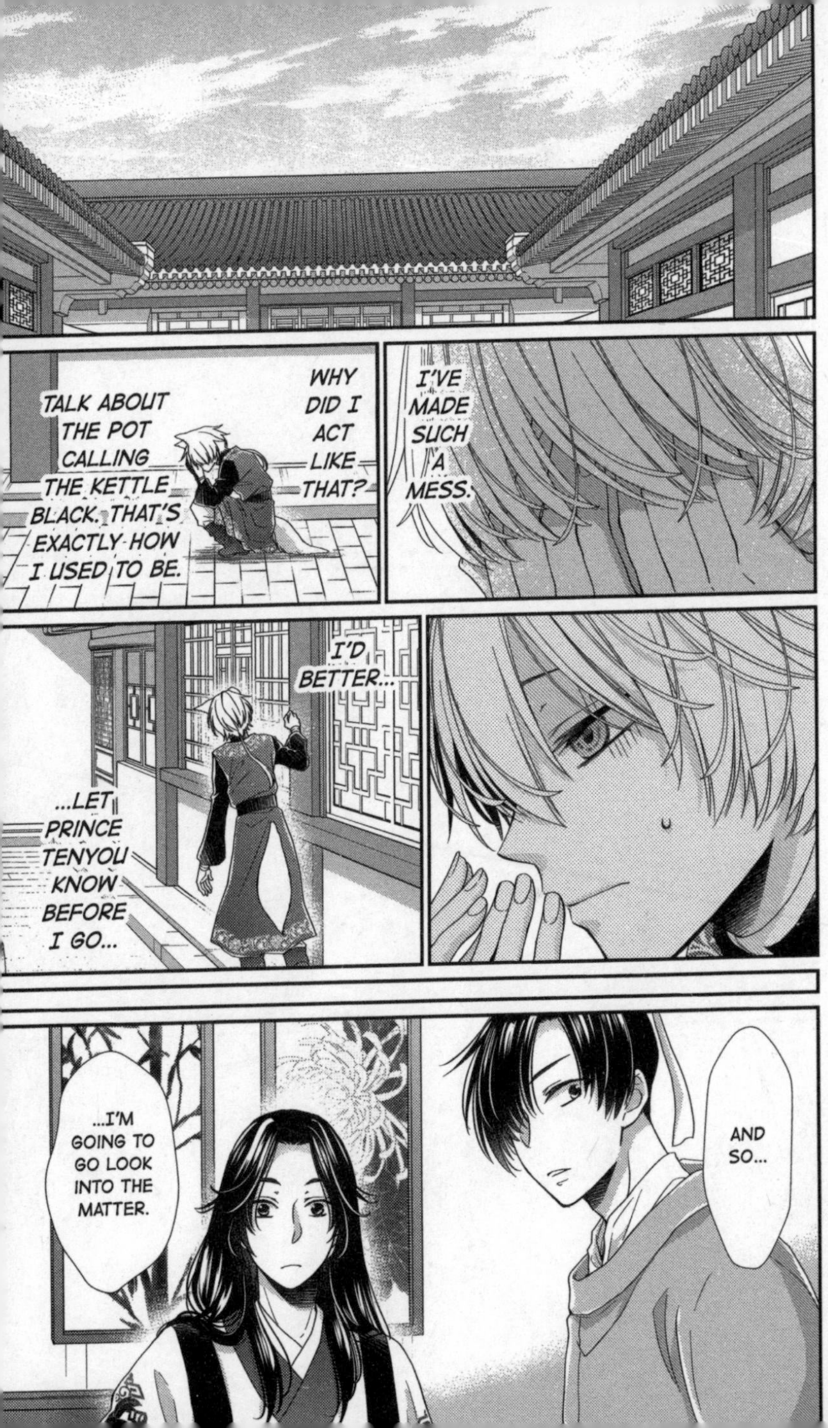
I'VE MADE SUCH A MESS.
WHY DID I ACT LIKE THAT?
TALK ABOUT THE POT CALLING THE KETTLE BLACK. THAT'S EXACTLY HOW I USED TO BE.
I'D BETTER...
...LET PRINCE TENYOU KNOW BEFORE I GO...
AND SO...
...I'M GOING TO GO LOOK INTO THE MATTER.

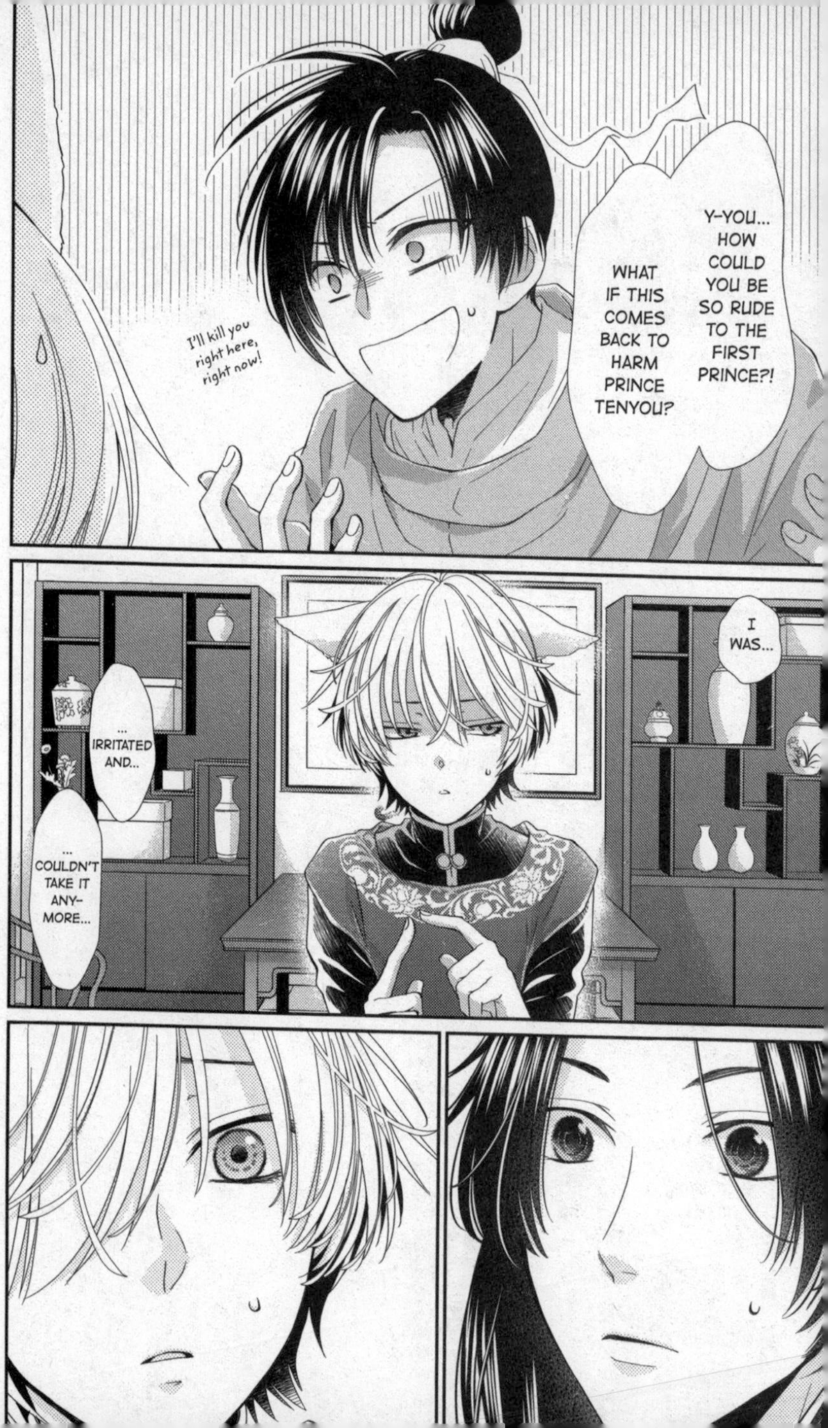
Y-YOU... HOW COULD YOU BE SO RUDE TO THE FIRST PRINCE?!
WHAT IF THIS COMES BACK TO HARM PRINCE TENYOU?
I'll kill you right here, right now!
I WAS...
... IRRITATED AND...
... COULDN'T TAKE IT ANYMORE...

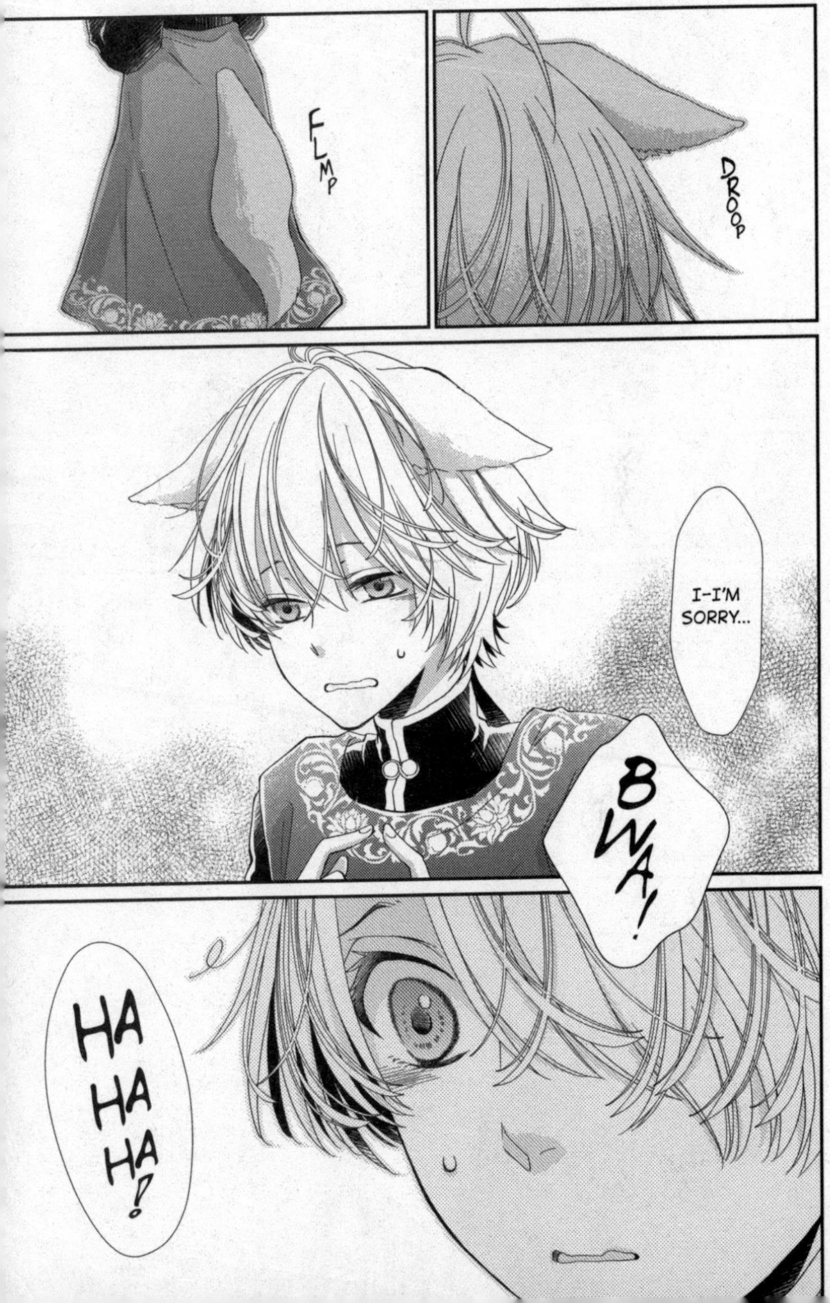
DROOP
FLMP
I-I'M SORRY...
BWA!
HA HA HA HA!

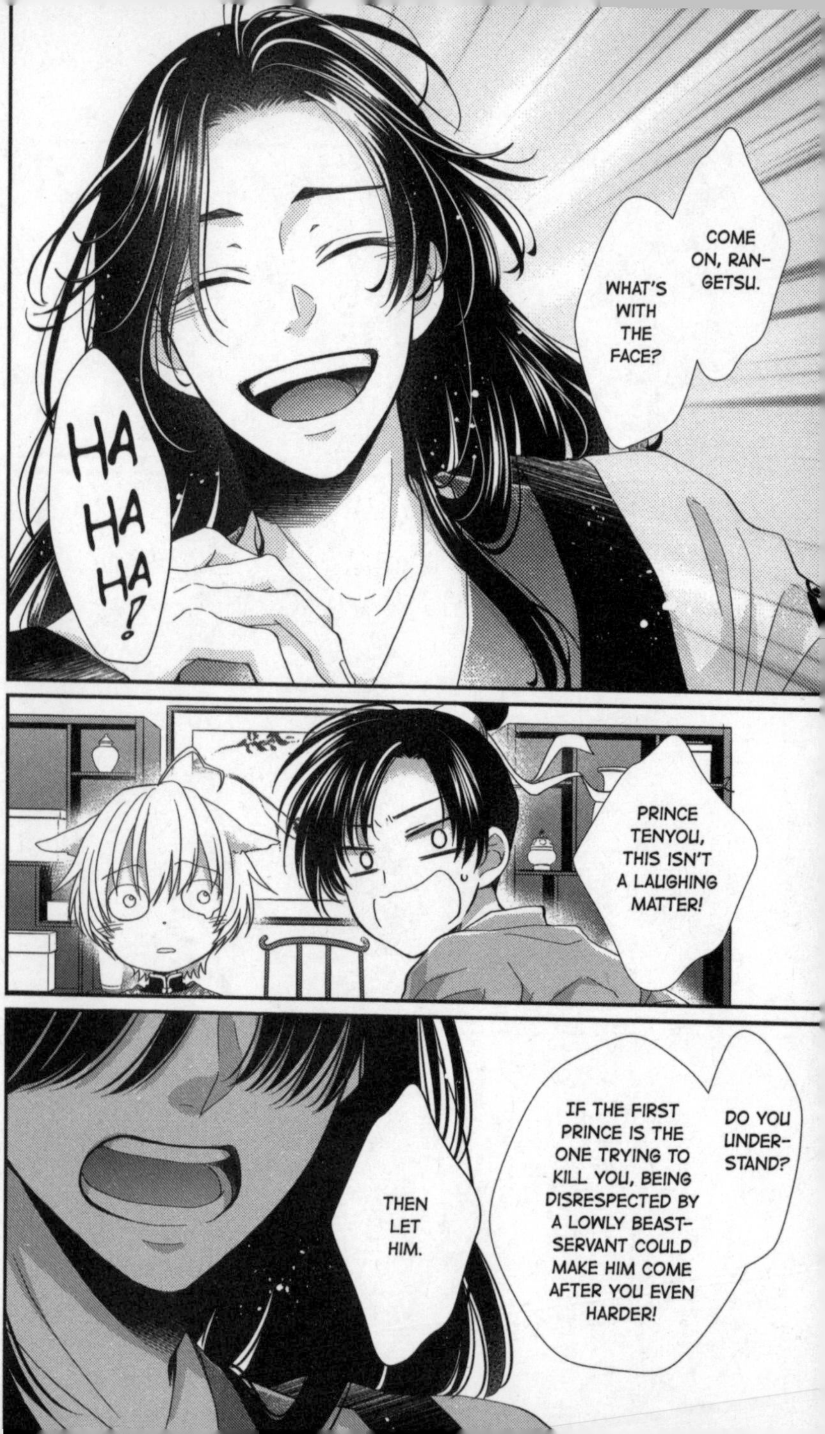
COME ON, RAN-GETSU.
WHAT'S WITH THE FACE?
HA HA HA!
PRINCE TENYOU, THIS ISN'T A LAUGHING MATTER!
DO YOU UNDER-STAND?
IF THE FIRST PRINCE IS THE ONE TRYING TO KILL YOU, BEING DISRESPECTED BY A LOWLY BEAST-SERVANT COULD MAKE HIM COME AFTER YOU EVEN HARDER!
THEN LET HIM.

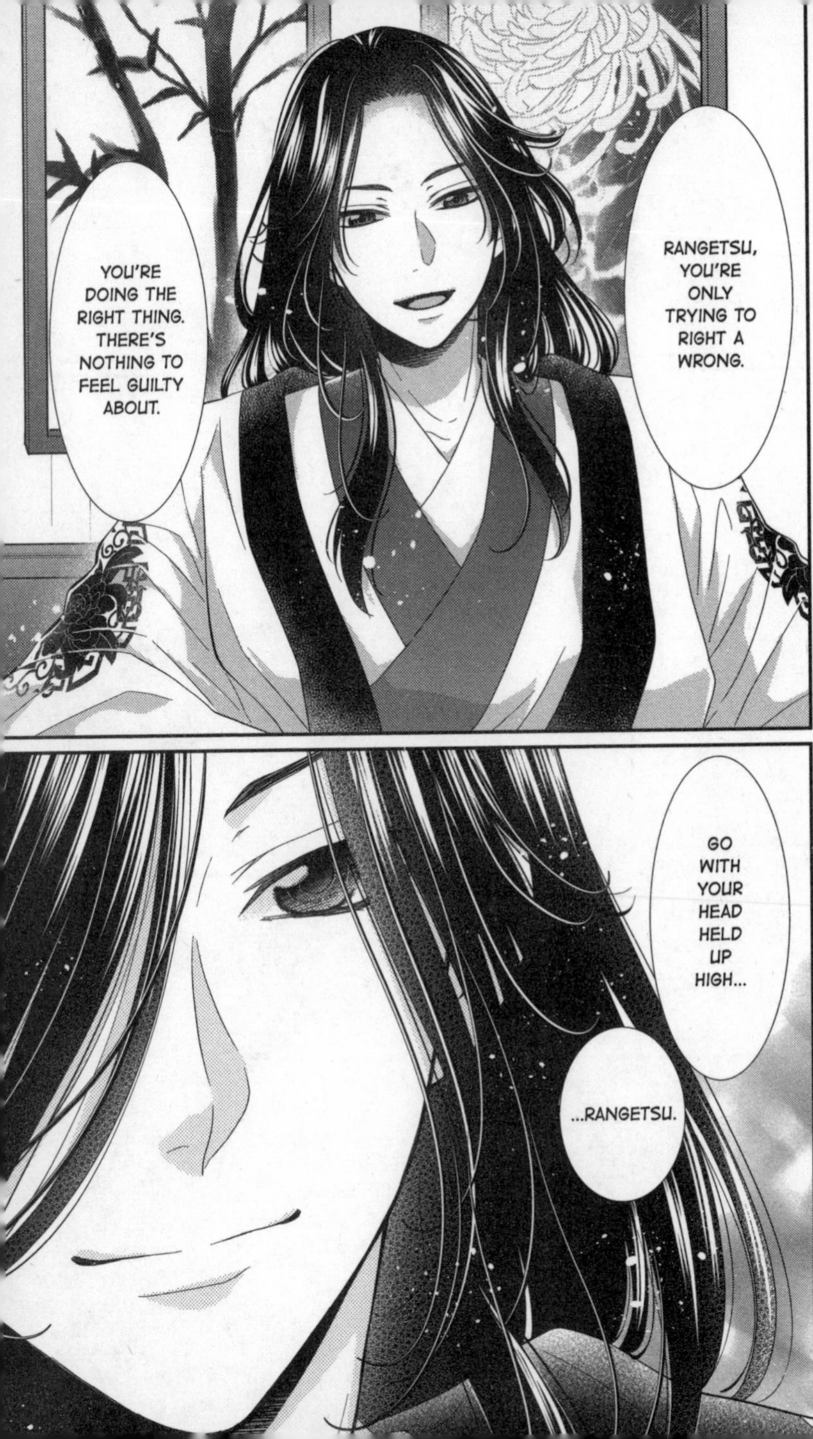
RANGETSU, YOU'RE ONLY TRYING TO RIGHT A WRONG.
YOU'RE DOING THE RIGHT THING. THERE'S NOTHING TO FEEL GUILTY ABOUT.
GO WITH YOUR HEAD HELD UP HIGH...
...RANGETSU.

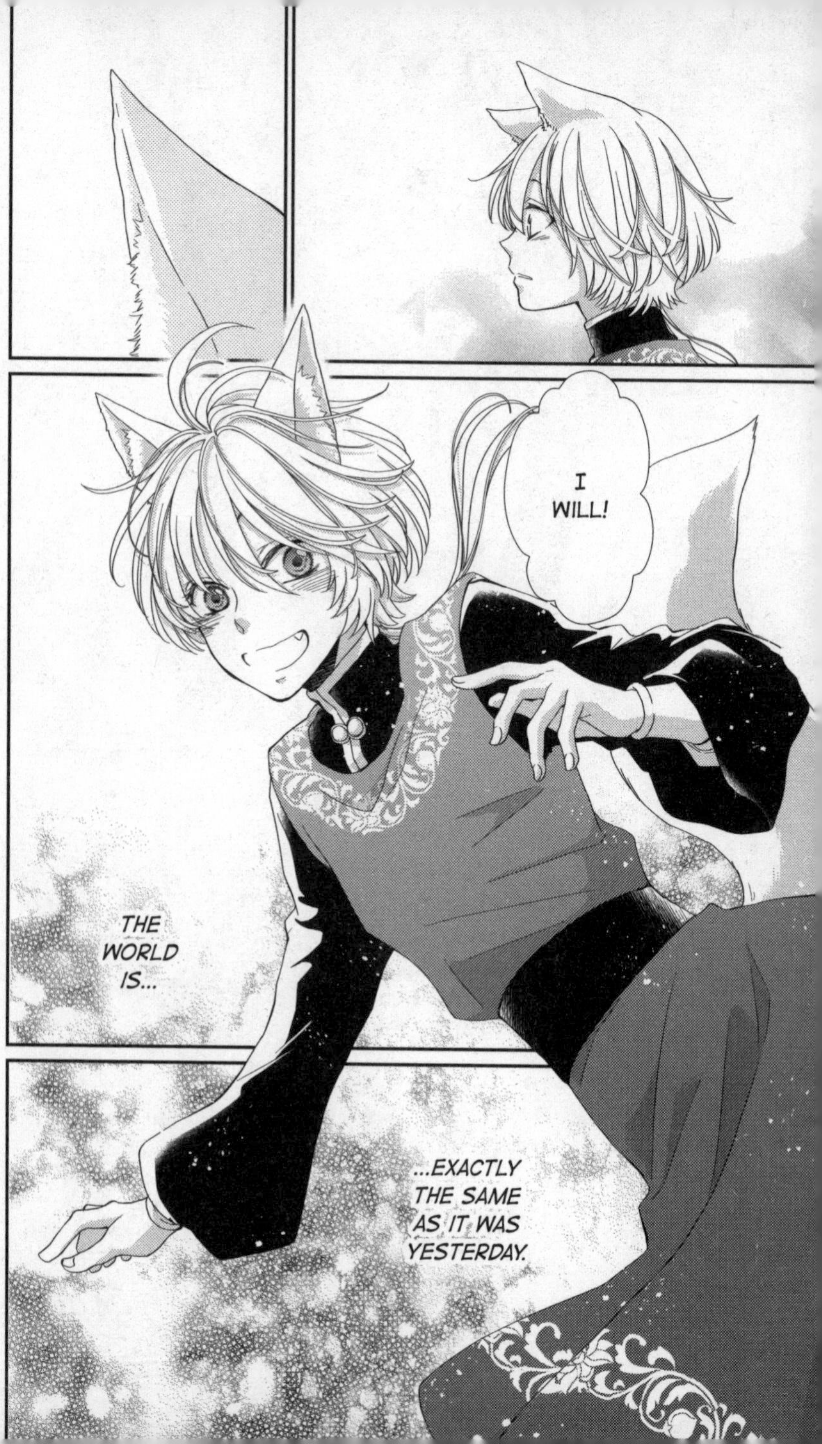
I WILL!
THE WORLD IS...
...EXACTLY THE SAME AS IT WAS YESTERDAY.

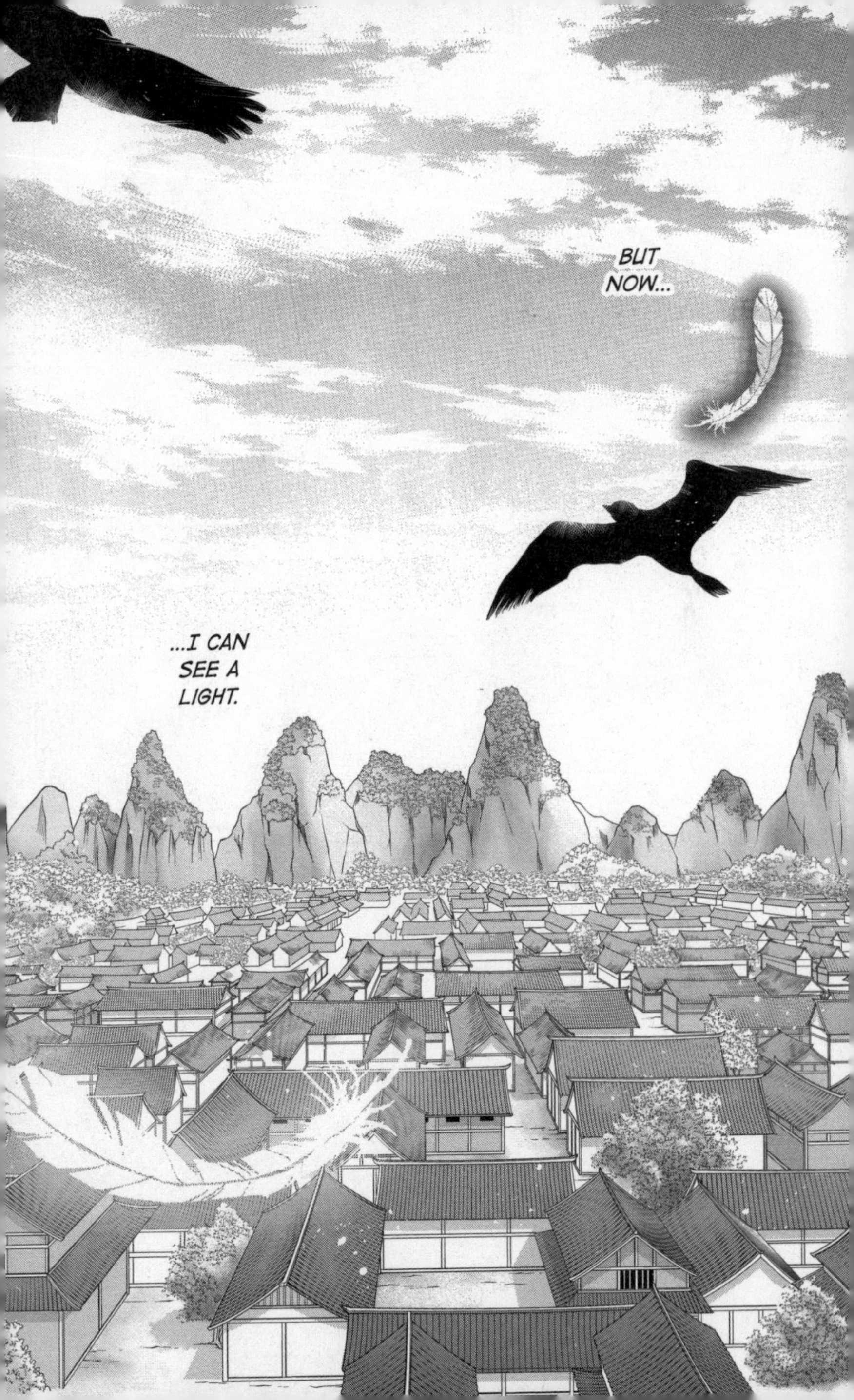
BUT NOW...
...I CAN SEE A LIGHT.

THE KING'S *Beast* 麗

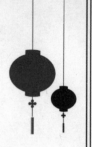

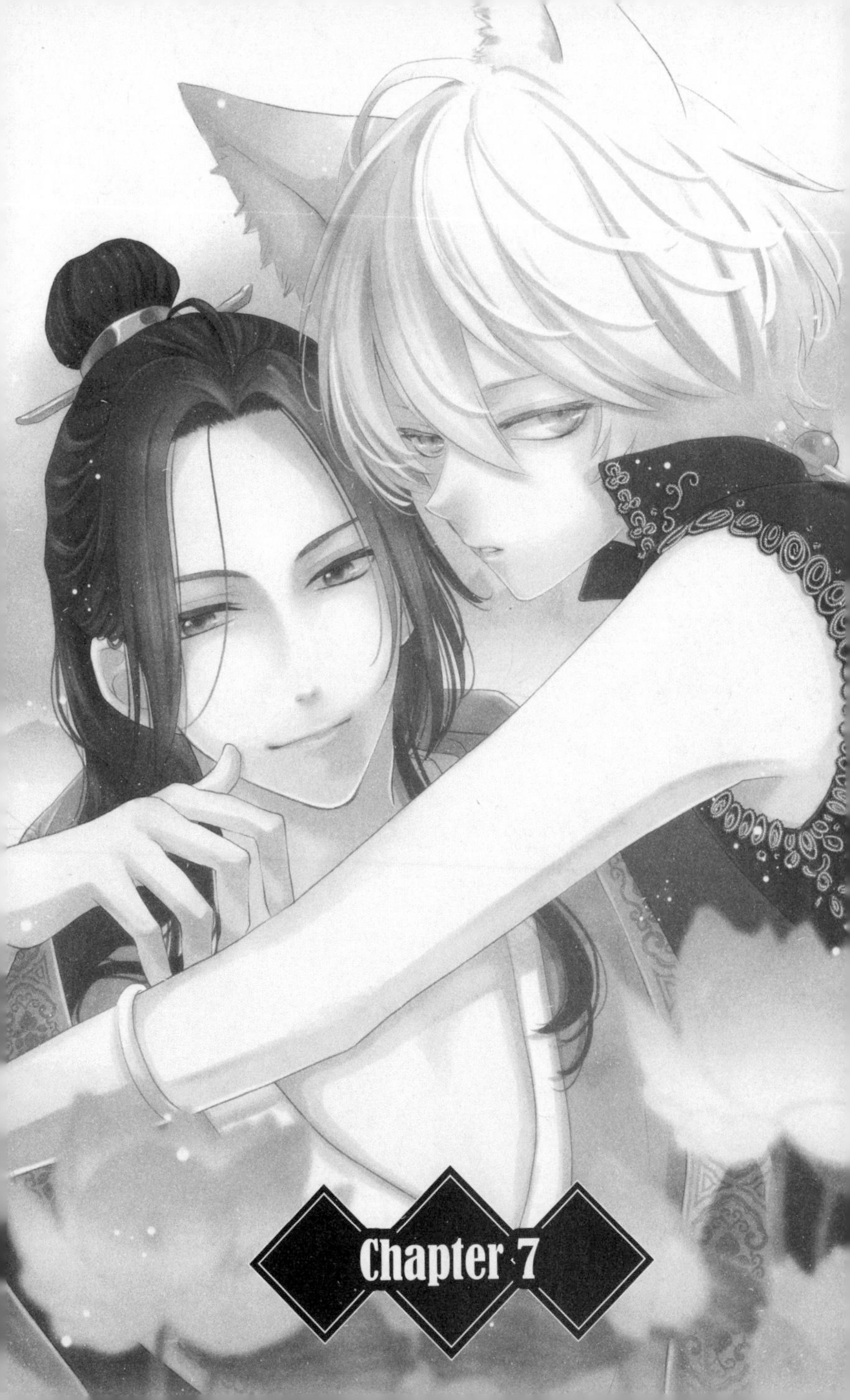
Chapter 7

THE KING'S *Beast*

麗

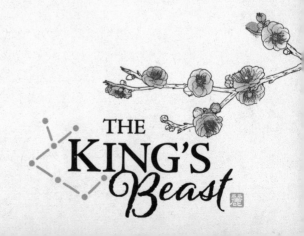

I...

...HAVE SPECIAL ABILITIES...

STARTING TODAY, YOU WILL BE...

...THE FIRST PRINCE'S BEAST-SERVANT.

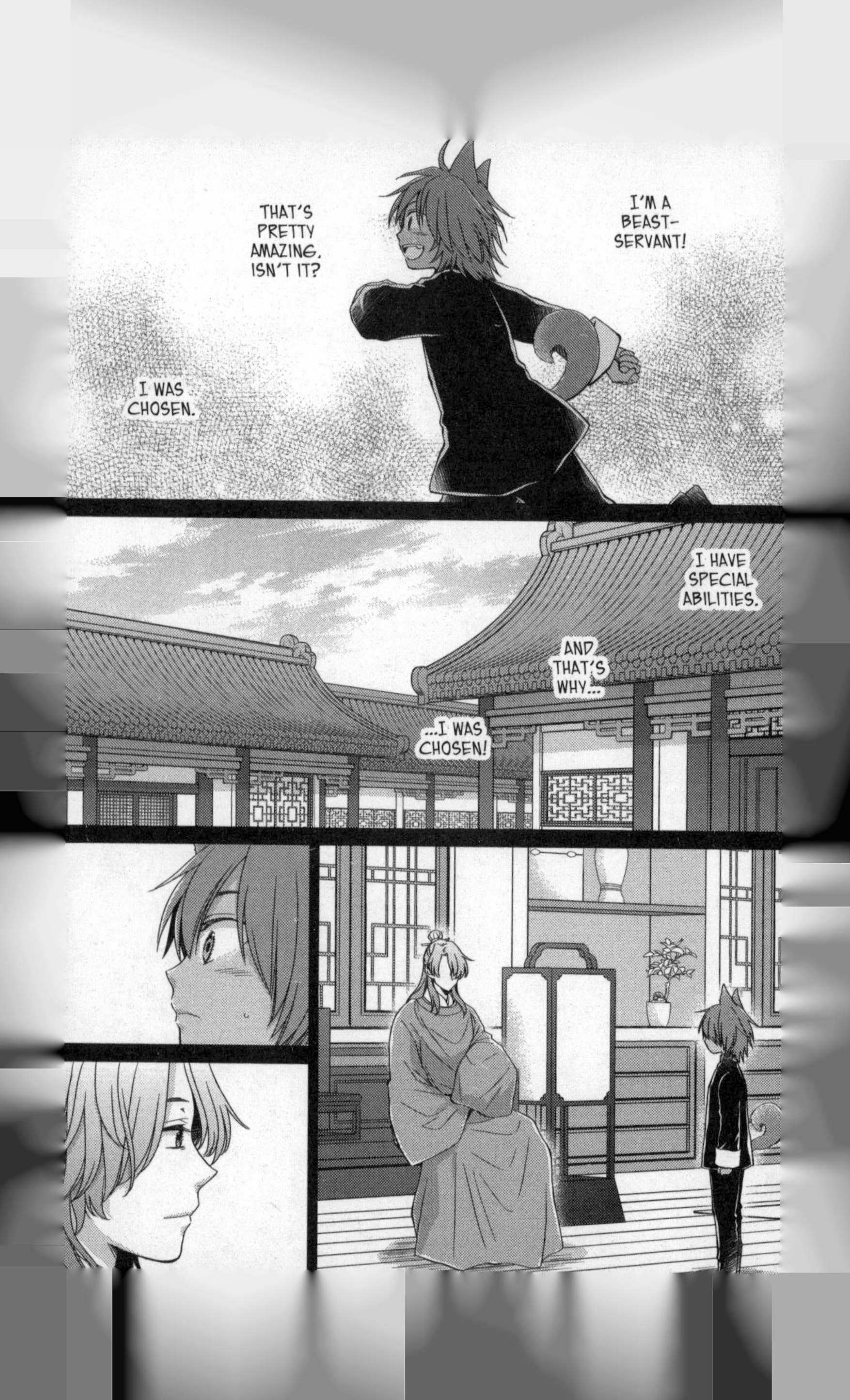
I'M A BEAST-SERVANT!
THAT'S PRETTY AMAZING, ISN'T IT?
I WAS CHOSEN.
I HAVE SPECIAL ABILITIES.
AND THAT'S WHY...
...I WAS CHOSEN!

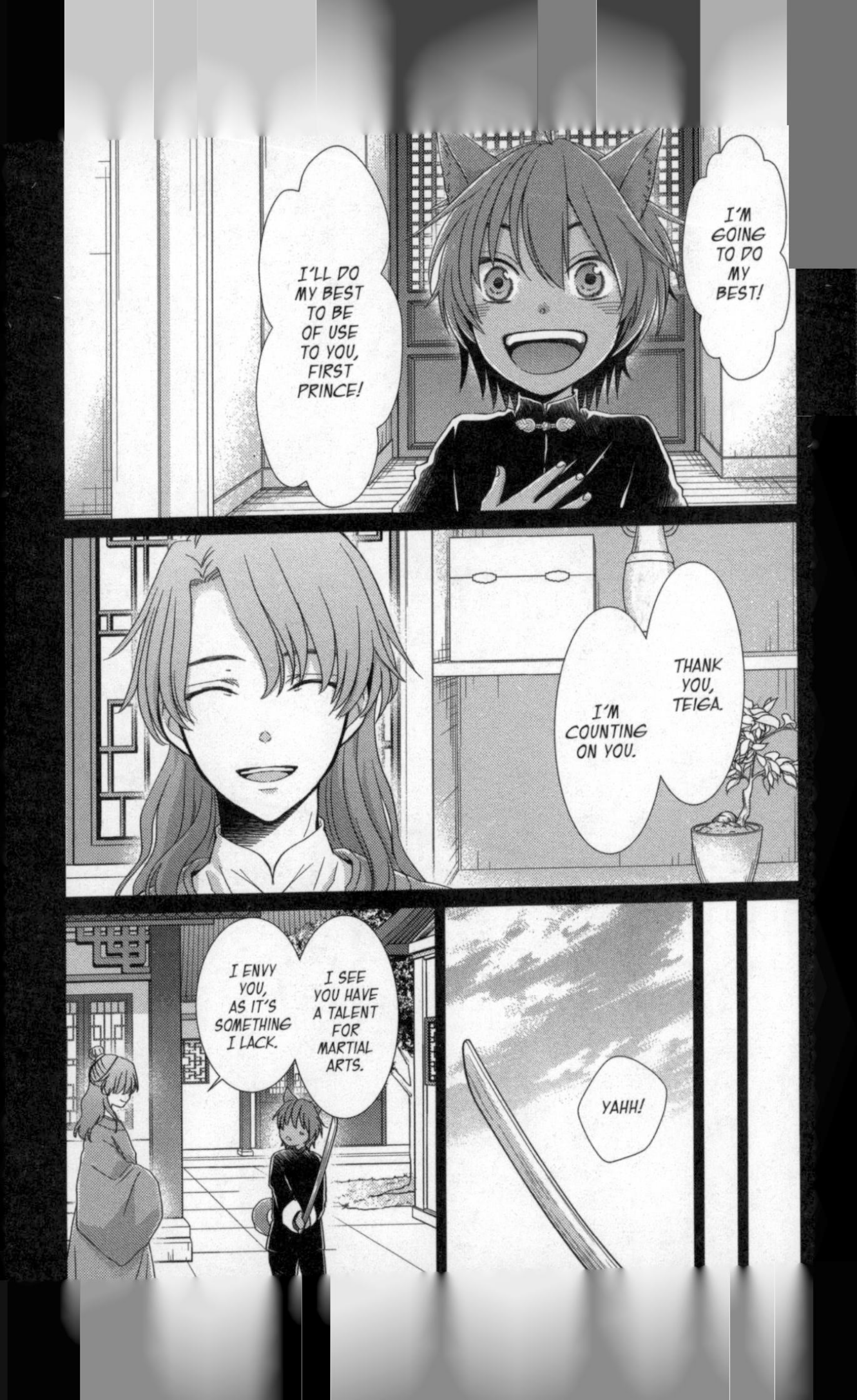
I'M GOING TO DO MY BEST!
I'LL DO MY BEST TO BE OF USE TO YOU, FIRST PRINCE!
THANK YOU, TEIGA.
I'M COUNTING ON YOU.
YAHH!
I SEE YOU HAVE A TALENT FOR MARTIAL ARTS.
I ENVY YOU, AS IT'S SOMETHING I LACK.

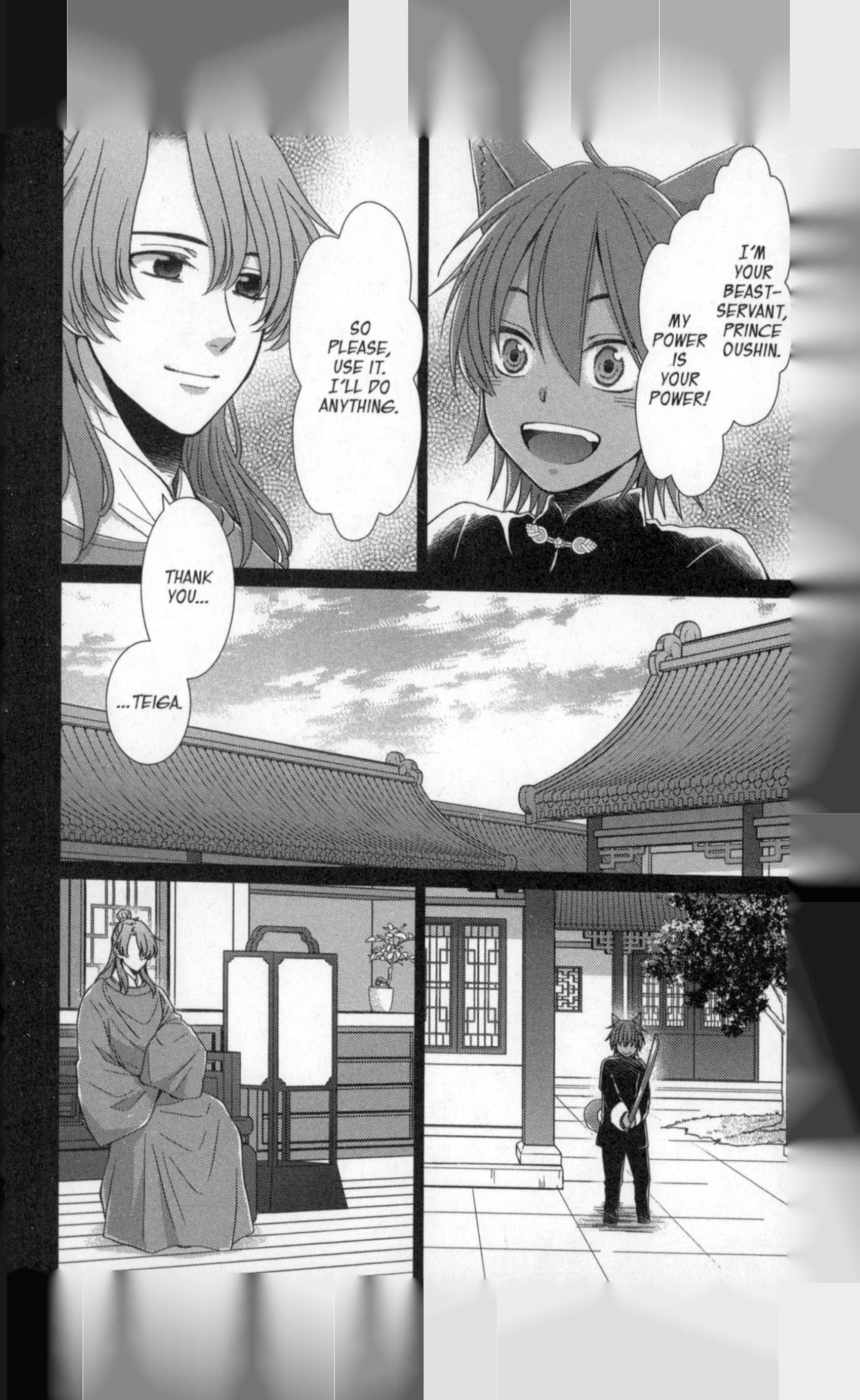
I'M YOUR BEAST-SERVANT, PRINCE OUSHIN.
MY POWER IS YOUR POWER!
SO PLEASE, USE IT. I'LL DO ANYTHING.
THANK YOU...
...TEIGA.

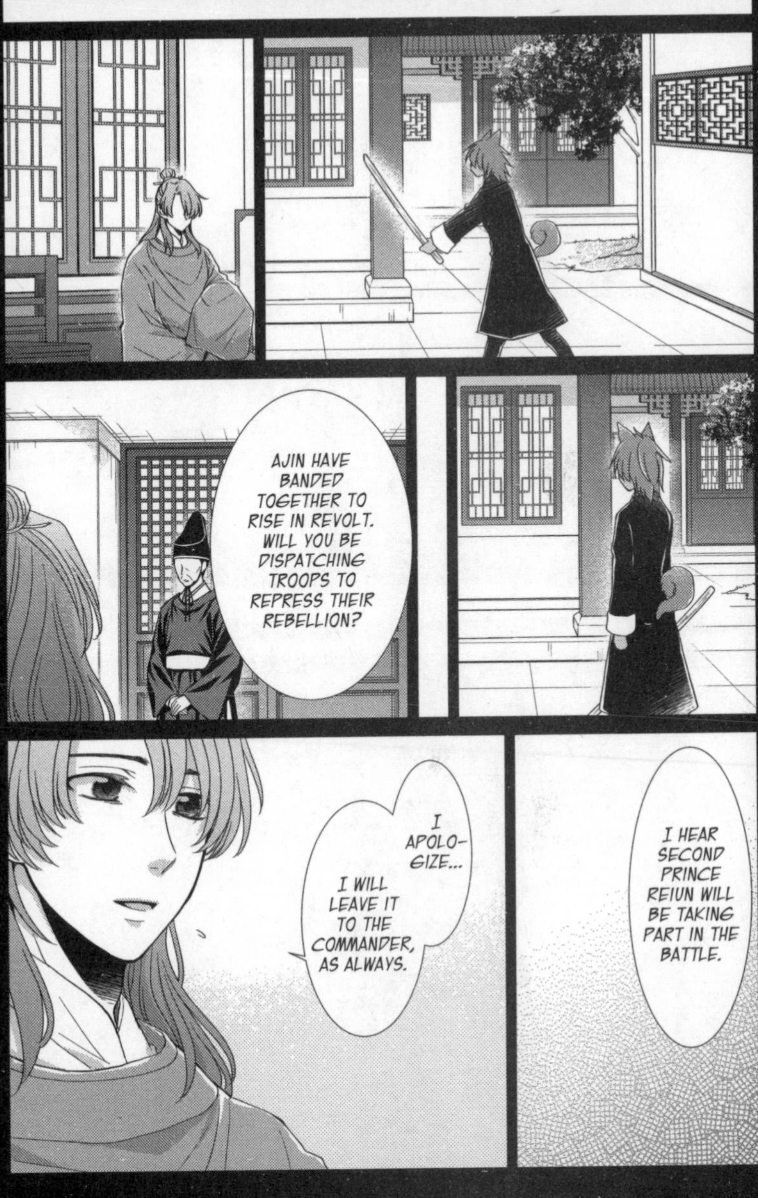
AJIN HAVE BANDED TOGETHER TO RISE IN REVOLT. WILL YOU BE DISPATCHING TROOPS TO REPRESS THEIR REBELLION?
I HEAR SECOND PRINCE REIUN WILL BE TAKING PART IN THE BATTLE.
I APOLOGIZE...
I WILL LEAVE IT TO THE COMMANDER, AS ALWAYS.

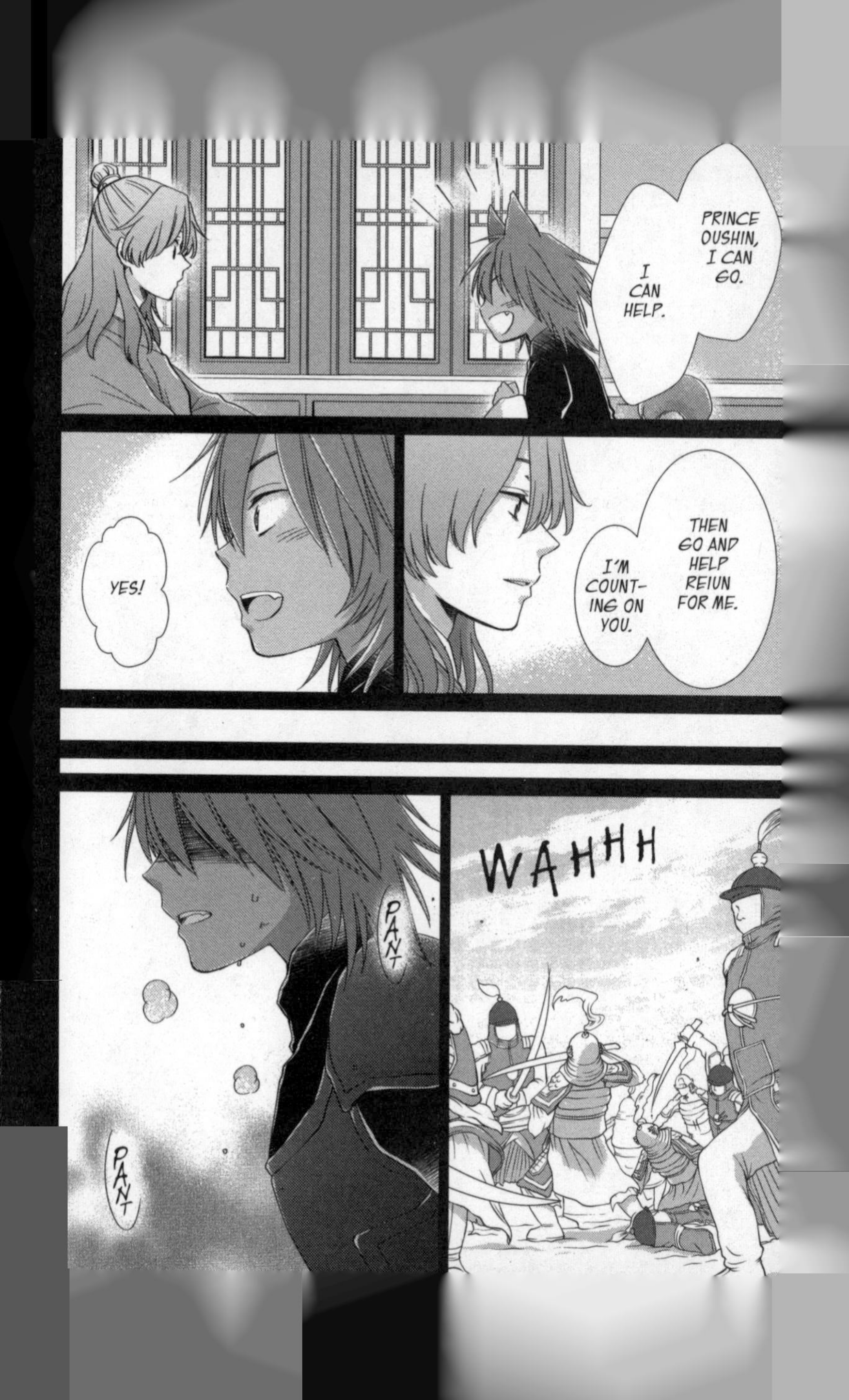
PRINCE OUSHIN, I CAN GO.
I CAN HELP.
THEN GO AND HELP REIUN FOR ME.
I'M COUNTING ON YOU.
YES!
WAHHH
PANT
PANT

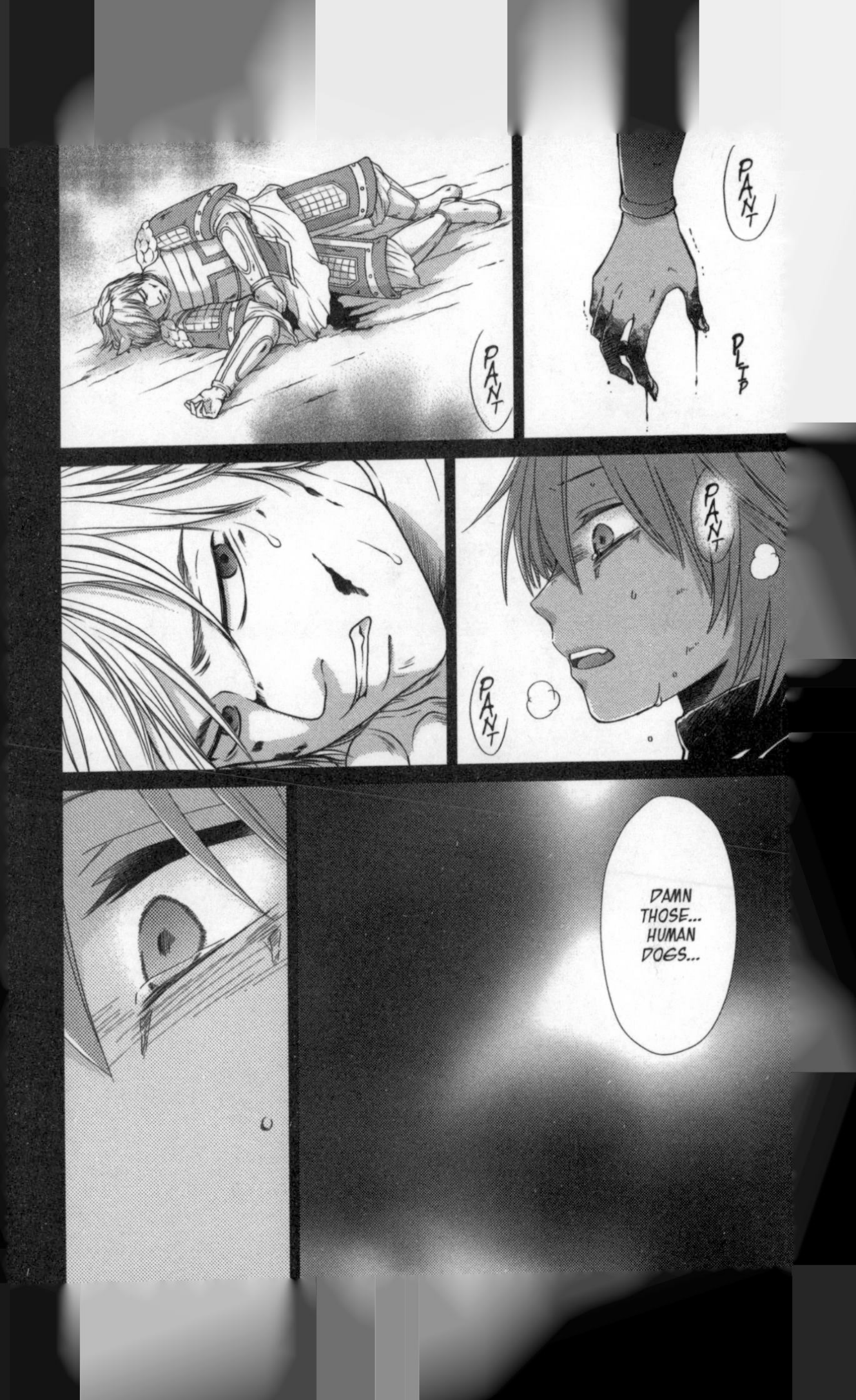
PANT
PLIP
PANT
PANT
PANT
DAMN THOSE... HUMAN DOGS...

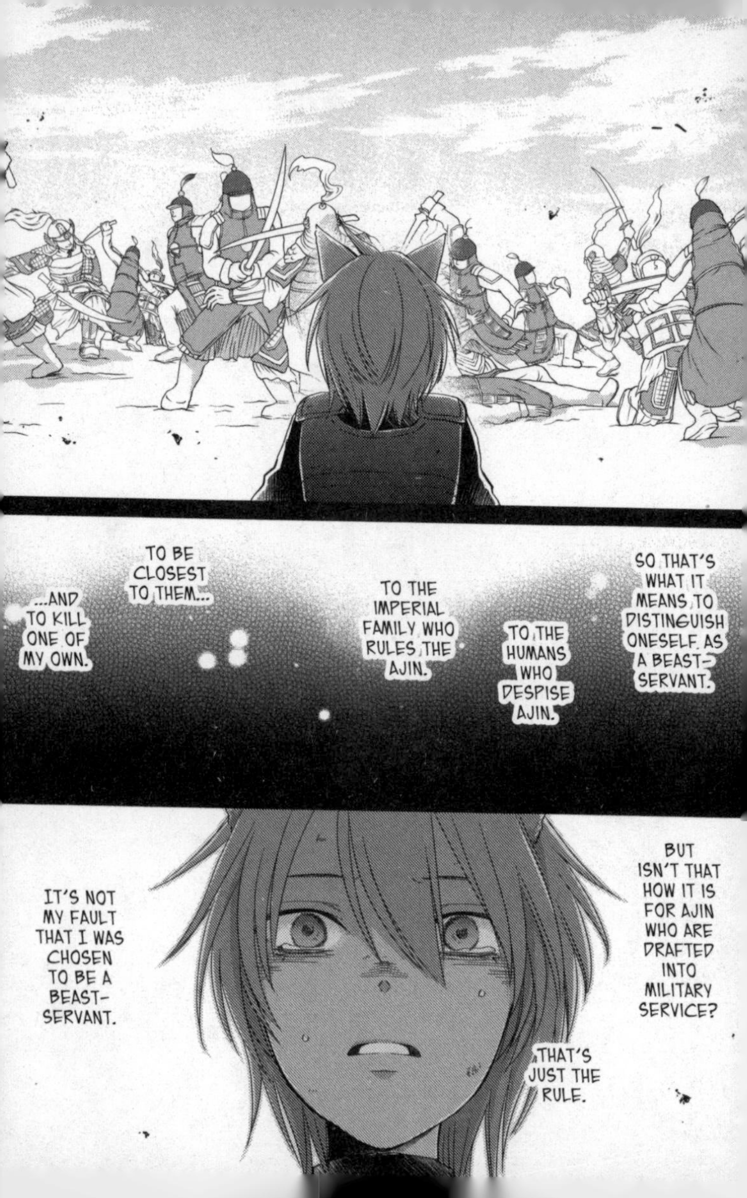
SO THAT'S WHAT IT MEANS TO DISTINGUISH ONESELF AS A BEAST-SERVANT.
TO THE HUMANS WHO DESPISE AJIN.
TO THE IMPERIAL FAMILY WHO RULES THE AJIN.
TO BE CLOSEST TO THEM...
...AND TO KILL ONE OF MY OWN.
BUT ISN'T THAT HOW IT IS FOR AJIN WHO ARE DRAFTED INTO MILITARY SERVICE?
THAT'S JUST THE RULE.
IT'S NOT MY FAULT THAT I WAS CHOSEN TO BE A BEAST-SERVANT.

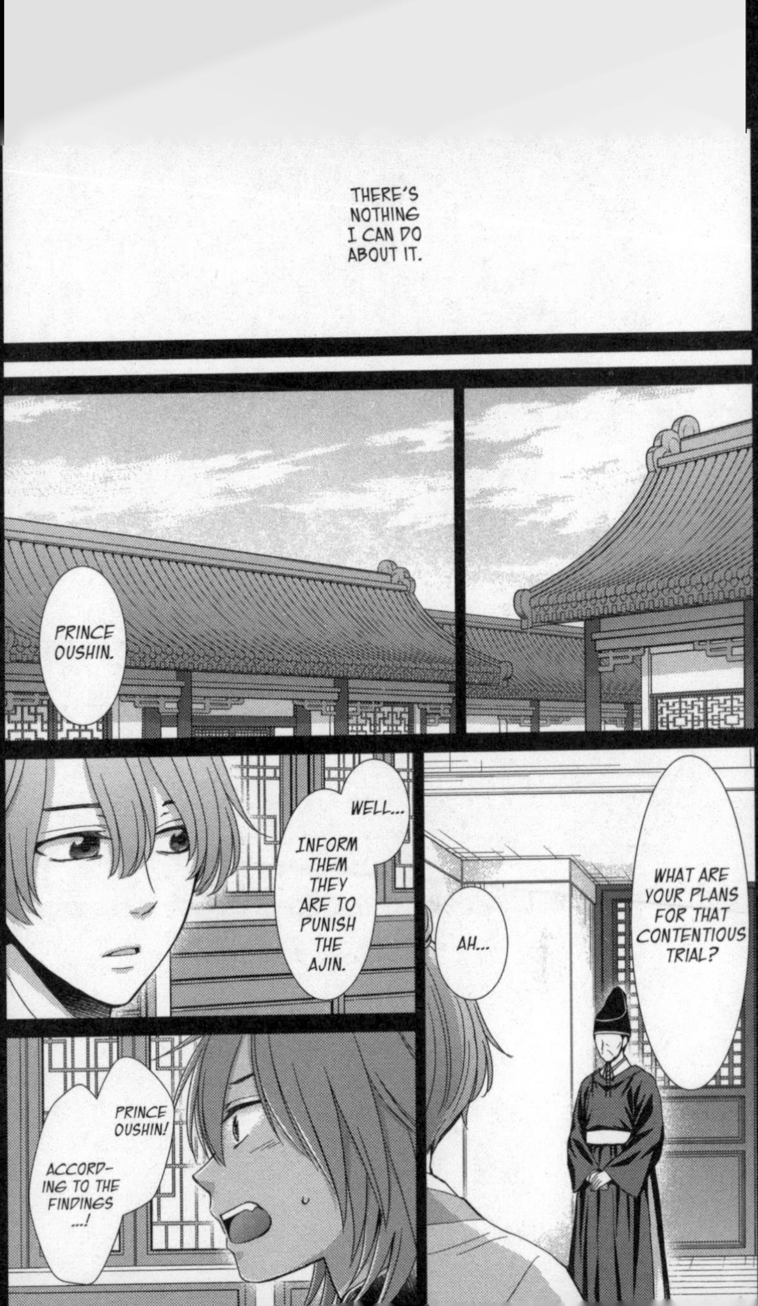
THERE'S NOTHING I CAN DO ABOUT IT.
PRINCE OUSHIN.
WHAT ARE YOUR PLANS FOR THAT CONTENTIOUS TRIAL?
AH...
WELL...
INFORM THEM THEY ARE TO PUNISH THE AJIN.
PRINCE OUSHIN!
ACCORD-ING TO THE FINDINGS ...!

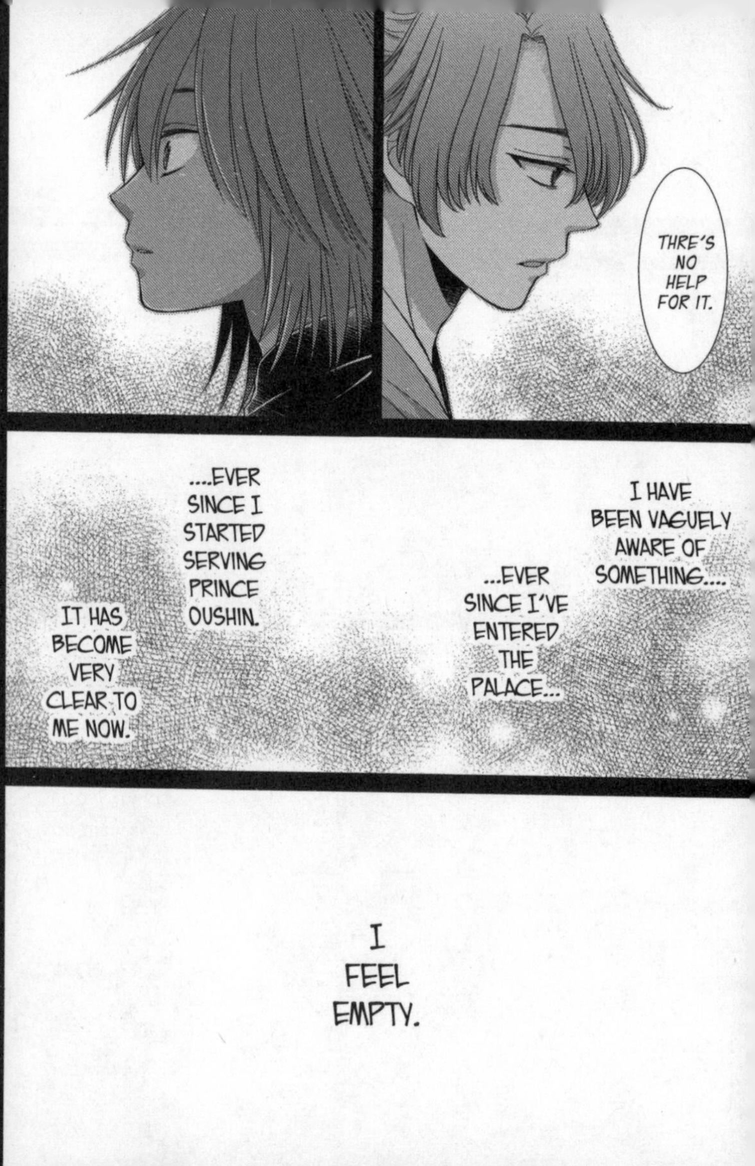
THRE'S NO HELP FOR IT.
I HAVE BEEN VAGUELY AWARE OF SOMETHING....
...EVER SINCE I'VE ENTERED THE PALACE...
....EVER SINCE I STARTED SERVING PRINCE OUSHIN.
IT HAS BECOME VERY CLEAR TO ME NOW.
I FEEL EMPTY.

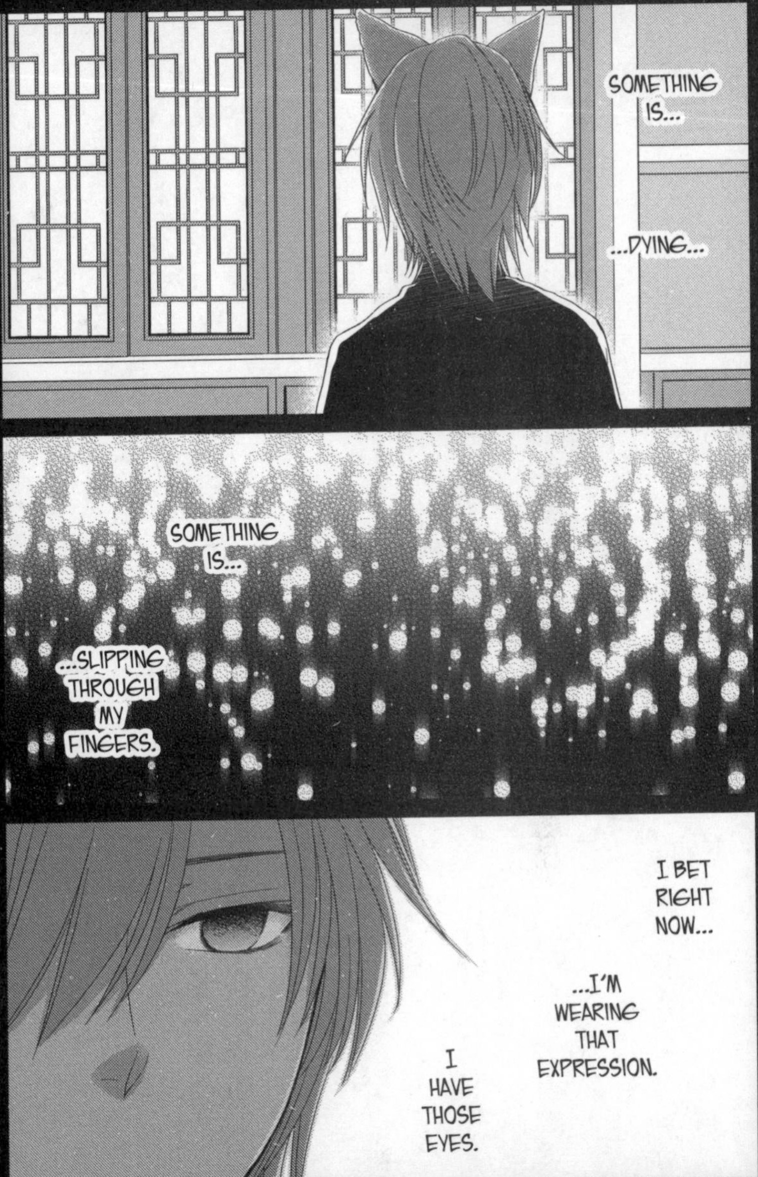
SOMETHING IS...
...DYING...
SOMETHING IS...
...SLIPPING THROUGH MY FINGERS.
I BET RIGHT NOW...
...I'M WEARING THAT EXPRESSION.
I HAVE THOSE EYES.

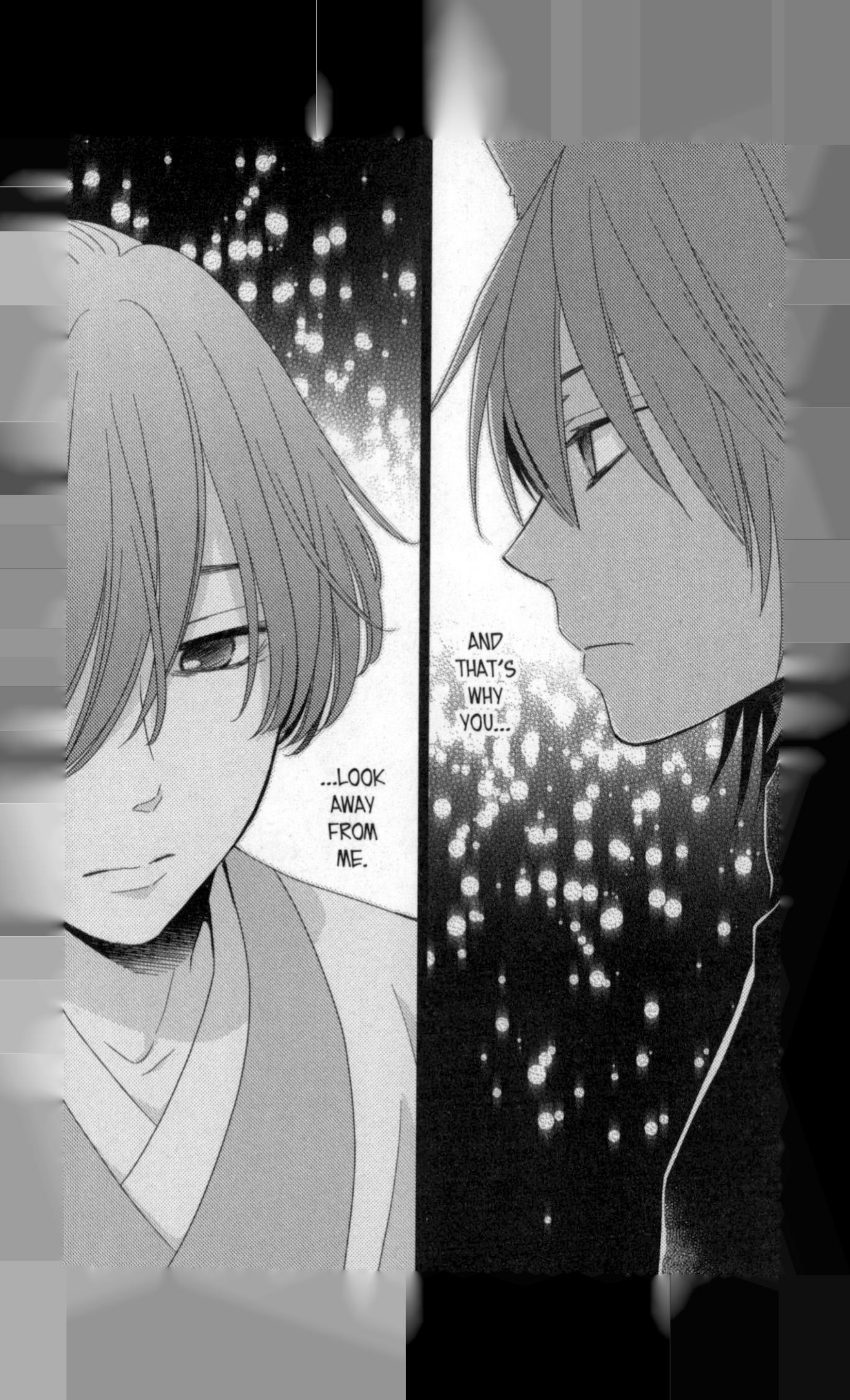
AND THAT'S WHY YOU...
...LOOK AWAY FROM ME.

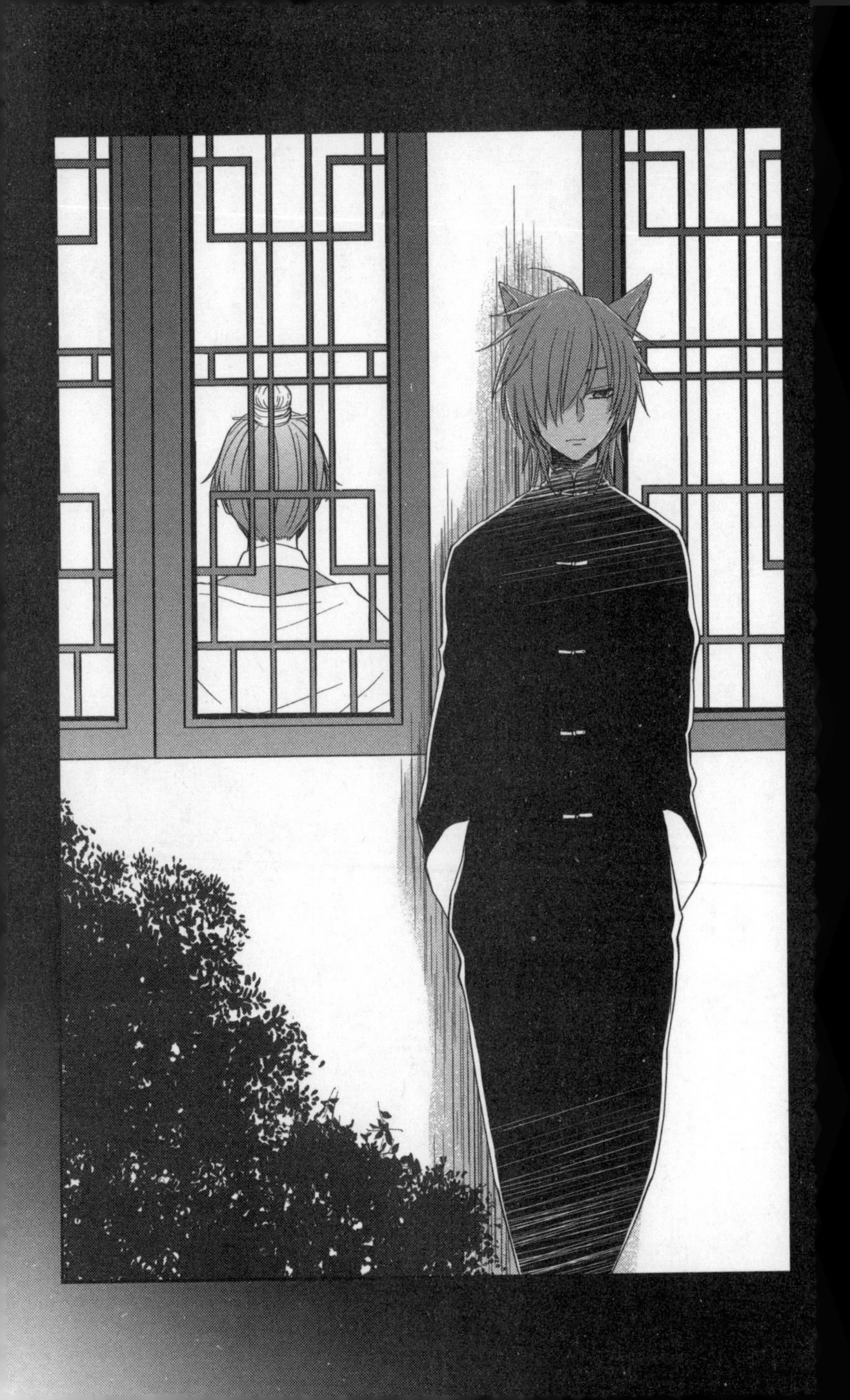

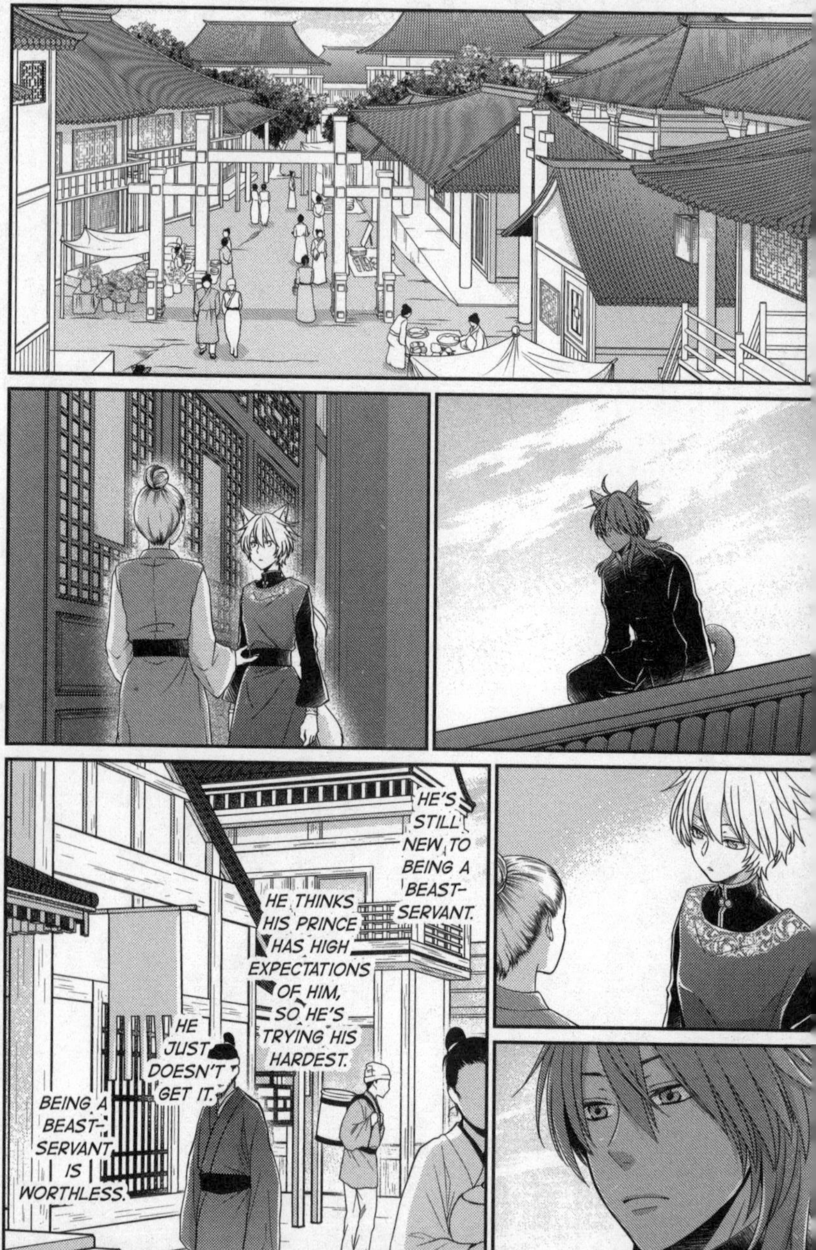
HE'S STILL NEW TO BEING A BEAST-SERVANT.
HE THINKS HIS PRINCE HAS HIGH EXPECTATIONS OF HIM, SO HE'S TRYING HIS HARDEST.
HE JUST DOESN'T GET IT.
BEING A BEAST-SERVANT IS WORTHLESS.

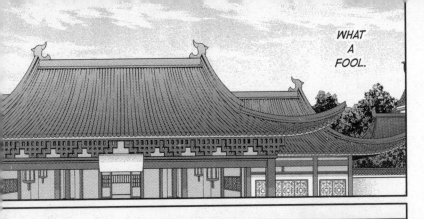

WHAT
A
FOOL.

"THE
MURDER
AT THAT
NOBLE
HOUSE
OVER
THERE?"

"THE HUSBAND
WAS QUITE A
WOMANIZER."

"HIS
MISTRESS WAS
SUMMONED TO
THE WIFE'S
ROOM AND
WAS KILLED."

"THE AJIN
WHO WORKED
FOR THE WIFE
WAS ARRESTED,
RIGHT? WELL...
I KNOW THE WIFE
WAS LOOKING
TO ACQUIRE
A YOUNGER,
HARDER-
WORKING AJIN
ANYWAY..."

ARE
YOU SURE
EVERYTHING
WILL BE ALL
RIGHT? I HEAR
THE FOURTH
PRINCE'S
BEAST-
SERVANT IS
LOOKING INTO
THE CASE.

MADAM
...

HMPH,
THERE'S
NO NEED
TO WORRY.
OUR
HOUSE
IS IN THE
FIRST
PRINCE'S
DIRECT
JURISDIC-
TION.

THERE'S
NO WAY
HE'D
WANT TO
MAKE AN
ENEMY
OF US.

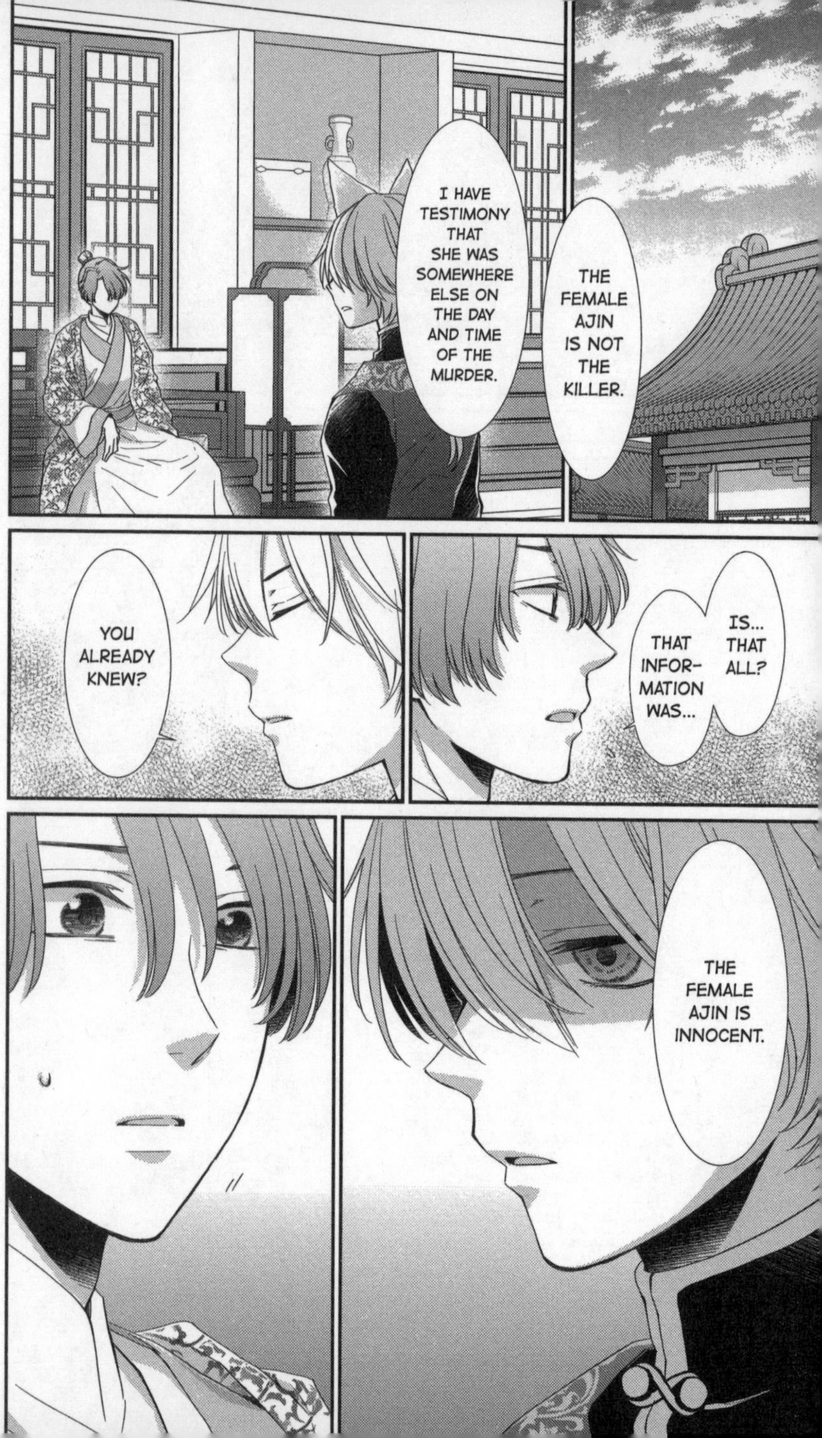
THE FEMALE AJIN IS NOT THE KILLER.
I HAVE TESTIMONY THAT SHE WAS SOMEWHERE ELSE ON THE DAY AND TIME OF THE MURDER.
THAT INFORMATION WAS...
IS... THAT ALL?
YOU ALREADY KNEW?
THE FEMALE AJIN IS INNOCENT.

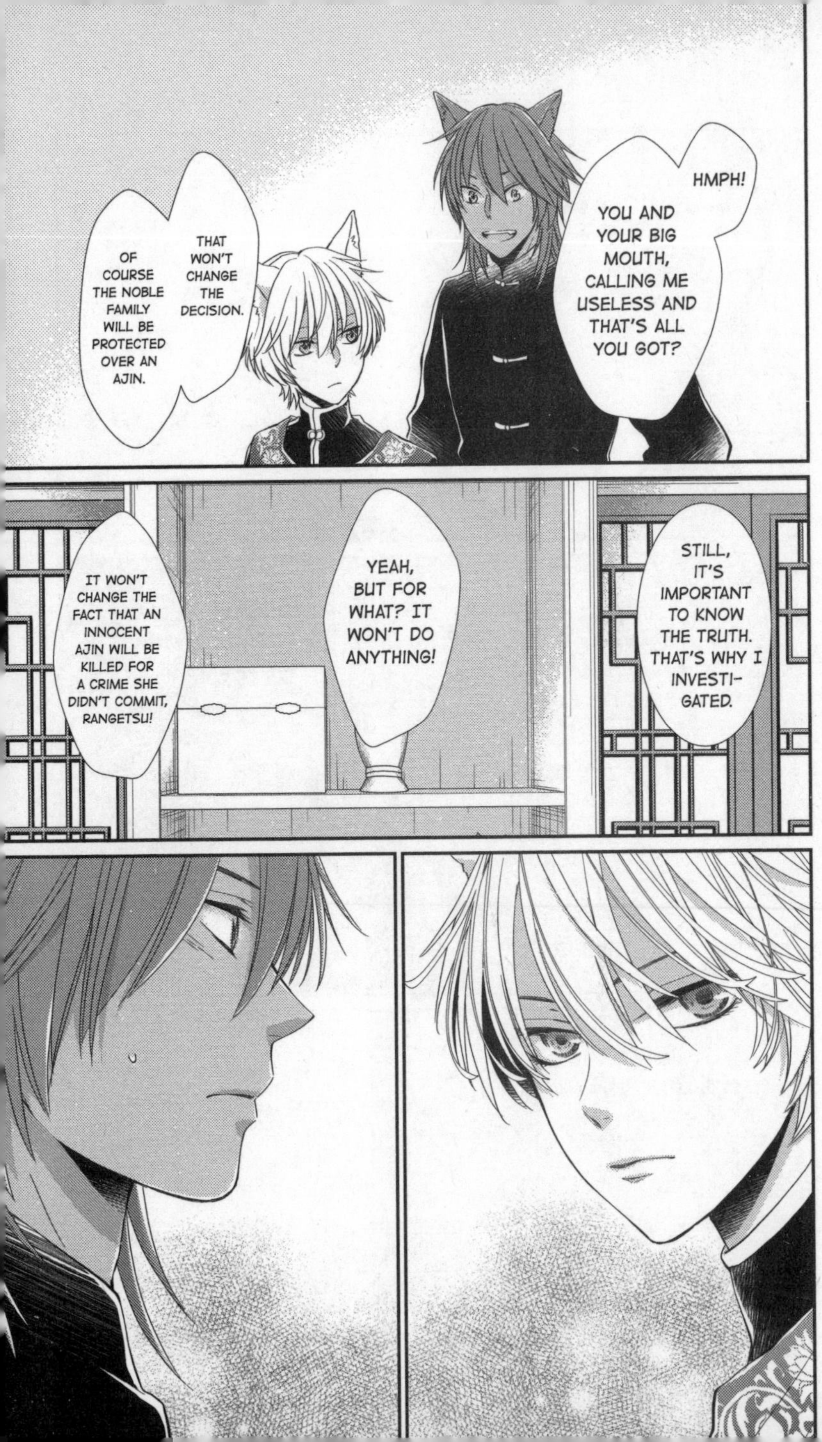
HMPH!
YOU AND YOUR BIG MOUTH, CALLING ME USELESS AND THAT'S ALL YOU GOT?
THAT WON'T CHANGE THE DECISION.
OF COURSE THE NOBLE FAMILY WILL BE PROTECTED OVER AN AJIN.
STILL, IT'S IMPORTANT TO KNOW THE TRUTH. THAT'S WHY I INVESTI-GATED.
YEAH, BUT FOR WHAT? IT WON'T DO ANYTHING!
IT WON'T CHANGE THE FACT THAT AN INNOCENT AJIN WILL BE KILLED FOR A CRIME SHE DIDN'T COMMIT, RANGETSU!

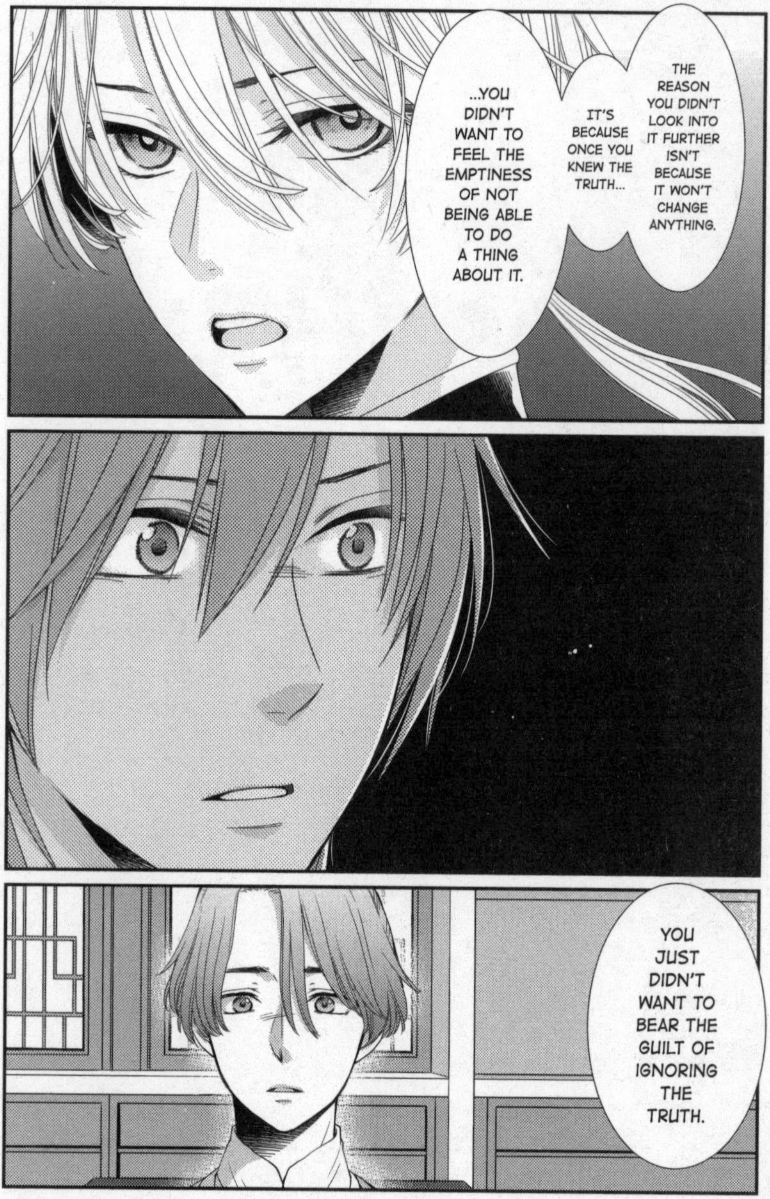
THE REASON YOU DIDN'T LOOK INTO IT FURTHER ISN'T BECAUSE IT WON'T CHANGE ANYTHING.
IT'S BECAUSE ONCE YOU KNEW THE TRUTH...
...YOU DIDN'T WANT TO FEEL THE EMPTINESS OF NOT BEING ABLE TO DO A THING ABOUT IT.
YOU JUST DIDN'T WANT TO BEAR THE GUILT OF IGNORING THE TRUTH.

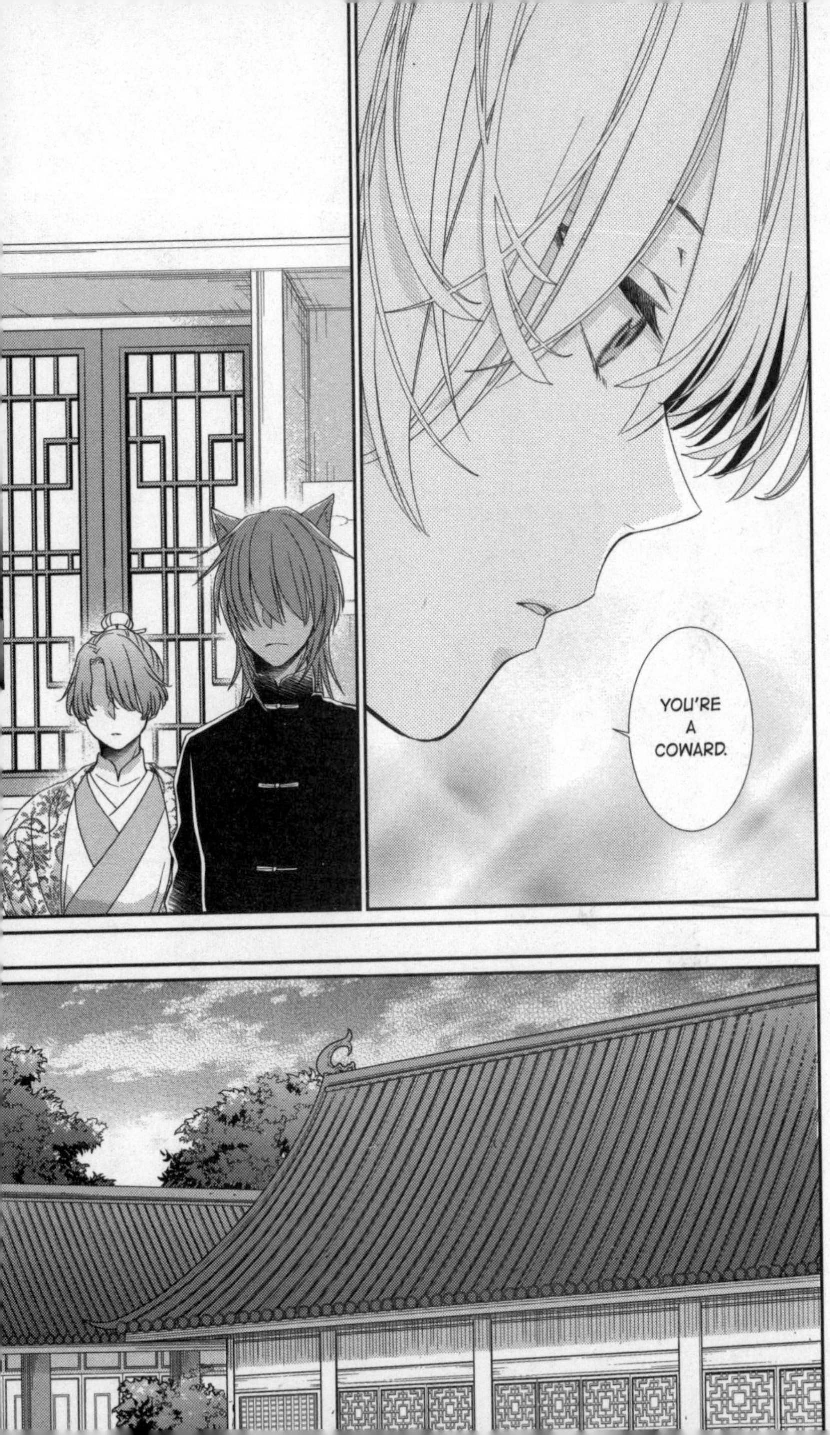
YOU'RE A COWARD.

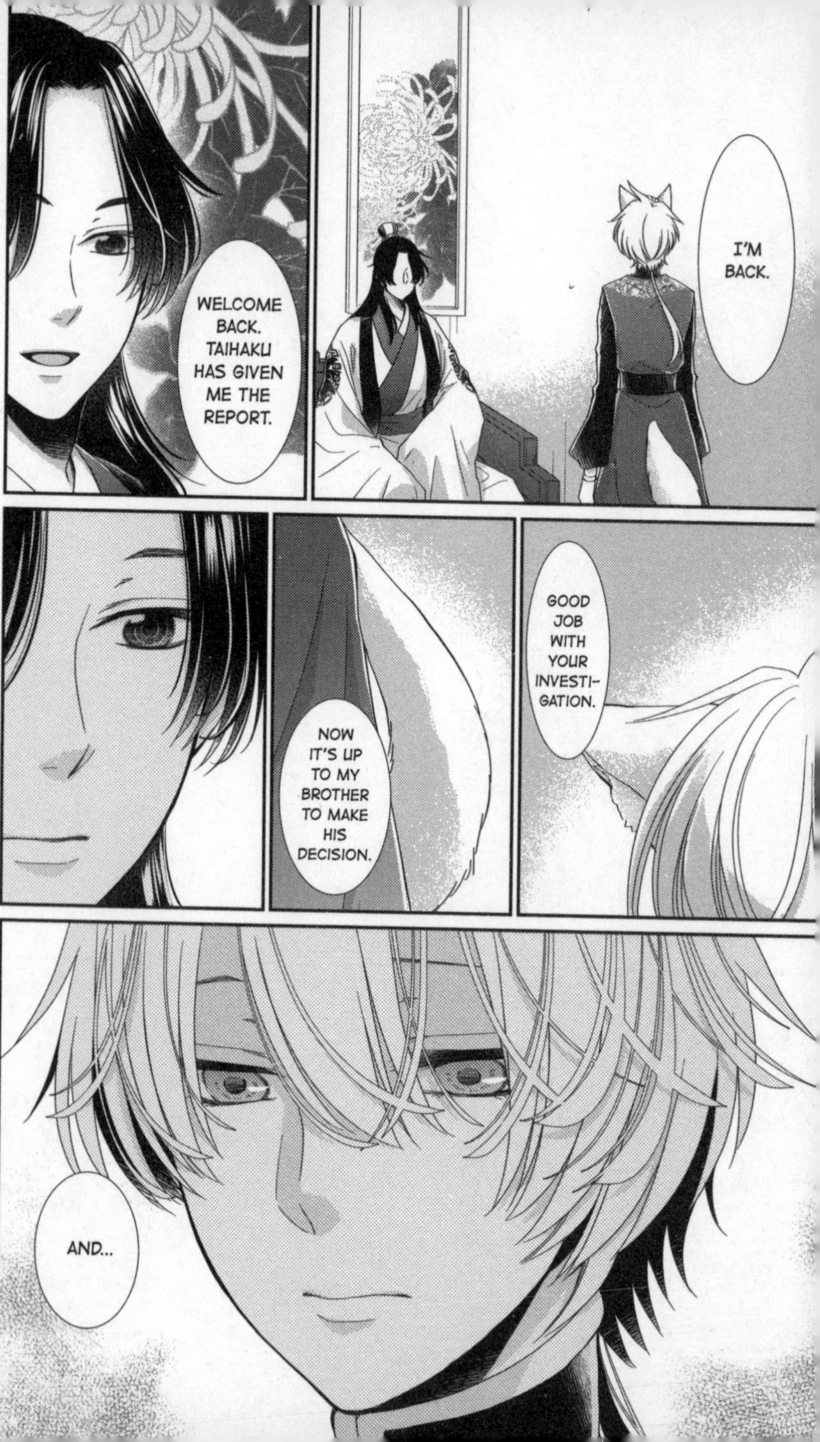
I'M BACK.
WELCOME BACK. TAIHAKU HAS GIVEN ME THE REPORT.
GOOD JOB WITH YOUR INVESTIGATION.
NOW IT'S UP TO MY BROTHER TO MAKE HIS DECISION.
AND...

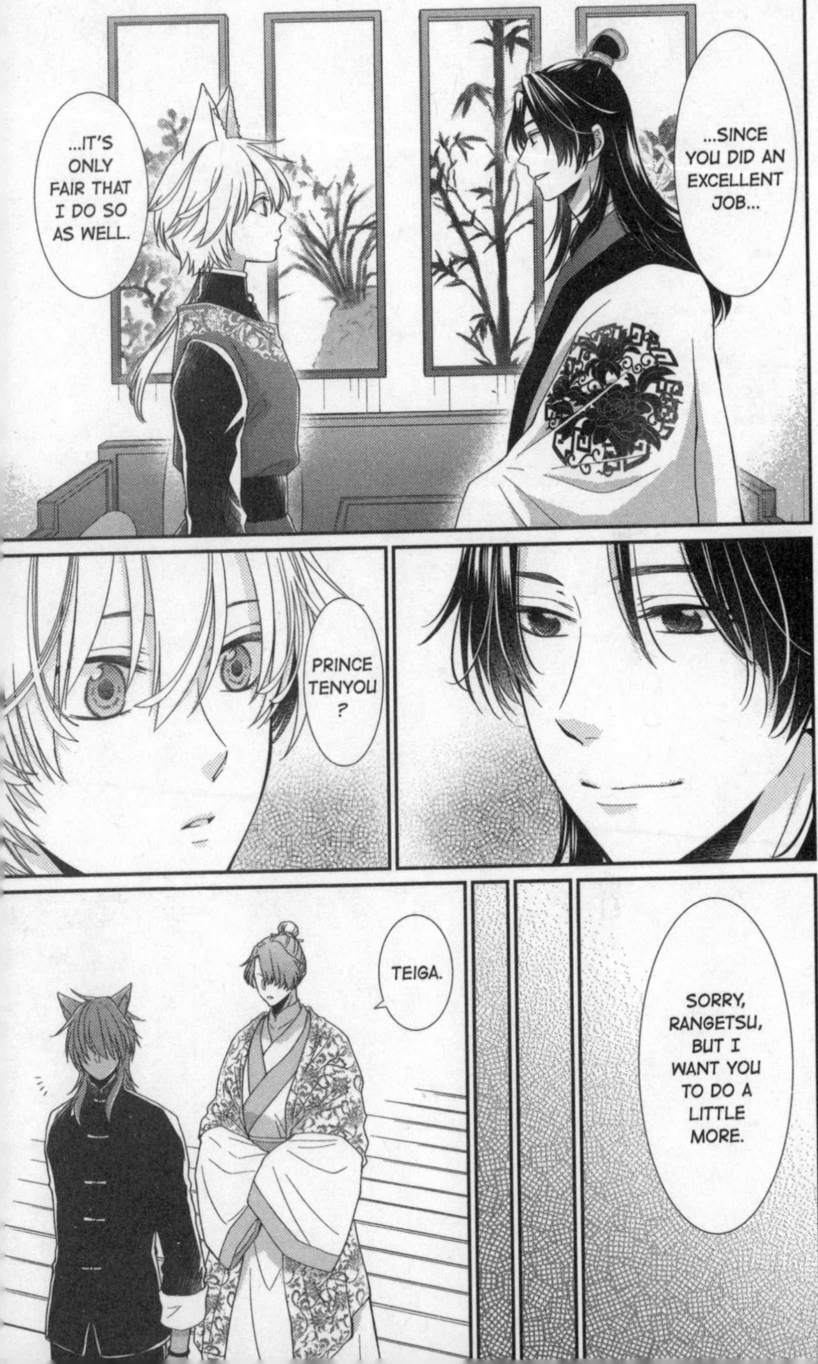
...SINCE YOU DID AN EXCELLENT JOB...
...IT'S ONLY FAIR THAT I DO SO AS WELL.
PRINCE TENYOU ?
SORRY, RANGETSU, BUT I WANT YOU TO DO A LITTLE MORE.
TEIGA.

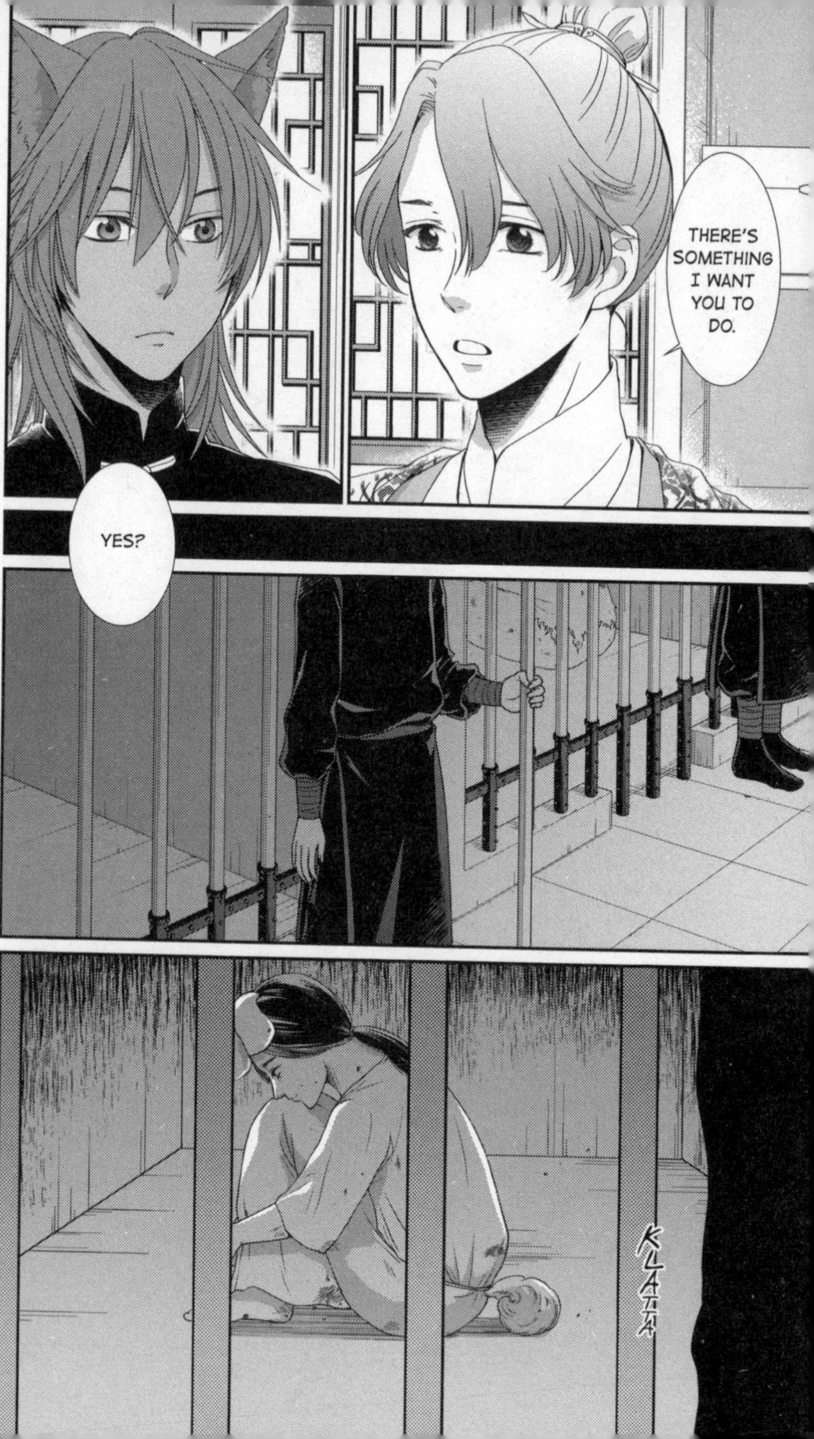
THERE'S SOMETHING I WANT YOU TO DO.
YES?
KLATTA

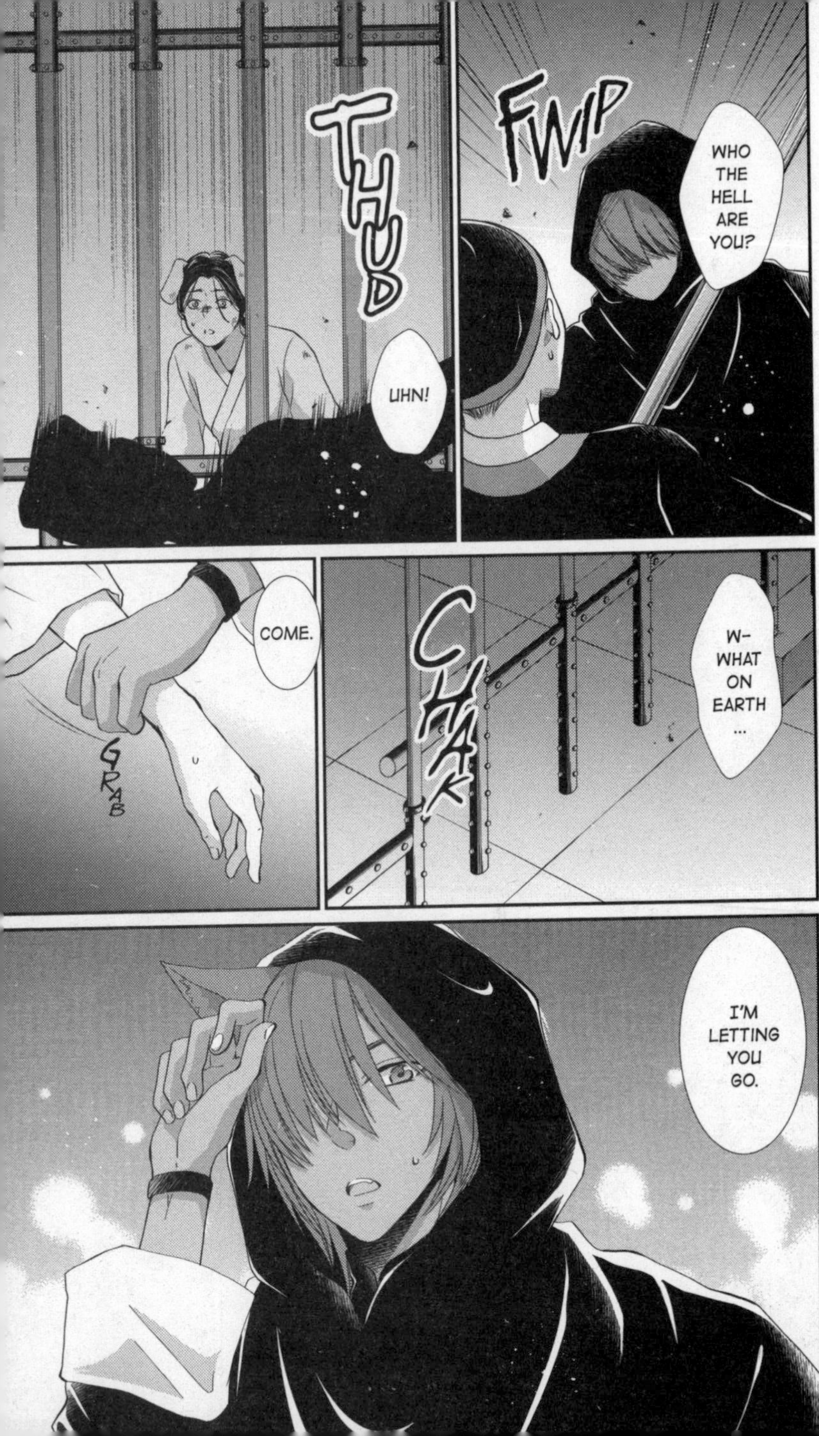
FWIP
WHO THE HELL ARE YOU?
THUD
UHN!
CHAK
W-WHAT ON EARTH...
COME.
GRAB
I'M LETTING YOU GO.

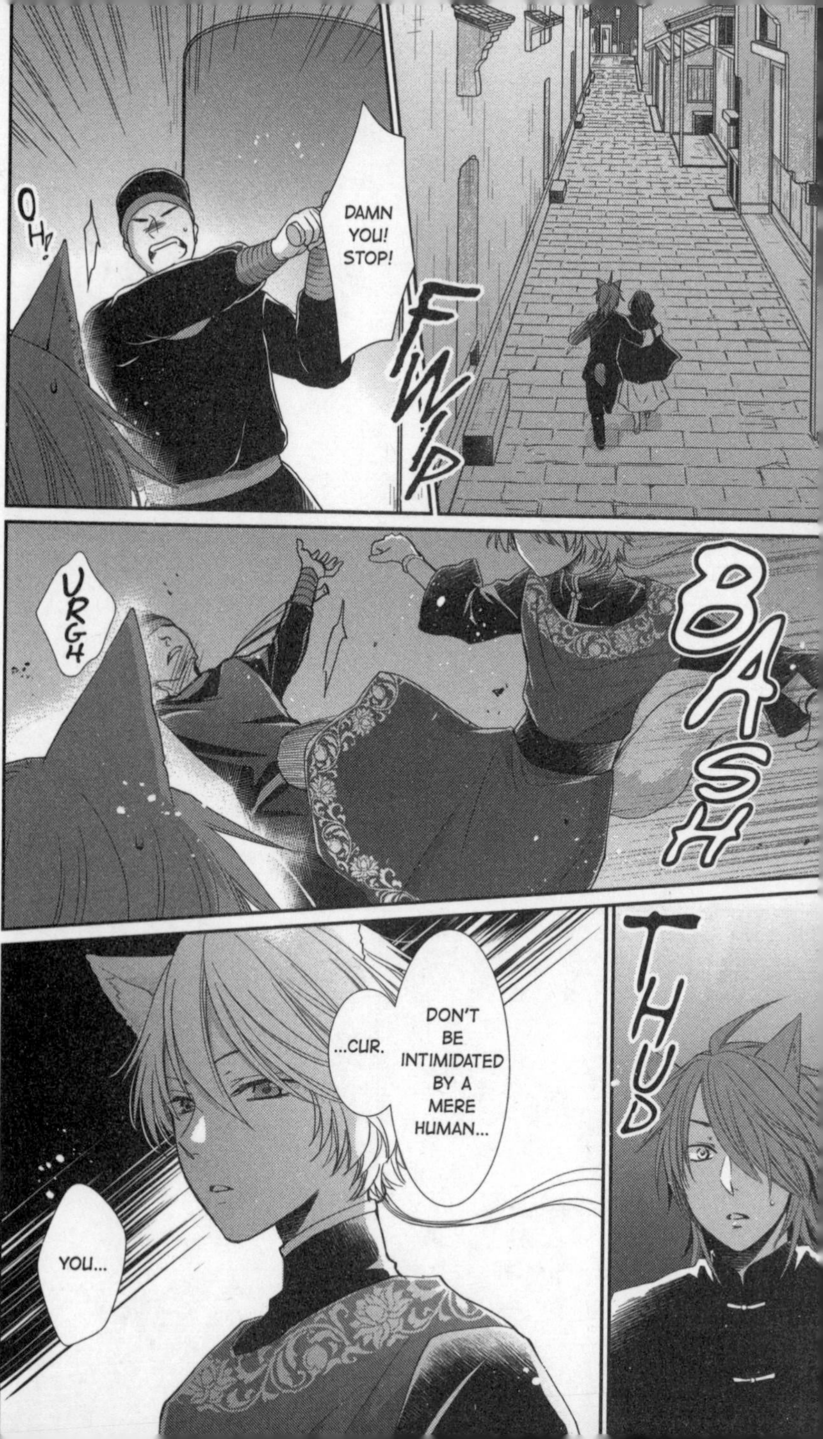
DAMN YOU! STOP!
FWIP
OH!?
BASH
URGH
THUD
DON'T BE INTIMIDATED BY A MERE HUMAN...
...CUR.
YOU...

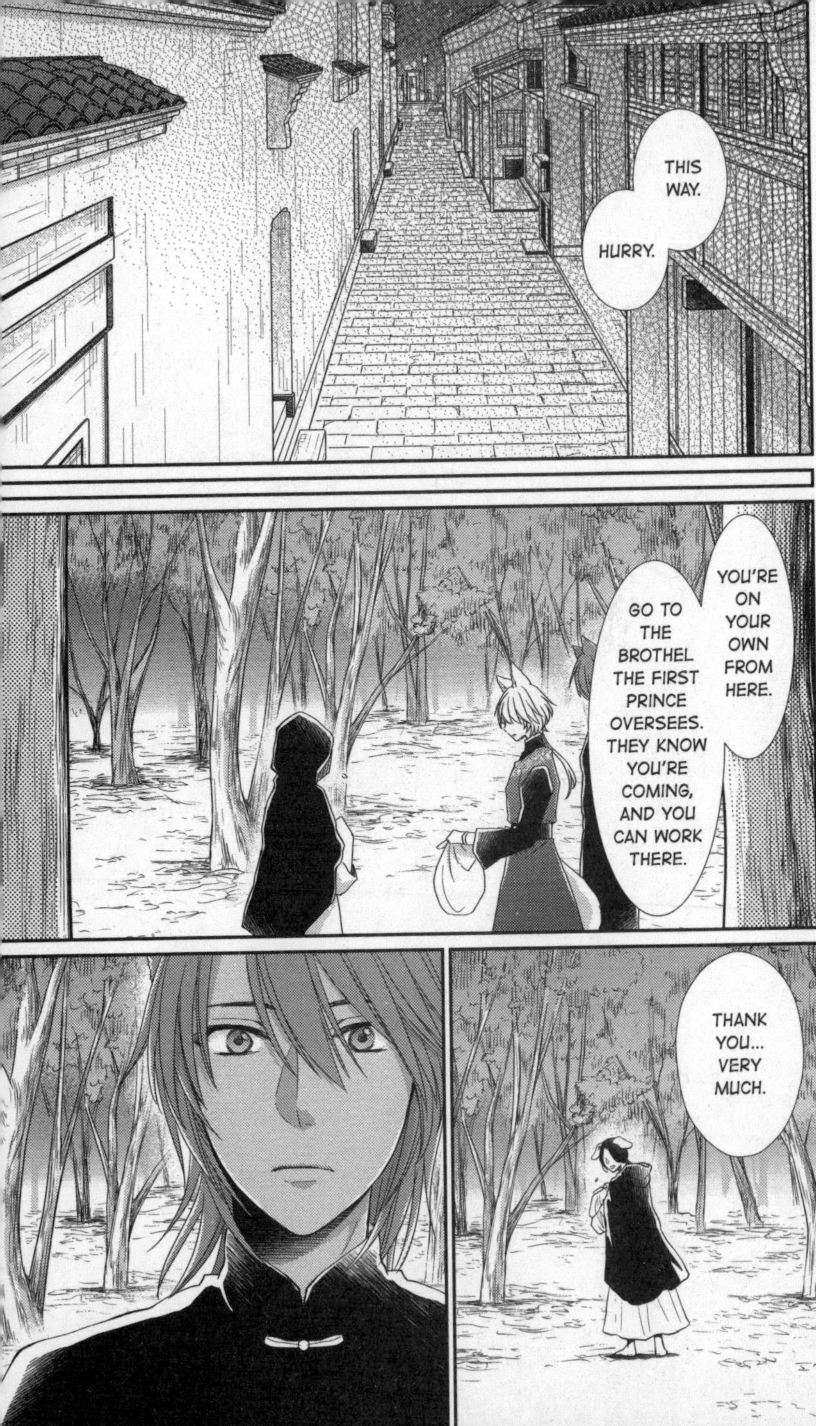
THIS WAY.
HURRY.
YOU'RE ON YOUR OWN FROM HERE.
GO TO THE BROTHEL THE FIRST PRINCE OVERSEES. THEY KNOW YOU'RE COMING, AND YOU CAN WORK THERE.
THANK YOU... VERY MUCH.

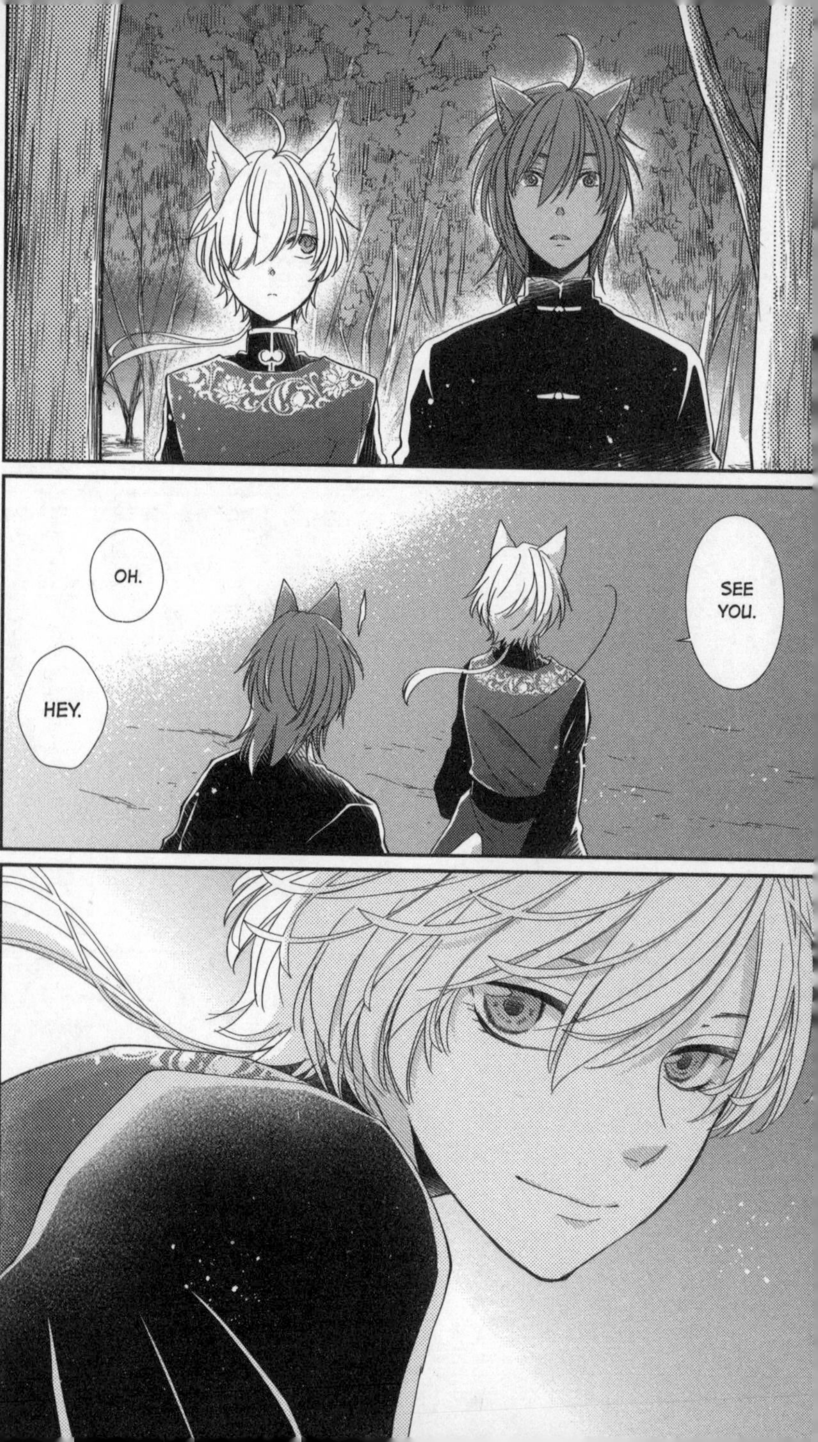
SEE YOU.
OH.
HEY.

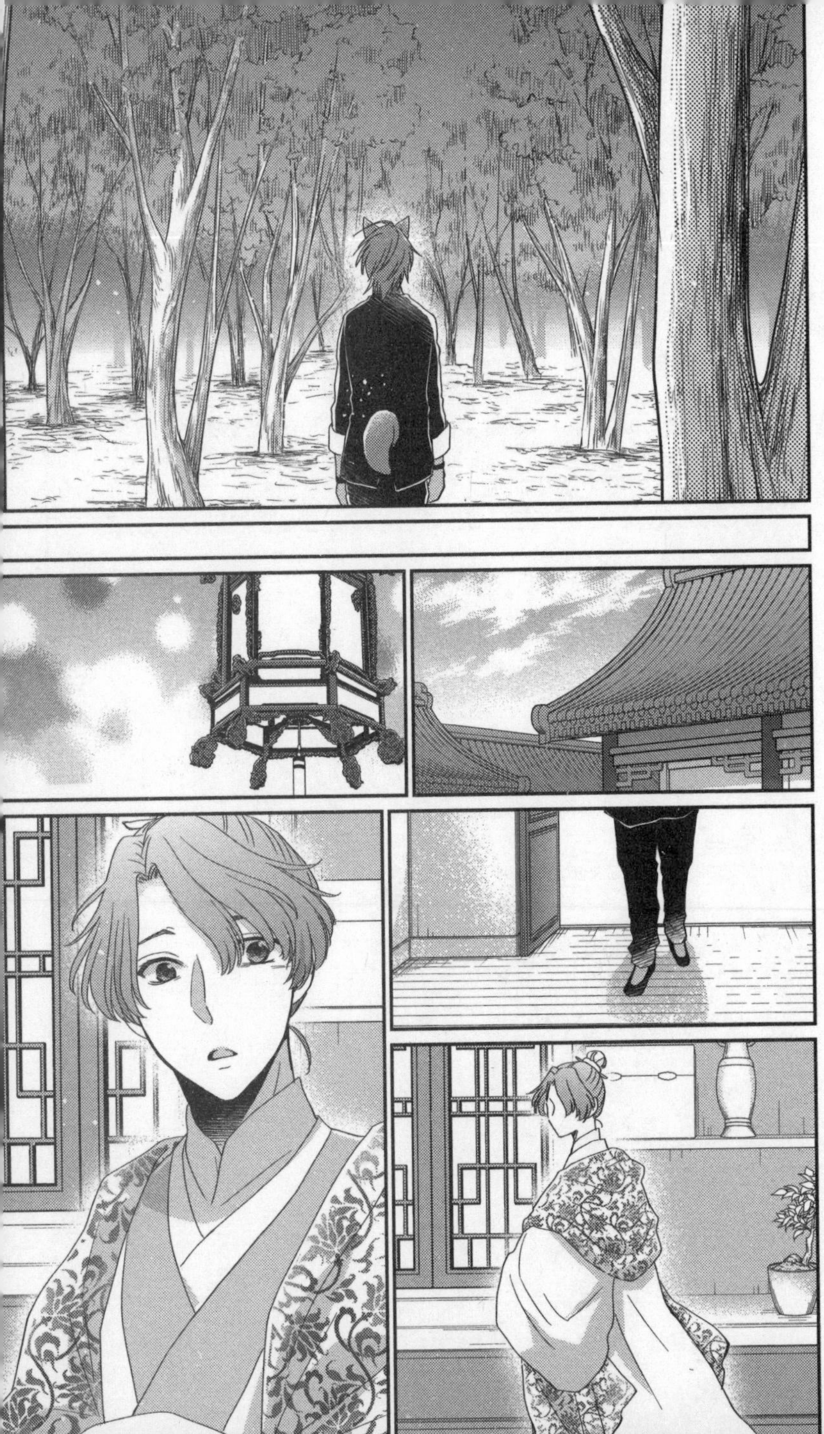

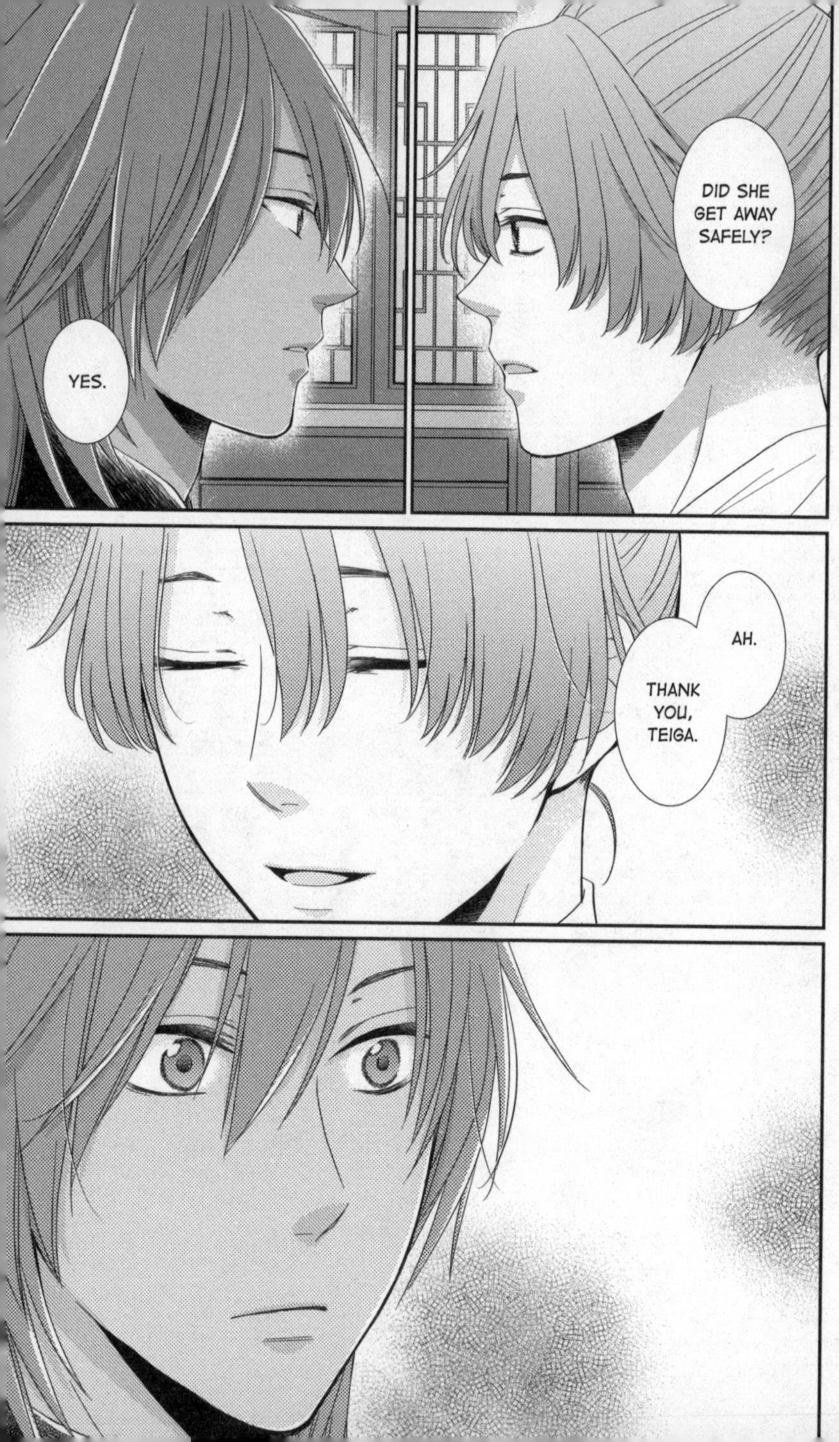
DID SHE GET AWAY SAFELY?
YES.
AH.
THANK YOU, TEIGA.

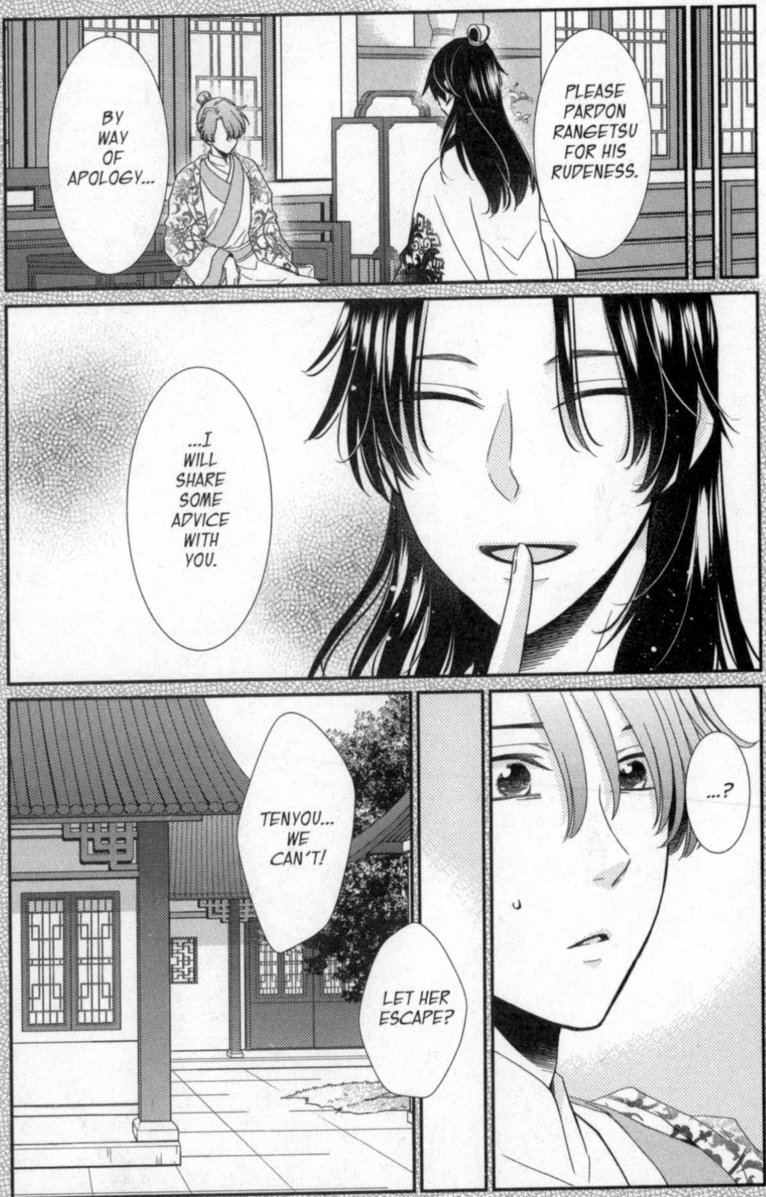
PLEASE PARDON RANGETSU FOR HIS RUDENESS.
BY WAY OF APOLOGY...
...I WILL SHARE SOME ADVICE WITH YOU.
...?
TENYOU... WE CAN'T!
LET HER ESCAPE?

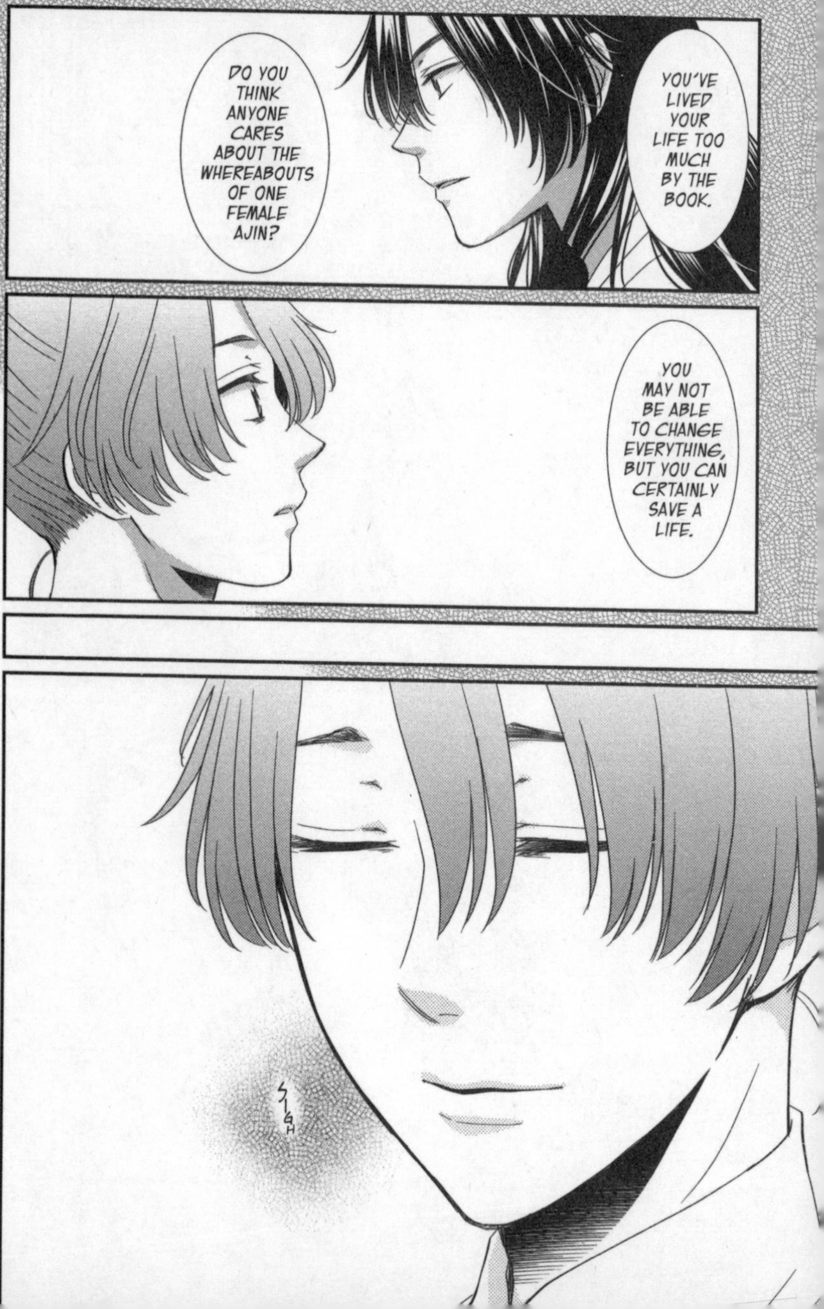
YOU'VE LIVED YOUR LIFE TOO MUCH BY THE BOOK.
DO YOU THINK ANYONE CARES ABOUT THE WHEREABOUTS OF ONE FEMALE AJIN?
YOU MAY NOT BE ABLE TO CHANGE EVERYTHING, BUT YOU CAN CERTAINLY SAVE A LIFE.
SIGH

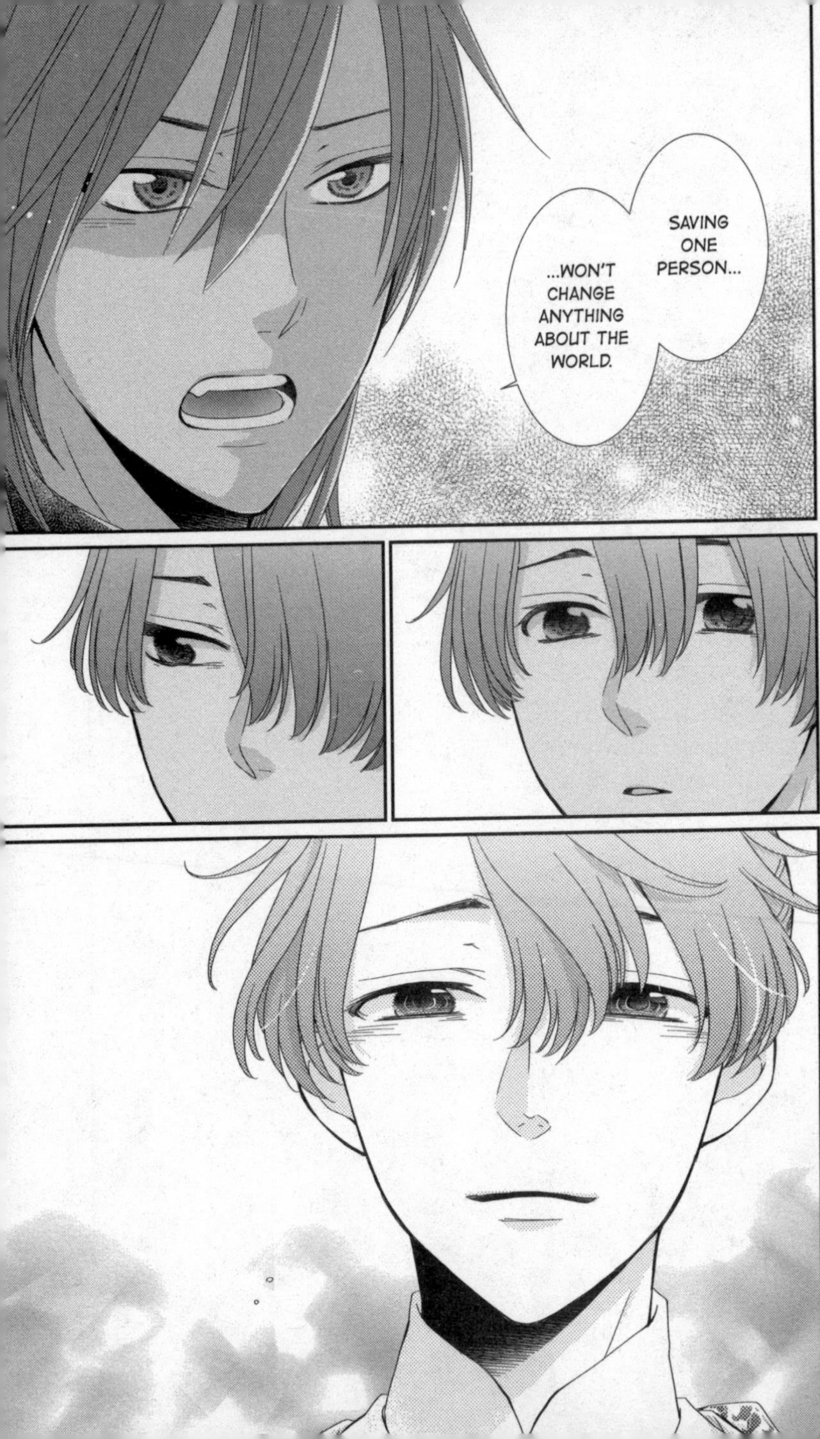
SAVING ONE PERSON...
...WON'T CHANGE ANYTHING ABOUT THE WORLD.

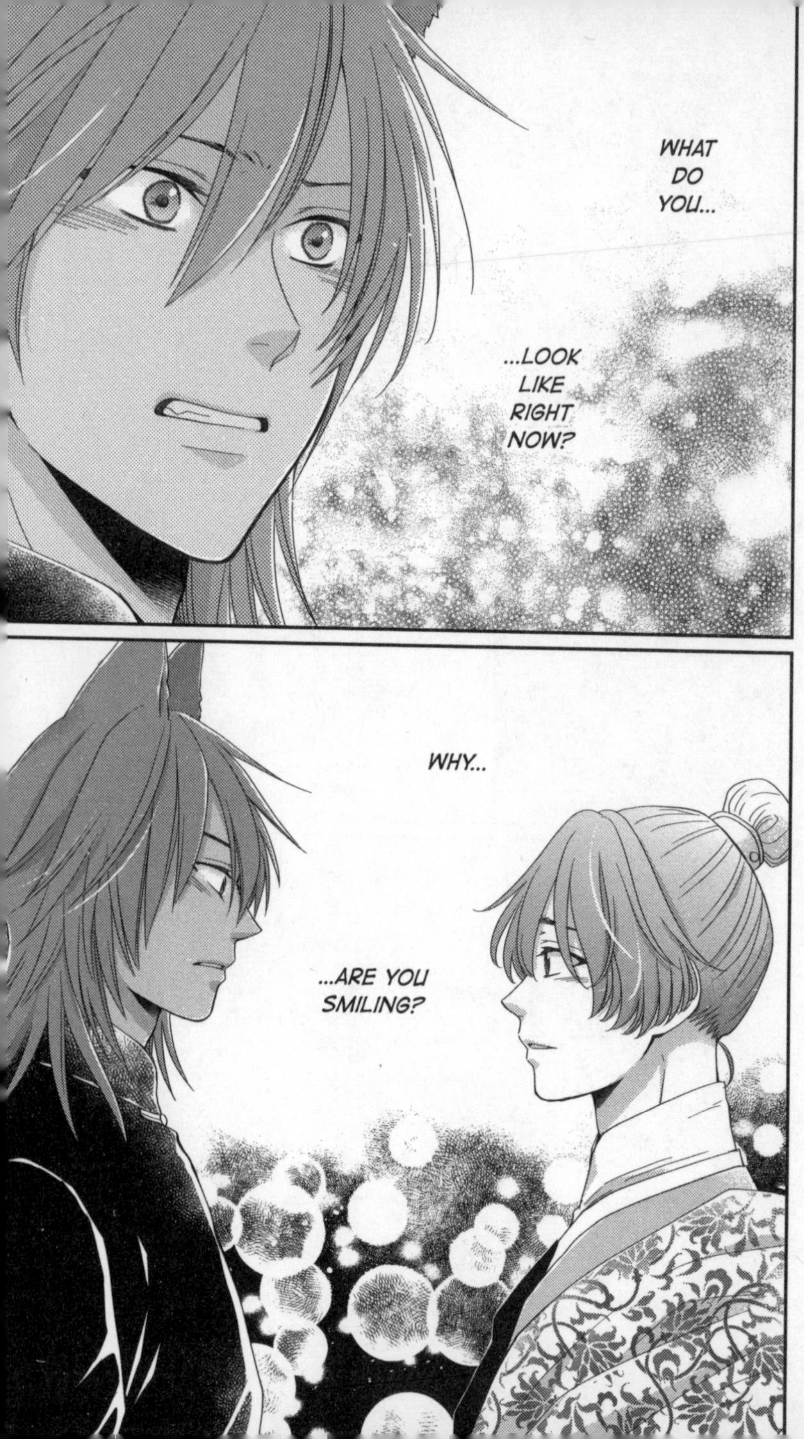
WHAT DO YOU...
...LOOK LIKE RIGHT NOW?
WHY...
...ARE YOU SMILING?

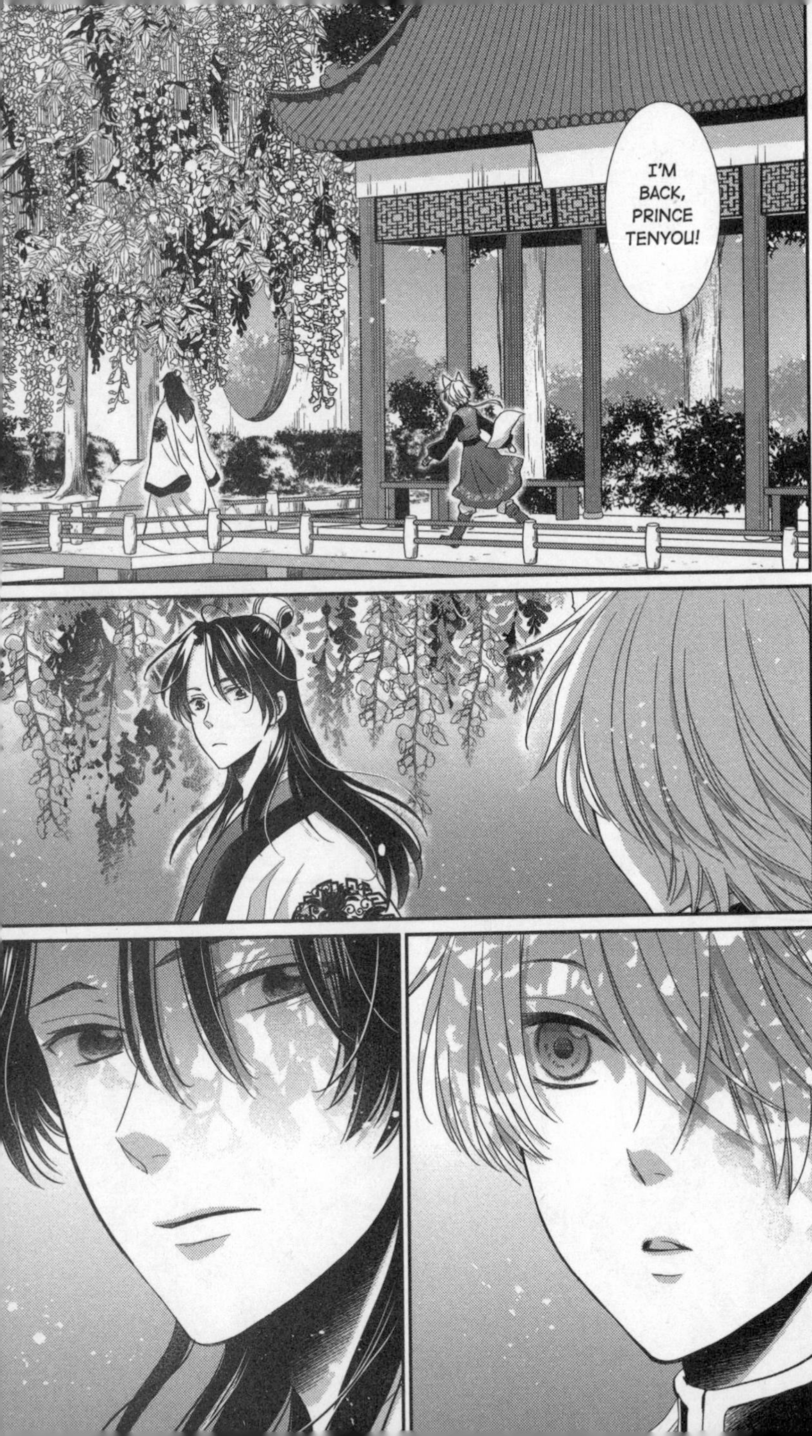
I'M BACK, PRINCE TENYOU!

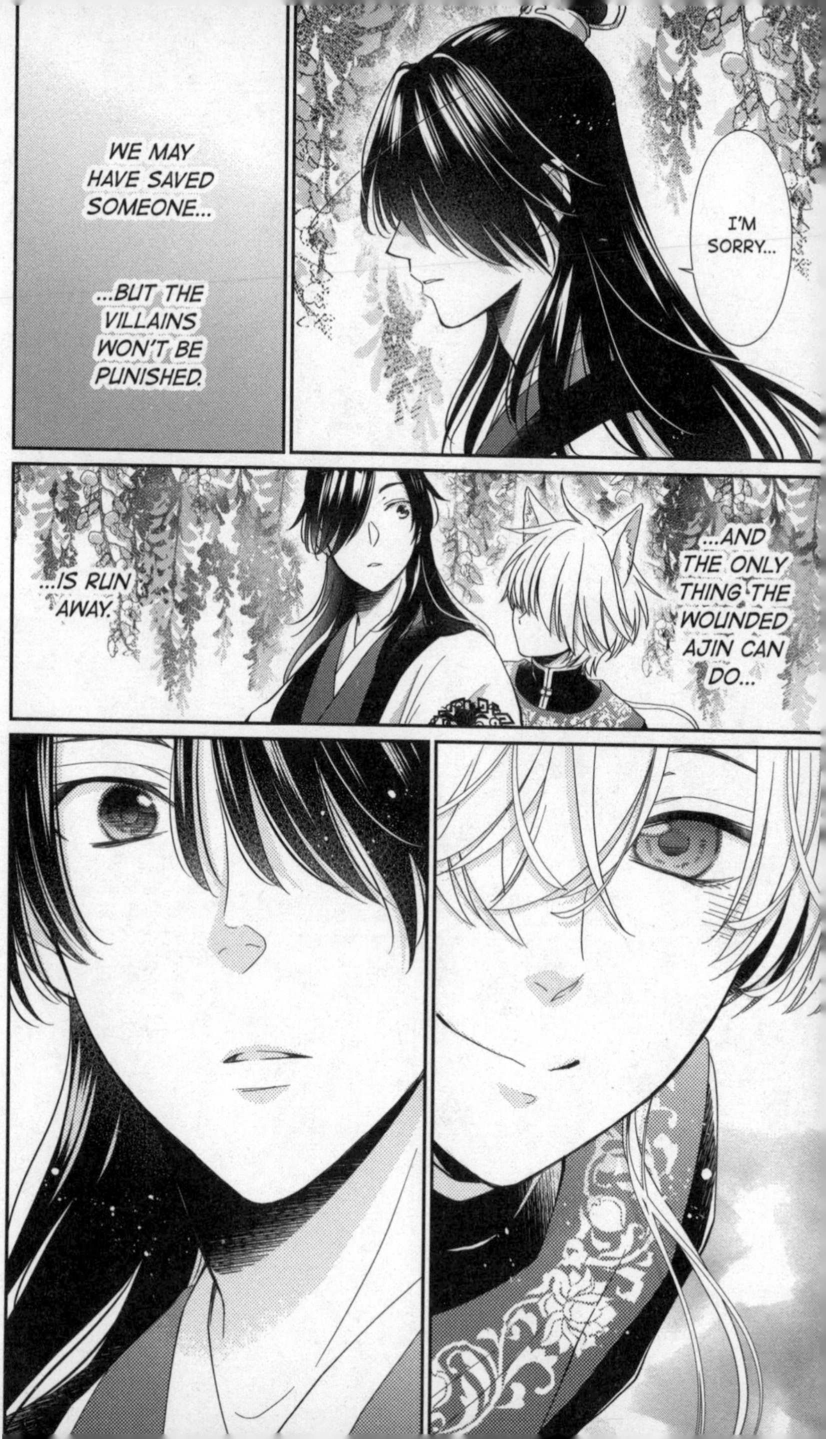
I'M SORRY...
WE MAY HAVE SAVED SOMEONE...
...BUT THE VILLAINS WON'T BE PUNISHED.
...AND THE ONLY THING THE WOUNDED AJIN CAN DO...
...IS RUN AWAY.

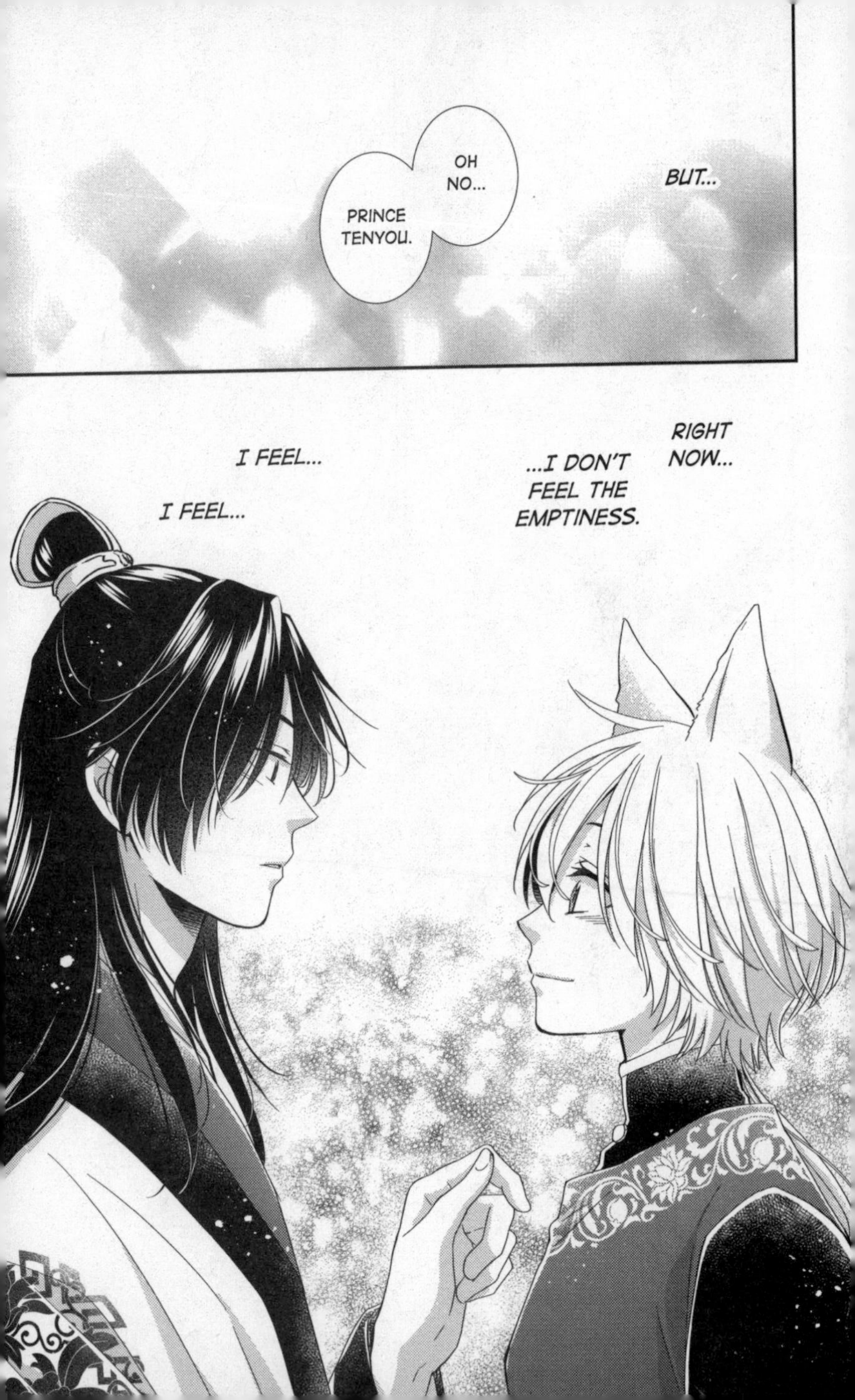
BUT...
OH NO... PRINCE TENYOU.
RIGHT NOW...
...I DON'T FEEL THE EMPTINESS.
I FEEL...
I FEEL...

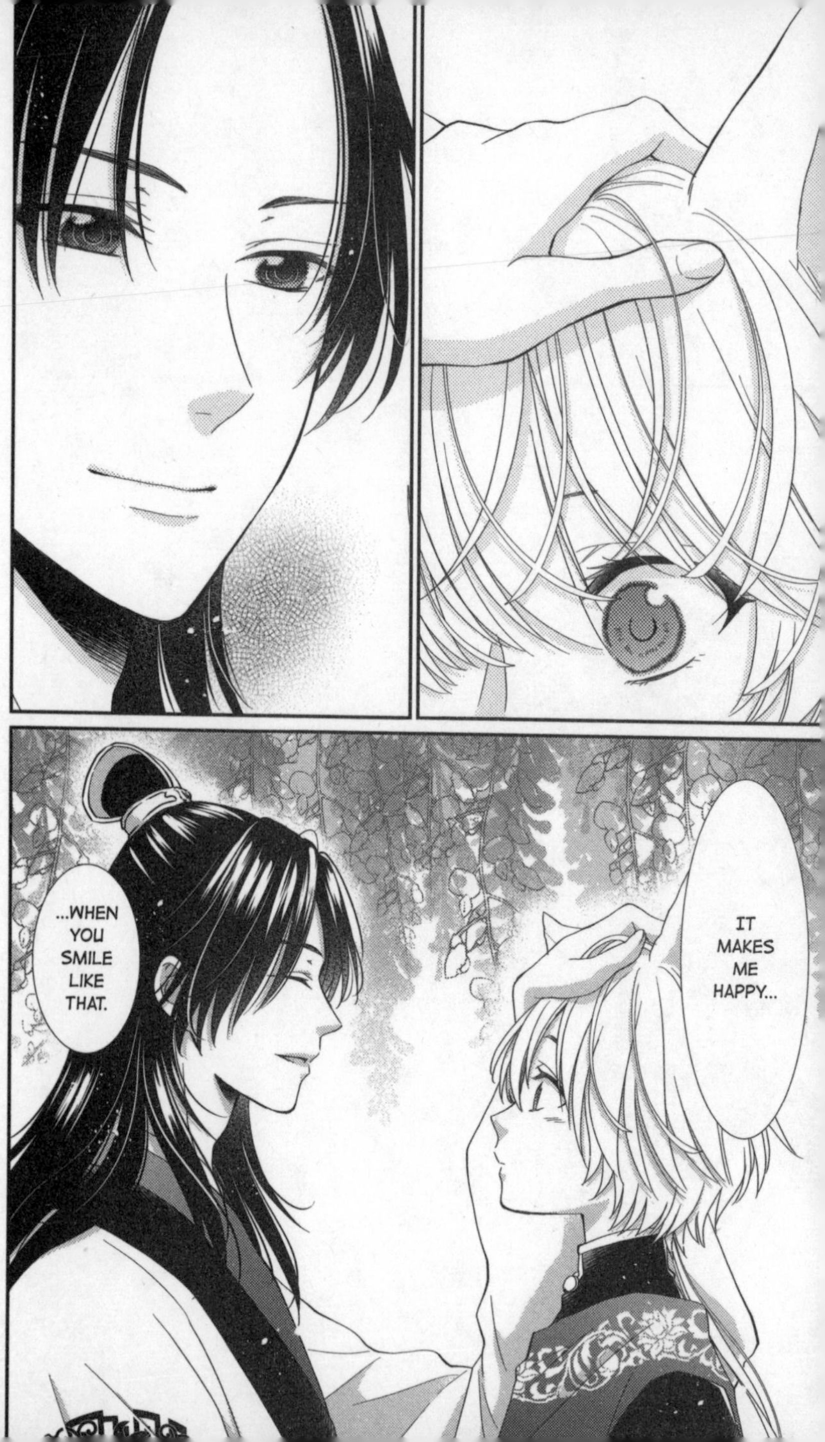
IT MAKES ME HAPPY...
...WHEN YOU SMILE LIKE THAT.

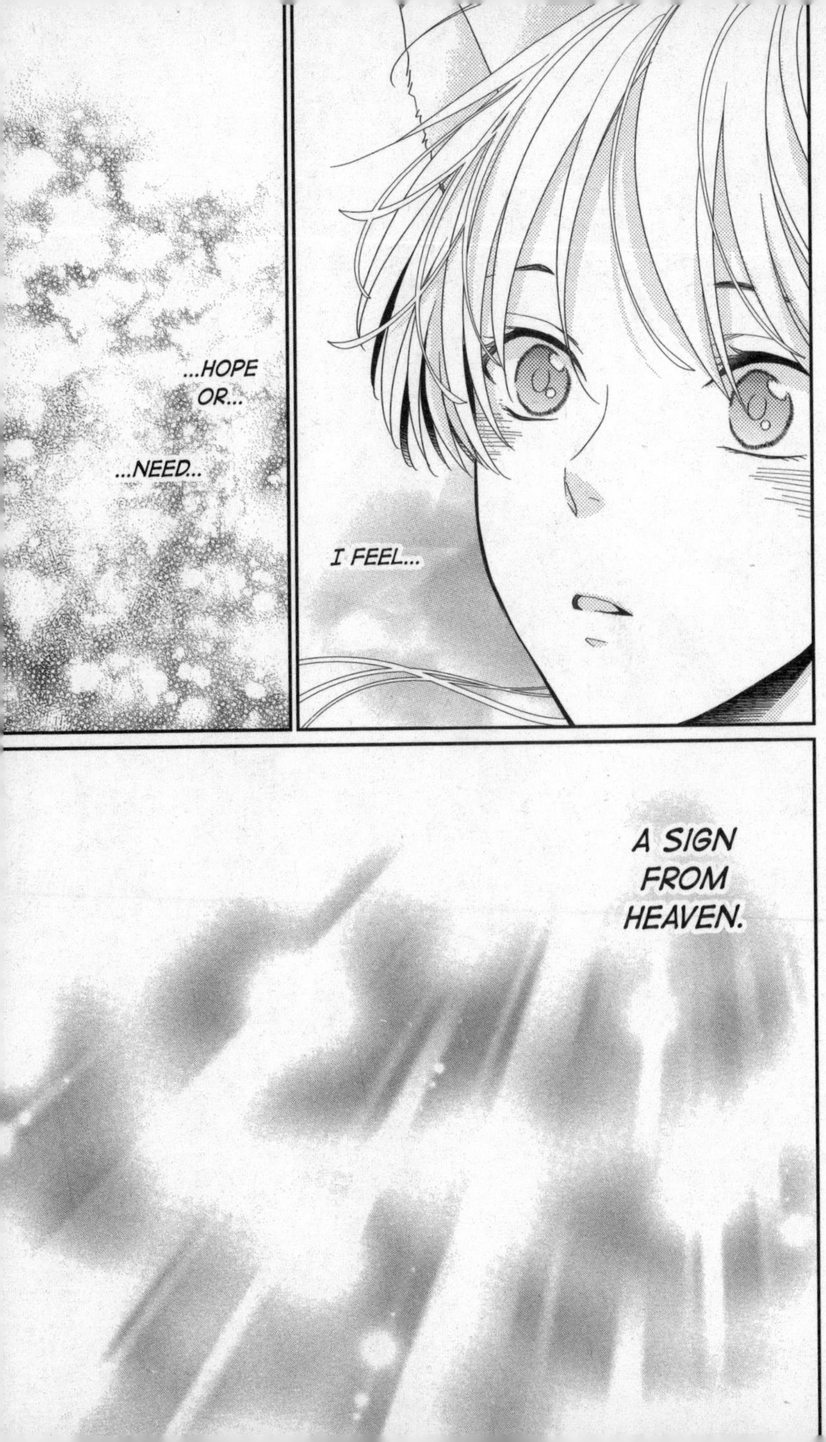
I FEEL...
...HOPE OR...
...NEED...
A SIGN FROM HEAVEN.

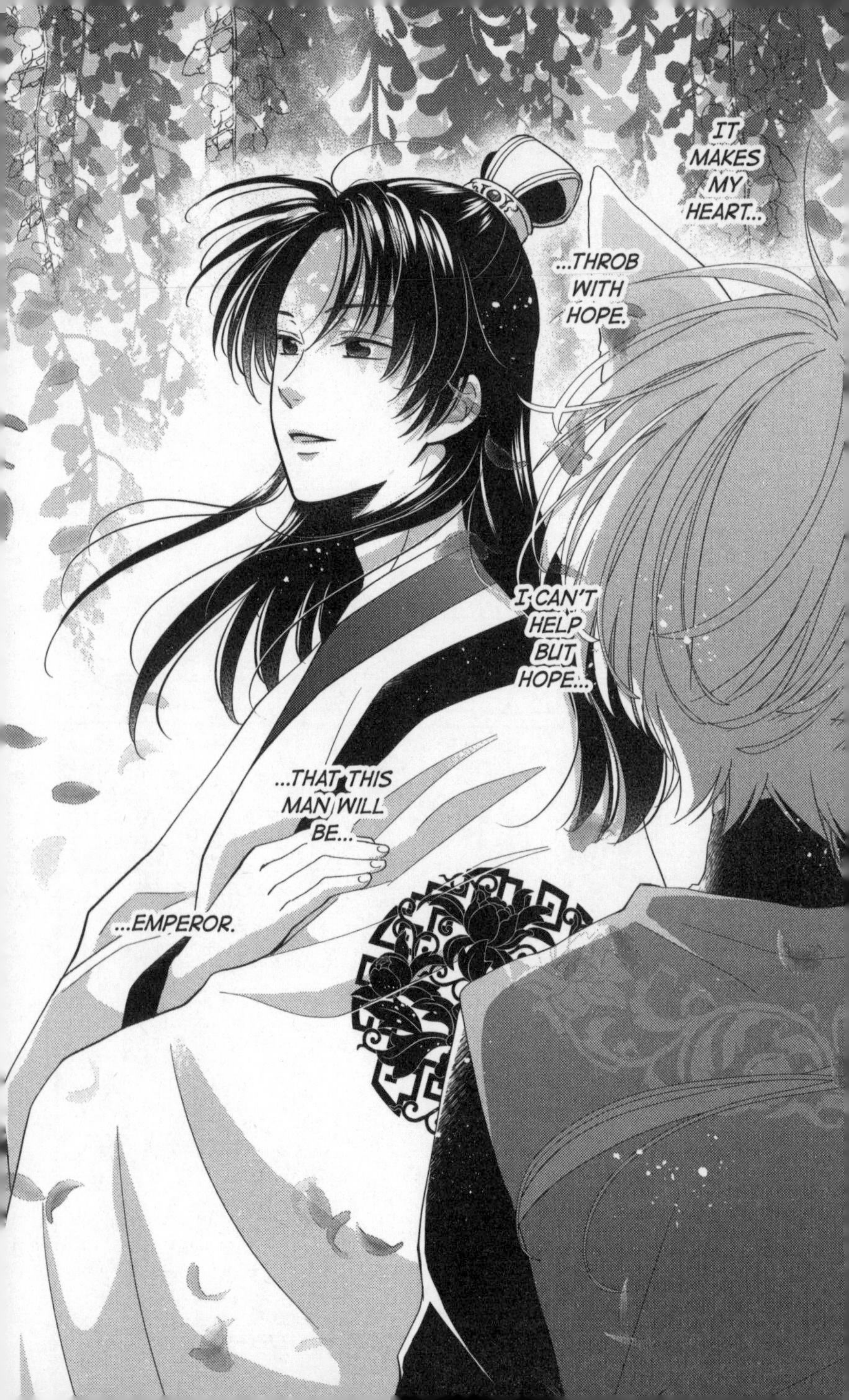
IT MAKES MY HEART...
...THROB WITH HOPE.
I CAN'T HELP BUT HOPE...
...THAT THIS MAN WILL BE...
...EMPEROR.

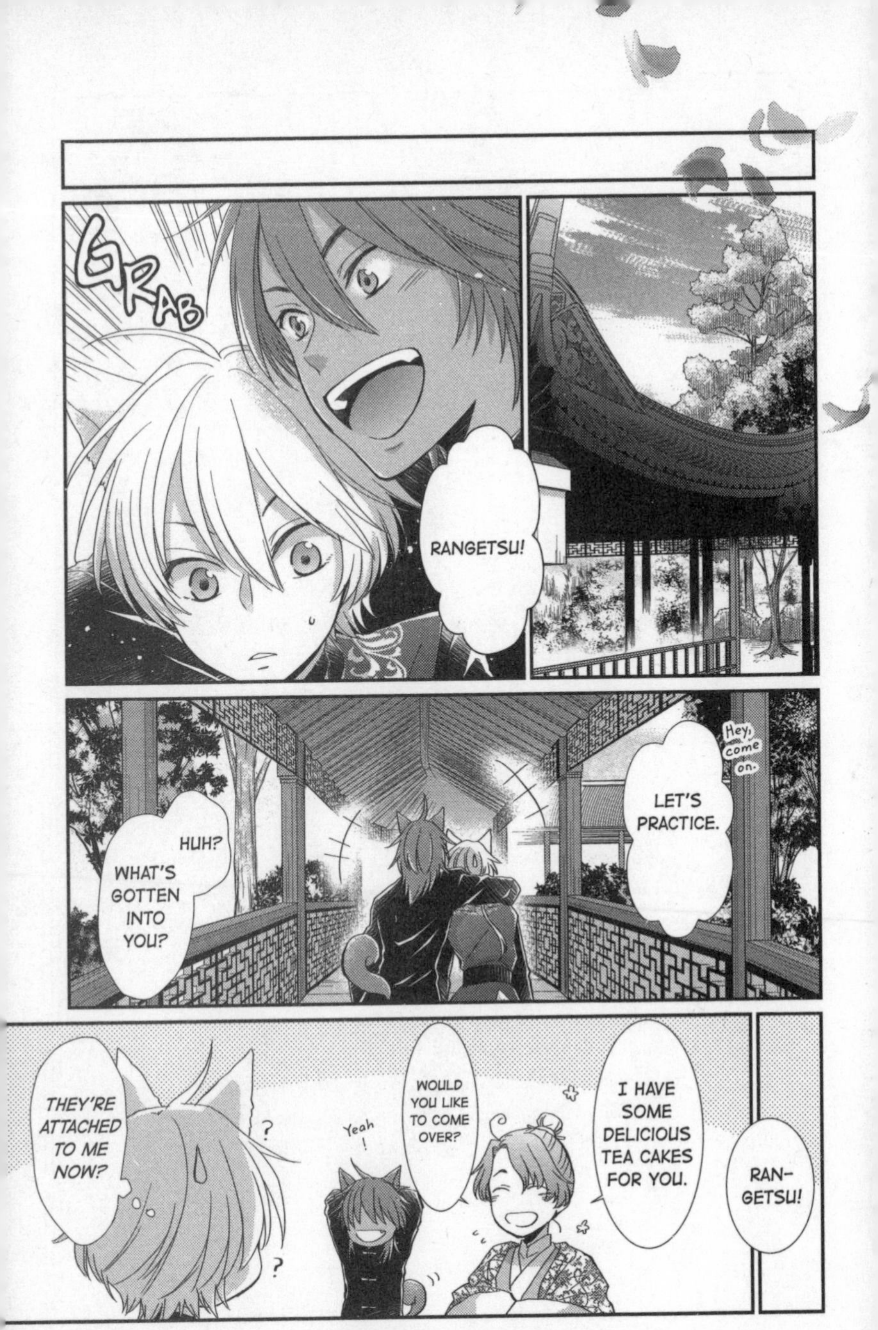
GRAB
RANGETSU!
Hey, come on.
LET'S PRACTICE.
HUH? WHAT'S GOTTEN INTO YOU?
RAN-GETSU!
I HAVE SOME DELICIOUS TEA CAKES FOR YOU.
WOULD YOU LIKE TO COME OVER?
Yeah!
THEY'RE ATTACHED TO ME NOW?

The King's Beast Volume 2 — The End

For all of you who may or may not be familiar with
Dawn of the Arcana…I hope you enjoy this!

—Rei Toma

Rei Toma has been drawing since childhood, and she
created her first complete manga for a graduation project
in design school. When she drew the short story manga
"Help Me, Dentist," it attracted a publisher's attention
and she made her debut right away. After she found
success as a manga artist, acclaim in other art fields
started to follow as she did illustrations for novels and
video game character designs. She is also the creator of
Dawn of the Arcana and *The Water Dragon's Bride*,
both available in English from VIZ Media.

THE KING'S Beast 2

SHOJO BEAT EDITION

STORY AND ART BY **Rei Toma**

ENGLISH TRANSLATION & ADAPTATION **JN Productions**
TOUCH-UP ART & LETTERING **Monaliza de Asis**
DESIGN **Joy Zhang**
EDITOR **Pancha Diaz**

OU NO KEMONO Vol. 2
by Rei TOMA
© 2019 Rei TOMA
All rights reserved.
Original Japanese edition published by SHOGAKUKAN.
English translation rights in the United States of America,
Canada, the United Kingdom, Ireland, Australia and New
Zealand arranged with SHOGAKUKAN.

Original Cover Design: Hibiki CHIKADA (fireworks. vc)

Printed in the U.S.A.

Published by VIZ Media, LLC
P.O. Box 77010
San Francisco, CA 94107

10 9 8 7 6 5 4 3 2 1
First printing, May 2021

PARENTAL ADVISORY
THE KING'S BEAST is rated T for Teen and is
recommended for ages 13 and up. This volume
contains death, violence and systemic oppression.

 MEDIA
viz.com

shojobeat.com

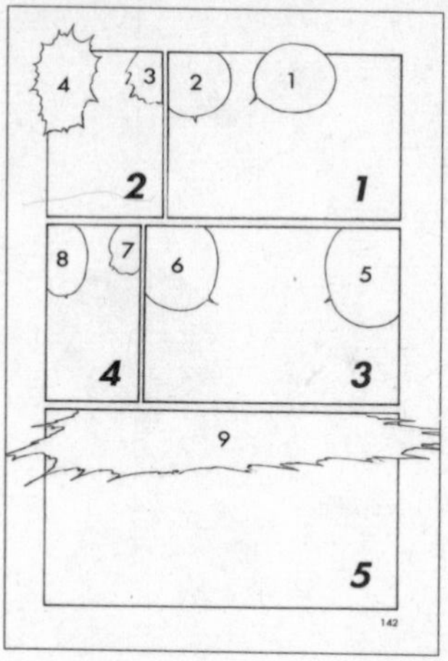

1
2
3
4
1
2
5
6
7
8
3
4
9
5
142

THIS IS THE LAST PAGE.

THE KING'S BEAST has been printed in the original Japanese format to preserve the orientation of the artwork.

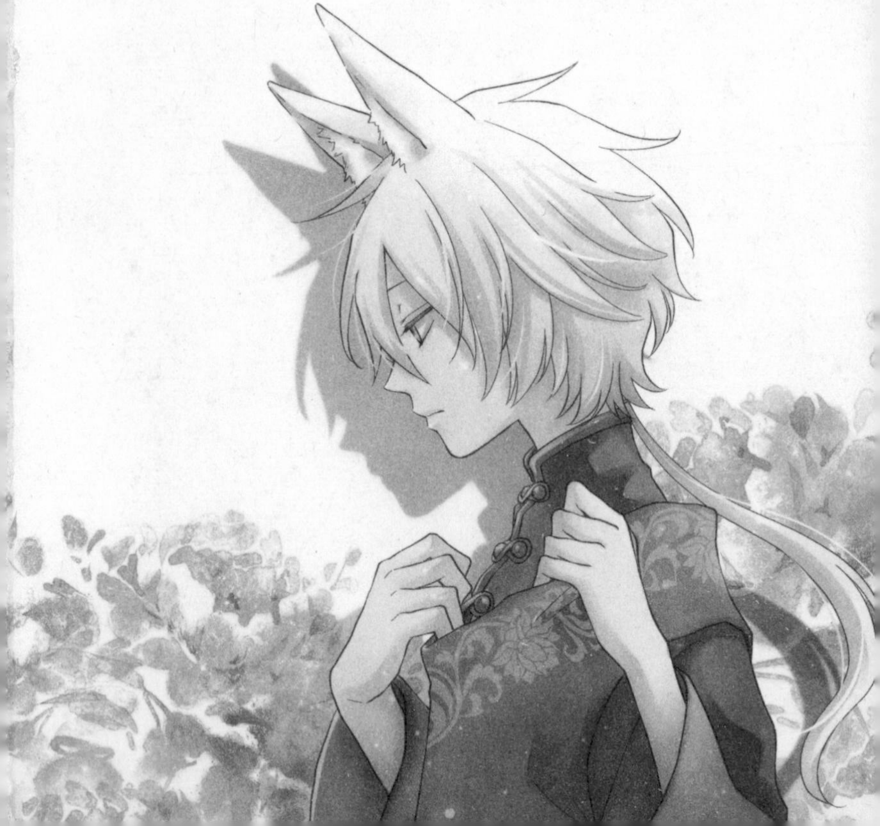